A–Z BOLD ACTION AND STRATEGIC IMPLEMENTATION

Transforming Business Competitive Ideas into Results

By

Michael Werki

COPYRIGHT NOTICE

TABLE OF CONTENTS

INTRODUCTION

In today's brutally competitive economic market, simple ideas are not enough to achieve triumph. It requires a daring mentality, tireless activity, and smart execution to translate those ideas into concrete outcomes. This is where "A-Z Bold Action and Strategic Implementation: Transforming Business Competitive Ideas into Results" comes into play.

This revolutionary book serves as your guide to managing the difficulties of current corporate competitiveness. Authored by an industry expert with a lot of knowledge, it is a complete resource that empowers you to unlock your business's full potential and exceed your competition.

By adopting the A-Z strategy explained inside these pages, you will start on a journey of daring and strategic thinking. The book digs deep into the key ideas of taking measured risks, questioning the status quo, and pushing beyond comfort zones. It offers you the skills and tactics required to capture opportunities and establish a compelling competitive edge.

However, this book goes beyond simple theory. It underlines the vital relevance of strategic implementation. You will learn how to examine your company environment, locate untapped potential, and develop a personalized route to success. With the book's direction, you will execute your strategy with precision, ensuring every activity matches your larger aims.

"A-Z Bold Action and Strategic Implementation" is an invaluable resource for startups, entrepreneurs, and established enterprises alike. It unveils the secrets of top industry performers, their tales of achievement, and the vital lessons learned along the road. It offers you the knowledge and insights required to handle the difficulties of today's corporate world and emerge successful.

Don't let your thoughts sit dormant. Transform them into reality through the force of bold action and smart execution. Let this book be your trusty companion on your way to reaching unequaled achievement. Prepare to disrupt, innovate, and leave your opponent in amazement.

CHAPTER 1: SETTING THE STAGE FOR SUCCESS

This is about Building Bridges to Triumph in Business as a business person.

In the ruthless world of business, setting the scene for success is the foundation upon which greatness is built. As intelligent entrepreneurs, we realize that every victory starts with a perfectly built stage, where aspirations change into reality. To soar above the competition and attain unparalleled heights, it is necessary to take decisive action, establish a compelling vision, and effectively manage resources.

In this write up, we will look into essential techniques and practical insights that can help you set the scene for victory in your entrepreneurial path.

Setting the stage for success in a corporate environment refers to the process of creating the essential circumstances, tactics, and foundation to accomplish desired objectives and long-term success. It entails establishing a favorable climate, aligning resources, identifying goals and objectives, and executing successful strategies to generate corporate development and profitability.

Unleashing Your Potential(Crafting The Perfect Foundation)

"Unleashing your potential" is all about tapping into your inner skills, talents, and qualities to accomplish remarkable achievements. It entails unlocking the full range of your potential and pushing beyond self-imposed restrictions to achieve new heights of accomplishment.

When it comes to setting the groundwork for business success, unlocking your potential plays a significant role. It begins with identifying and appreciating your unique talents, abilities, and interests. Take the time to examine your skills and weaknesses, finding areas where you thrive and those that may require work. By identifying your strengths, you may harness them to your advantage, enabling you to flourish in areas that coincide with your natural skills.

Unleashing your potential sometimes means moving beyond your comfort zone and taking deliberate risks. Growth and achievement can lie outside the borders of familiarity. Embrace obstacles and perceive them as opportunities for personal and professional progress. Push yourself to attempt new things, gain new information, and build new talents. Embracing an attitude of constant learning and growth helps you to unleash latent potential and find new opportunities for success.

Moreover, establishing the foundation for success demands a strong conviction in your ability and the courage to pursue your objectives. Believe in yourself and your goal, even when confronted with hurdles or failures. Develop a positive mentality that focuses on solutions rather than concentrating on difficulties. Surround yourself with a supporting network of mentors, coworkers, and friends who uplift and motivate you. By growing self-belief and building a supportive atmosphere, you empower yourself to release your full potential and accomplish exceptional achievements.

Unleashing your potential also includes establishing bold objectives and committing to a plan of action. Take the time to explain your goals and design a plan that describes the activities required to attain them. Break down your long-term objectives into smaller, doable milestones that you can monitor and assess along the way. By creating specific objectives and building a roadmap, you generate a feeling of direction and purpose that pulls you ahead on your path to success.

Ultimately, releasing your potential in business demands a mix of self-awareness, boldness, confidence, and unrelenting perseverance. It is about identifying and appreciating your unique traits, moving beyond your comfort zone, believing in yourself, and creating ambitious objectives. By tapping into your genuine potential and using your skills, you set the foundation for outstanding accomplishments and open up endless prospects for success in the corporate world.

Building Bridges To Success

Building bridges to success entails developing connections, collaborations, and partnerships that support development and move you toward accomplishing your objectives. It is about using the talents, resources, and networks of others to strengthen your capabilities and increase your reach in the corporate world.

One of the major parts of establishing bridges to success is developing strategic alliances. Identify persons, organizations, or suppliers who share your vision, beliefs, and ambitions. Look for partners that have complementary talents, experience, or resources that can boost your strengths. Collaborating with the proper partners may give reciprocal advantages, providing a win-win scenario where both parties can achieve more success than they could on their own.

Strategic partnerships may take numerous forms, including joint ventures, co-marketing activities, or supplier agreements. They may help you tap into new markets, reach new client groups, and extend your product or service offerings. By teaming forces with partners that have established networks and market presence, you may expand your reach and utilize their experience to drive your development.

Building bridges to success also entails networking and relationship-building. Attend industry events, conferences, and seminars to network with like-minded individuals, possible clients, and industry leaders. Actively participate in networking opportunities both online and offline, employing platforms such as LinkedIn or industry-specific forums. Cultivate connections with people who may give direction, mentoring, or partnership possibilities that move your firm ahead.

In addition to external ties, developing bridges inside your firm is vital. Foster a culture of cooperation and teamwork, fostering cross-functional communication and knowledge-sharing. Break down silos and offer chances for workers to cooperate on projects, share ideas, and exploit each other's talents. By building strong internal connections, you may leverage the pooled skills and experience inside your business to generate innovation and create success.

Building bridges to success also entails keeping open lines of communication with stakeholders, investors, and consumers. Regularly connect with these groups to obtain input, understand their requirements, and create trust. Actively explore ways to communicate with consumers via surveys, focus groups, or social media interactions. By building good connections with stakeholders and consumers, you may get useful insights, boost your reputation, and create loyalty that supports your long-term success.

Charting The Course To Triumph

Charting the route to success entails formulating a well-defined plan of action and executing it strategically to reach your company objectives. It comprises defining clear goals, building a roadmap, and regularly analyzing and altering your strategy to manage hurdles and exploit opportunities.

To map the route to victory, start by defining precise, measurable, attainable, relevant, and time-bound (SMART) objectives. Clearly explain what you intend to achieve and develop metrics to measure your progress. Break down your long-term goals into smaller, practical milestones that serve as checkpoints along your path.

Once you have identified your objectives, build a roadmap or action plan that explains the activities necessary to attain them. Identify the primary strategies, actions, and resources required to attain each milestone. Assign duties to team members and establish deadlines to guarantee responsibility and progress.

Regularly analyze and change your methods as you navigate your route to success. Monitor your progress, measure key performance metrics, and get feedback from consumers, stakeholders, and team members. Stay updated about industry trends, competition, and upcoming opportunities. Be flexible in altering your plans depending on the insights you acquire and the changing business scenario.

Effective communication and teamwork are vital while mapping the route to victory. Ensure that your team is aligned with the broader goals and objectives. Foster open communication lines, promote feedback, and establish a culture that supports innovation and ongoing development. Collaboration among team members provides for varied viewpoints, stimulates creativity, and boosts problem-solving ability.

In addition, it is crucial to be adaptable and flexible in your approach. The corporate world is dynamic, and unanticipated difficulties or opportunities may occur. Embrace change, adjust swiftly, and exploit your capacity to pivot when required. This flexibility enables you to capitalize on new trends and alter your plans to retain a competitive edge.

Regularly monitor and analyze your progress against the milestones and targets you have established. Celebrate wins and milestones reached along the road to preserve motivation and momentum. Learn from setbacks and disappointments, considering them as useful lessons that contribute to your growth and development.

By planning the route to victory, you provide a clear direction and structure for achievement. It helps you remain focused, make educated choices, and efficiently manage resources. By regularly analyzing and adapting your plans, you can overcome hurdles, grasp opportunities, and position your organization for long-term success. Remember, the route to victory is rarely linear, and flexibility and adaptation are vital as you negotiate the ever-changing business world.

Empowering Excellence(Cultivating a Winning Mindset)

Empowering greatness entails developing an atmosphere and culture that encourages the growth, development, and empowerment of people inside your business. It emphasizes providing the essential support, resources, and chances for your team members to flourish, develop, and accomplish their maximum potential.

To enable greatness begins with investing in your people. Provide them with the tools, training, and resources they need to increase their skills and expertise. Offer professional development programs, seminars, and training sessions that match their career ambitions and the organization's objectives. By investing in their development, you not only boost their competencies but also generate a feeling of worth and loyalty to the firm.

Encourage open communication and cooperation among your team. Create a secure and inclusive workplace where everyone feels comfortable expressing their ideas, thoughts, and comments. Foster a culture that honors varied opinions and fosters healthy debates. Actively listen to your team members' opinions and offer them the opportunity to add their unique views to projects and decision-making processes.

Empower your team by distributing responsibility and giving them autonomy in their tasks. Trust your team members to make choices and take responsibility for their job. Allow them to explore new ideas, take reasonable chances, and learn from both triumphs and disappointments. Encouraging autonomy not only empowers people but also leads to improved creativity, innovation, and problem-solving inside the business.

Recognize and appreciate successes. Acknowledge the successes of your team members publicly, whether via team meetings, newsletters, or company-wide announcements. Providing recognition and incentives for excellent achievement creates a culture of excellence and pushes others to strive for greatness. Celebrate both individual and communal triumphs, generating a spirit of friendship and togetherness.

Create mentoring and coaching initiatives inside your business. Pair experienced personnel with novice team members to give advice, support, and opportunity for advancement. Mentors may give useful ideas, share experiences, and assist negotiate problems. Additionally, encourage workers to participate in peer-to-peer learning and information sharing, where team members may benefit from one another's skills and experiences.

Lead by example. As a leader, exemplify the attributes you wish to see in your team members. Demonstrate honesty, enthusiasm, and a dedication to excellence. Encourage a good work-life balance and emphasize employee well-being. Foster a friendly and supportive work atmosphere that encourages cooperation and personal development.

By enabling greatness, you establish a culture that appreciates and fosters the potential of each employee inside your firm. This not only leads to improved work satisfaction and employee retention but also cultivates a high-performing team that is motivated, engaged, and driven to deliver excellent outcomes. When employees feel empowered and respected, they are more inclined to go above and beyond, boosting the success of the business as a whole.

As dedicated company leaders, we recognize that setting the groundwork for success is a complicated process.

By establishing a strong foundation, coordinating resources efficiently, and executing well-defined plans, we create the road for our company to develop and achieve excellence. However, success is not a final destination; it is a continual journey. Continuously adapt, innovate, and embrace chances to remain one step ahead. With steadfast dedication, endurance, and a clear vision, we may set the scene for victory and make an unforgettable impression in the corporate world.

CHAPTER 2:THE POWER OF VISION

In today's dynamic business landscape, vision is the secret ingredient that fuels exceptional success. Visionary leaders possess a unique ability to transcend the present and envision a future that is bold, innovative, and transformative. It is this power of vision that propels businesses towards greatness, enabling them to break barriers, embrace change, and achieve remarkable results. In this article, we dive into the vital role of vision in the world of business and explore how it can elevate your organization to unparalleled heights.

The Concept Of The Power Of Vision In The Business

Ignite Growth: As visionary leaders, we possess the extraordinary foresight to anticipate industry trends, identify emerging opportunities, and craft strategic roadmaps that ignite growth. Our ability to envision a compelling future empowers us to align our teams, resources, and actions towards a common goal. A well-defined vision provides clarity and direction, enabling us to navigate challenges, make informed decisions, and seize lucrative growth prospects.

Igniting growth is a crucial aspect of leveraging the power of vision in business. When we talk about igniting growth, we refer to the strategic actions and initiatives taken to propel our business forward, capitalize on opportunities, and achieve sustainable expansion.

__Here are some key points to further explain how the power of vision ignites growth:__

1. Anticipating Industry Trends: As visionary leaders, we possess the ability to anticipate industry trends and market dynamics. By staying informed about emerging technologies, shifts in consumer behavior, regulatory changes, and competitive landscapes, we position ourselves to identify growth opportunities before others do. This foresight enables us to align our business strategies and leverage our vision to capitalize on emerging trends, staying ahead of the curve and driving growth.

2. Identifying Emerging Opportunities: A clear and compelling vision enables us to identify and seize emerging opportunities. By envisioning the future and understanding the needs and desires of our target audience, we can proactively identify gaps in the market and develop innovative products, services, or business models that address those needs. This proactive approach positions us as market leaders and allows us to capture new markets, expand our customer base, and fuel business growth.

3. Developing Strategic Roadmaps: A visionary leader understands that a vision without a plan is merely a dream. To ignite growth, we develop strategic roadmaps that outline the steps and actions required to achieve our vision. These roadmaps provide a clear path forward, guiding our teams towards specific goals, milestones, and performance targets. Strategic roadmaps ensure that everyone in the organization is

aligned, focused, and working towards common objectives, fostering growth and accelerating progress.

4. Allocating Resources Wisely: Growth requires the effective allocation of resources. Visionary leaders understand the importance of resource optimization and ensure that resources such as capital, talent, and technology are strategically deployed to drive growth initiatives. By aligning resources with the areas of the business that have the highest potential for growth, we maximize efficiency, minimize waste, and unlock the full potential of our organization.

5. Embracing Innovation: The power of vision encourages us to think outside the box and embrace innovation as a key driver of growth. By fostering a culture of innovation, we encourage our teams to generate and implement new ideas, explore disruptive technologies, and challenge the status quo. This mindset of continuous improvement and adaptation enables us to stay agile, seize market opportunities, and propel our business towards sustained growth.

6. Navigating Challenges and Risks: Growth is often accompanied by challenges and risks. However, visionary leaders view these obstacles as opportunities for growth and learning. By anticipating potential challenges and developing contingency plans, we mitigate risks and navigate through uncertain times more effectively. Our vision acts as a compass, guiding us through challenges and keeping us focused on long-term growth objectives.

7. Seizing Strategic Partnerships: Visionary leaders understand the value of strategic partnerships in driving growth. By identifying potential partners who share our vision and complement our strengths, we can leverage their expertise, resources, and networks to accelerate growth initiatives. Strategic partnerships open doors to new markets, enhance our competitive advantage, and enable us to achieve collective growth that may not be possible alone.

See Beyond Limits: Visionary leaders are not bound by the confines of conventional thinking or limited possibilities. We possess a disruptive mindset that thrives on pushing boundaries and challenging the status quo. Obstacles are merely stepping stones, and setbacks are opportunities for growth. By fostering a culture of innovation and creativity, we unleash our business's true potential, embracing bold ideas and pioneering groundbreaking solutions that set us apart from the competition.Seeing beyond limits is a key aspect of harnessing the power of vision in business. It involves cultivating a mindset that goes beyond conventional thinking and challenges perceived boundaries.

Here's a deeper explanation of what it means to see beyond limits:

1. Challenging Conventional Thinking: Visionary leaders have the ability to question existing norms and challenge the status quo. Instead of accepting limitations or following established practices, they seek innovative and alternative approaches to problem-solving. By encouraging their teams to

think outside the box and question assumptions, visionary leaders create an environment that fosters creativity and opens up new possibilities.

2. Embracing a Growth Mindset: Seeing beyond limits requires cultivating a growth mindset. This mindset emphasizes the belief that talents, abilities, and intelligence can be developed through dedication, effort, and continuous learning. Visionary leaders encourage their teams to embrace challenges, persevere in the face of setbacks, and view failures as opportunities for growth and learning. By promoting a growth mindset, leaders create a culture that empowers individuals to push past limitations and unlock their full potential.

3. Embracing Change and Adaptability: Visionary leaders understand that in a rapidly evolving business landscape, change is inevitable. They embrace change as an opportunity rather than a threat, and they encourage their teams to do the same. By fostering an environment that values adaptability, visionary leaders empower their organizations to navigate uncertainty, seize emerging opportunities, and stay ahead of the competition.

4. Encouraging Risk-Taking and Innovation: Seeing beyond limits involves taking calculated risks and fostering a culture of innovation. Visionary leaders encourage their teams to explore new ideas, experiment with different approaches, and take calculated risks to drive innovation. They create an environment where failure is seen as a stepping stone towards

success, fostering a culture that supports and rewards creativity, exploration, and entrepreneurship.

5. Encouraging Continuous Improvement: Visionary leaders promote a mindset of continuous improvement. They recognize that there is always room for growth and progress, even when goals are achieved. By setting high standards, providing feedback, and promoting a culture of learning and development, visionary leaders inspire their teams to constantly challenge themselves and strive for excellence. This commitment to continuous improvement enables organizations to push boundaries and exceed expectations.

6. Fostering a Culture of Possibility: Seeing beyond limits involves creating a culture that believes in the potential for greatness. Visionary leaders instill confidence and optimism in their teams, fostering a belief that anything is possible. They encourage individuals to dream big, set ambitious goals, and pursue their aspirations with determination. By nurturing a culture of possibility, visionary leaders inspire their organizations to transcend limitations and achieve extraordinary outcomes.

The Visionary Advantage: In a cutthroat marketplace, having a clear and compelling vision provides us with a distinct competitive advantage. It acts as a magnetic force, attracting top talent, inspiring customer loyalty, and fostering strategic partnerships.

Our visionary organization exudes confidence and purpose, radiating an irresistible energy that draws stakeholders towards our mission. By effectively communicating our vision, we rally our teams and stakeholders around a common cause, fostering collaboration and driving collective efforts towards achieving extraordinary outcomes.

The visionary advantage refers to the unique benefits and competitive edge that visionary leaders and organizations gain by harnessing the power of vision.

Here's a closer look at the elements that contribute to the visionary advantage:
1. Strategic Clarity: Visionary leaders possess a clear and compelling vision that outlines the future direction of their organizations. This vision serves as a strategic compass, providing a sense of purpose, direction, and long-term goals. By communicating this vision effectively, leaders align their teams, stakeholders, and resources towards a common objective. The strategic clarity offered by a visionary leader enables everyone to understand the organization's mission, values, and strategic priorities, creating a focused and unified workforce.

2. Inspiration and Motivation: A powerful vision inspires and motivates individuals within the organization. It taps into their aspirations, instills a sense of meaning and purpose in their work, and fuels their commitment to achieving extraordinary results. Visionary leaders have the ability to paint a vivid picture of the future, compelling others to invest their time,

energy, and talents into realizing that vision. The inspiration and motivation derived from a compelling vision often lead to increased employee engagement, loyalty, and productivity.

3. Attraction and Retention of Top Talent: The visionary advantage attracts top talent to an organization. A clear and inspiring vision acts as a magnet, drawing individuals who share similar values and ambitions. Visionary leaders have the ability to articulate their vision in a way that resonates with potential employees, attracting those who are passionate about contributing to a greater purpose. This advantage in attracting top talent gives visionary organizations a competitive edge in acquiring the best resources and skills to drive their growth and innovation initiatives.

4. Innovation and Adaptability: Visionary leaders foster a culture of innovation and adaptability within their organizations. They encourage creativity, risk-taking, and the exploration of new ideas. By aligning their vision with a commitment to innovation, visionary leaders inspire their teams to think outside the box, challenge assumptions, and embrace change. This culture of innovation and adaptability enables organizations to stay ahead of market trends, anticipate disruptions, and seize opportunities for growth and competitive advantage.

5. Resilience in Times of Change: The visionary advantage provides organizations with resilience in the face of change and adversity. A well-defined vision serves as a guiding light during times of uncertainty, helping leaders and employees

navigate challenges with clarity and determination. By anchoring decisions and actions to the vision, visionary leaders instill confidence and stability within the organization, enabling it to adapt, pivot, and thrive in dynamic business environments.

6. Long-Term Strategic Alignment: Visionary leaders possess the ability to foster long-term strategic alignment within their organizations. They ensure that all initiatives, projects, and actions are aligned with the overarching vision. This alignment prevents fragmentation and ensures that everyone is working towards a common goal. By maintaining strategic focus and unity, visionary organizations optimize their resources, streamline decision-making processes, and achieve greater efficiency and effectiveness in executing their strategies.

Chart Your Course: A vision without action is merely a daydream. To harness the full power of our visionary outlook, we must translate our vision into actionable plans and initiatives. By setting measurable goals, creating strategic roadmaps, and executing with precision, we transform our vision into tangible results. A well-executed vision empowers our teams, builds momentum, and establishes a culture of achievement that propels our organization towards sustainable success.

Charting your course refers to the process of setting a clear direction and creating a strategic roadmap to achieve your business vision and goals. It involves careful planning, defining objectives, and mapping out the steps required to reach those objectives.

Here's a deeper explanation of what it means to chart your course:

1. Defining Objectives: To chart your course, you first need to clearly define your objectives. These objectives should align with your overarching vision and be specific, measurable, achievable, relevant, and time-bound (SMART). By setting clear objectives, you provide a concrete target to work towards and establish a foundation for your strategic roadmap.

2. Strategic Planning: Once you have defined your objectives, the next step is strategic planning. This involves identifying the key strategies, initiatives, and actions necessary to achieve your objectives. It requires a thorough analysis of internal and external factors that impact your business, such as market trends, competitive landscape, customer needs, and internal capabilities. Strategic planning enables you to make informed decisions and prioritize the most effective paths to success.

3. Developing a Roadmap: A strategic roadmap serves as a visual guide that outlines the major milestones, activities, and timelines needed to achieve your objectives. It breaks down the strategic plan into actionable steps and provides a clear path for your team to follow. The roadmap should include specific tasks, responsibilities, and resources required at each stage, ensuring that everyone understands their roles and the overall timeline for implementation.

4. Resource Allocation: Charting your course involves allocating resources effectively to support the implementation of your strategic roadmap. This includes financial resources, human capital, technology, and other necessary assets. By strategically allocating resources, you ensure that you have the necessary means to execute your plans and achieve your objectives in a timely manner.

5. Monitoring and Adjusting: Once your strategic roadmap is in motion, it is important to regularly monitor progress and make adjustments as needed. This involves tracking key performance indicators (KPIs) and milestones, evaluating the effectiveness of your strategies, and identifying any deviations or obstacles that may arise. By monitoring progress, you can proactively address challenges, adapt your plans, and keep your course on track.

6. Communication and Alignment: Effective communication is essential when charting your course. You need to ensure that your vision, objectives, and strategic roadmap are clearly communicated to all stakeholders, including employees, customers, investors, and partners. Transparent and consistent communication helps build alignment, fosters engagement, and keeps everyone focused on the common goal.

7. Flexibility and Agility: While charting your course involves careful planning, it is also important to maintain flexibility and agility. Business environments are dynamic, and unexpected opportunities or challenges may arise. Being open to adjustments and adapting your course when necessary

allows you to seize emerging opportunities and navigate changing circumstances effectively.

Elevate Your Business: The power of vision is not limited to top-level executives; it can permeate all levels of our organization. By fostering a culture that values and rewards visionary thinking, we tap into the collective creativity and ingenuity of our employees. Encouraging an environment that nurtures innovative ideas allows us to unlock untapped potential, fuel breakthrough results, and drive continuous improvement.

Elevating your business involves taking deliberate actions and implementing strategies to enhance its overall performance, competitiveness, and success. It's about pushing boundaries, surpassing expectations, and reaching new heights.

Here's a deeper explanation of what it means to elevate your business:

1. Strategic Differentiation: To elevate your business, you need to differentiate it from competitors.

This involves identifying and highlighting your unique value proposition, the factors that set your business apart and make it stand out in the market. By understanding your target audience's needs and preferences, you can develop strategies that emphasize your strengths, differentiate your offerings, and create a compelling reason for customers to choose your business over others.

2. Customer-Centric Approach: Elevating your business requires a strong focus on customer satisfaction and creating exceptional customer experiences. By putting customers at the center of your strategies, you can anticipate their needs, exceed their expectations, and build long-term relationships. This includes providing personalized services, actively seeking feedback, and continuously improving your products, processes, and interactions based on customer insights.

3. Innovation and Adaptability: Elevating your business involves embracing innovation and staying adaptable in a rapidly changing business landscape. Innovation can take various forms, such as developing new products, introducing disruptive technologies, or improving operational efficiency. By fostering a culture of creativity and experimentation, you can continuously innovate and adapt to evolving customer demands, industry trends, and emerging opportunities.

4. Operational Excellence: Elevating your business requires a commitment to operational excellence. This involves optimizing processes, enhancing productivity, and delivering consistent quality in your products or services. By streamlining operations, eliminating waste, and implementing efficient systems, you can improve profitability, customer satisfaction, and overall business performance.

5. Talent Development: Elevating your business goes hand in hand with developing your human capital. It involves attracting, nurturing, and retaining top talent. By investing in employee training, career development programs, and

fostering a positive work environment, you can build a skilled and motivated workforce. Engaged employees contribute to increased productivity, innovation, and customer satisfaction, ultimately elevating the overall performance of your business.

6. Strategic Partnerships: Elevating your business often involves forming strategic partnerships with other organizations. By collaborating with complementary businesses, you can access new markets, share resources, and leverage each other's strengths. Strategic partnerships can lead to increased brand visibility, expanded customer base, and enhanced capabilities, ultimately elevating the overall competitiveness and growth potential of your business.

7. Continuous Improvement: To elevate your business, you need to embrace a mindset of continuous improvement. This involves regularly assessing your business performance, identifying areas for enhancement, and implementing changes accordingly. By fostering a culture of learning, encouraging feedback, and seeking innovative solutions, you can continually refine and optimize your operations, products, and strategies.

CHAPTER 3: STRATEGIC SYNERGY(YOUR PURPOSE)

In today's tough commercial field, having a crystal-clear sense of purpose, connected with a well-defined vision and strong values, is not simply a lofty idea; it's a strategic need.

Defining your mission and integrating it with your business's vision and values produces a strong synergy that drives development, draws consumers, and fuels staff productivity. In this post, we dig into the relevance of identifying your purpose and present practical techniques to integrate your vision and values, ensuring your company surges forward in a purpose-driven industry.

Strategic synergy refers to the harmonic alignment and integration of diverse aspects inside a company or organization to achieve a bigger combined impact than the sum of their separate parts. It entails utilizing the interconnection of multiple components to enhance performance, competitive advantage, and overall company success.

In the context of identifying your mission, aligning your vision, and adopting your values, strategic synergy emerges as the coherent integration of these factors across your company strategy and operations. It is the strategic alignment of purpose, vision, and values that help your firm to prosper in a purpose-driven marketplace.

Strategic synergy works on multiple levels within a business:

1. Internal Alignment:
Strategic synergy begins inside the company, ensuring that all internal stakeholders, including executives, workers, and teams, are on the same page. By unifying the mission, vision, and values, everyone has a shared understanding of the organization's broad direction and the principles that govern its activities. This internal alignment encourages unity, teamwork, and a common motivation toward attaining the business's objectives.

2. External Alignment:
Strategic synergy goes beyond the internal workings of the company. It entails integrating mission, vision, and values with the expectations and demands of external stakeholders, including customers, suppliers, partners, and the wider community. When external stakeholders connect with and support the mission, vision, and values of a company, it develops relationships, generates trust, and boosts brand reputation, eventually driving growth and consumer loyalty.

3. Strategic Decision-Making:
Strategic synergy impacts the decision-making process at every level of the company. When purpose, vision, and values are well-defined and incorporated into the strategic planning

process, they serve as guiding principles that guide company choices. By continually analyzing possible opportunities, initiatives, and collaborations against these guiding principles, strategic choices become more focused, coherent, and aligned with the overall direction of the firm.

4. Competitive Advantage:
Strategic synergy generates a distinct competitive edge for firms. When mission, vision, and values are properly articulated and incorporated into the company plan, they distinguish the brand and resonate with consumers seeking deeper connections and shared beliefs. This alignment promotes brand positioning, attracts a devoted client base, and sets the firm apart from rivals.

5. Organizational Culture:
Strategic synergy leads to the establishment of purposeful and values-driven company culture. When purpose and values are interwoven in the fabric of the business, they impact the behavior, attitudes, and conventions inside the workplace. A purpose-driven culture supports employee engagement, productivity, and a strong feeling of belonging, recruiting top talent and establishing a great work environment.

The Power Of Purpose

The strength of purpose rests in its capacity to offer a distinct sense of direction, meaning, and drive to people and organizations. It goes beyond just financial aims or operational objectives and delves into a deeper, essential cause for existing. Purpose provides companies with a convincing response to the basic issue of "why" they exist and what influence they aspire to create.

Here are several essential factors that demonstrate the power of purpose:

1. Meaning and Fulfillment:
Purpose fills labor with a feeling of purpose and satisfaction. When people understand and connect with the goal of their job, they are more likely to feel deeper happiness and receive a sense of fulfillment from their efforts. This internal desire may lead to improved engagement, inventiveness, and a willingness to go the additional mile.

2. Guiding North Star:
Purpose operates as a guiding light, offering a clear direction for decision-making and strategic decisions. It acts as a filter that helps prioritize opportunities and match activities with the greater goal and vision of the business. When confronted with challenging decisions, a well-defined purpose helps direct the company towards options that are compatible with its fundamental values and long-term aims.

3. Inspiring Stakeholders:
Purpose has the potential to inspire and engage numerous stakeholders, including workers, consumers, investors, and partners. When a business's mission connects with these stakeholders, it fosters a feeling of shared values and a closer relationship. Purpose-driven firms generally attract loyal

consumers who identify with their goal and workers who are enthusiastic about making a significant difference.

4. Differentiation and Competitive Advantage:
A well-defined mission sets a firm different from its rivals. Purpose-driven firms have a distinctive narrative to tell and a compelling rationale for consumers to select them over alternatives. The purpose may define a company, attract a particular target group, and build a stronger emotional connection with consumers. It helps build a unique character and positioning that goes beyond product features or cost.

5. Resilience and Adaptability:
Purpose gives a stable basis through times of transition and uncertainty. When confronted with problems or disruptions, purpose-driven enterprises are better positioned to adapt and navigate through the storm. Purpose works as an anchor that keeps the organization focused on its long-term goals, allowing it to weather short-term failures and make strategic changes while keeping faithful to its fundamental values and purpose.

6. Positive Social Impact:
Purpose-driven companies can have a beneficial influence on society and contribute to a bigger cause. By integrating their mission with social and environmental activities, companies can drive positive change and build a better world. This dedication to social responsibility not only draws socially aware customers but also develops trust and increases the company's reputation.

Crafting A Compelling Vision

To prevail in the corporate realm, we need a vision that transcends the banal. A well-crafted vision statement articulates the future we want to build, stirring enthusiasm and motivating action. It sets the framework for strategic planning, unites our team around a unified aim, and inspires the quest for excellence. A compelling vision pulls us ahead, pushing us to fight barriers and grasp opportunities with unyielding commitment.

Crafting a compelling vision includes providing a clear and inspirational depiction of the future state that a firm intends to reach. It extends beyond the day-to-day activities and defines a long-term orientation for the business. A captivating vision serves as a rallying point that catches the imagination of stakeholders and leads to strategic decision-making.

Here are some essential characteristics that demonstrate the relevance and advantages of building a compelling vision:

1. Clarity and Focus:
A compelling vision gives clarity and focus by outlining a desirable future condition. It helps executives and workers understand where the company is headed and what it seeks to achieve. This clarity facilitates alignment and guarantees that efforts are focused toward a unified objective, preventing distractions and encouraging a shared sense of purpose.

2. Inspiration & Motivation:
A well-crafted vision inspires and drives stakeholders. It provides a vision of a future that is attractive, significant, and worth pursuing. By defining a compelling vision, leaders can generate passion and excitement among their teams, igniting a collective desire to accomplish amazing achievements. It functions as a source of inspiration through hard times and fosters tenacity and resilience.

3. Strategic Direction:
A vision offers strategic direction, providing a guide for decision-making and resource allocation. When presented with alternatives, a compelling vision helps leaders assess solutions based on their alignment with the intended future state. It fosters strategic thinking and allows proactive planning, ensuring that choices are made in keeping with the long-term objectives of the company.

4. Differentiation and Competitive Advantage:
A compelling vision helps separate a firm from its competition. It establishes a distinctive position in the market and sets the firm apart by articulating its distinct value offer. A vision that connects with clients may attract dedicated followers who agree with the organization's objectives and are attracted to its purpose. This distinction might lead to competitive advantage and greater market share.

5. Alignment and Engagement:
A compelling vision aligns and engages stakeholders. It provides a sense of shared purpose and develops a feeling of

belonging and dedication among workers, customers, and partners. When people consider themselves as contributors to a broader vision, they are more likely to be interested, involved, and eager to work jointly toward its fulfillment.

6. Measurement and Accountability:
A compelling vision gives a framework for assessment and responsibility. It creates key performance indicators (KPIs) that fit with the planned future state, enabling progress to be monitored and evaluated. By frequently assessing performance against the goal, companies may discover areas of improvement, recognize accomplishments, and hold people and teams responsible for their contributions.

7. Adaptability and Innovation:
Crafting a compelling vision stimulates flexibility and creativity. It should not be a static declaration, but rather a dynamic and changing guidepost that accepts change and fosters innovative thinking. A vision that supports innovation allows workers to explore new ideas and techniques to attain the desired future state, allowing the firm to remain ahead of the curve and adapt effectively to market disruptions.

Identifying Core Values

Identifying core values entails understanding and articulating the essential ideas and beliefs that influence the behavior, choices, and culture of a company or organization. Core values serve as the moral compass and ethical underpinning, affecting how people and the company as a whole function.

Here are some major characteristics that show the relevance and advantages of recognizing core values:

1. Defining Organizational Identity:
Core values are a vital aspect of the identity and character of a company. They define its culture, identifying what it stands for and how it functions. By establishing core values, a firm establishes its essential beliefs and provides a framework for decision-making and conduct.

2. Guiding Principles:
Core values operate as guiding principles that guide activities, decisions, and relationships inside the business. They establish a set of criteria against which actions and decisions are judged. When fundamental values are clear and regularly respected, they generate a feeling of alignment and develop a shared understanding of what is expected from workers at all levels.

3. Building Trust and Reputation:
Core principles help to create trust and a favorable reputation. When a firm runs based on a set of clearly articulated and implemented values, it creates trust among customers, workers, and other stakeholders. Consistently adhering to fundamental principles promotes credibility, trustworthiness, and a feeling of integrity, which may increase brand reputation and attract loyal consumers.

4. Cultural Alignment:

Identifying fundamental principles helps develop a strong and coherent business culture. When core values are profoundly established in the organization's DNA, they govern the actions, conventions, and attitudes inside the workplace. A strong values-based culture draws workers who align with those values, generating a feeling of belonging, engagement, and dedication.

5. Decision-Making Framework:

Core values serve as a decision-making framework, allowing employees to make decisions that are compatible with the organization's beliefs. When confronted with issues or obstacles, workers may resort to fundamental principles to guide their actions. This consistent decision-making process encourages ethical conduct, supports integrity, and decreases the danger of behaviors that might hurt the organization's reputation.

6. Attracting and Retaining Talent:

Organizations that define and promote strong core principles are more likely to recruit and retain great personnel. Employees are increasingly seeking companies that correspond with their own beliefs and give a feeling of purpose beyond financial reward. Expressed core values may function as a magnet, pulling employees who connect with those principles and improving employee engagement and loyalty.

7. Differentiation in the Market:

Core principles may distinguish a firm in a competitive environment. When a company's values fit with the values of its target audience, it generates a deep emotional connection and develops brand loyalty. By stressing fundamental values in marketing and communication activities, a firm may separate itself from rivals and attract consumers who share those values.

8. Consistency and Long-Term Success:

Consistently respecting basic beliefs provides stability and long-term success. Organizations that stay loyal to their basic beliefs, especially in the face of adversities or external pressures, create a reputation for dependability, trustworthiness, and resilience. This consistency helps ongoing performance and the building of a strong corporate identity.

Strategies For Alignment

Strategies for alignment comprise practical measures and ways to ensure that the mission, vision, and values of a company are successfully integrated and aligned across the organization. Alignment is crucial to promote consistent behavior, decision-making, and activities that support the broader aims and ideals of the organization.

Here are important techniques to establish alignment:

1. Define and Refine:

Begin by clearly identifying the mission, vision, and values of the firm. Reflect on their correctness, relevance, and alignment with the developing demands of the company and its stakeholders. If required, tweak them to ensure they are appealing, clear, and connect with the anticipated future state.

2. Communicate and Cascade:
Effective communication is crucial for alignment. Ensure that the mission, vision, and values are consistently articulated across all levels of the business. This involves engaging leaders, managers, and workers via multiple channels including meetings, presentations, internal communications, and training sessions. Cascading the message ensures that everyone knows and adopts the guiding concepts.

3. Integrate into Strategy:
Align the mission, vision, and values with the organization's strategic planning procedures. Integrate them into the establishment of goals, objectives, and initiatives. Evaluate strategic choices and efforts against the guiding principles to ensure consistency and alignment. This integration guarantees that the organization's direction and activities are closely tied to its mission and vision.

4. Align Performance Measures:
Develop performance metrics and key performance indicators (KPIs) that match the mission, vision, and values. These measurements should represent the expected results and actions that support the guiding principles. Regularly monitor and analyze performance against these indicators, offering feedback and recognition to people and teams that reflect the linked values.

5. Empower and Engage Employees:

Empower workers to participate in the alignment process. contribute chances for them to contribute ideas, thoughts, and comments linked to the mission, vision, and values. Engage workers in conversations and activities that foster awareness, ownership, and commitment to the guiding values. Encourage them to connect their work and choices with the common values of the business.

6. Training and Development:

Offer training and development programs that reinforce the mission, vision, and values. Provide personnel with the information and abilities required to comprehend and implement the guiding principles in their day-to-day job. This training helps workers absorb the ideas and maintains a culture of alignment across the firm.

7. Review and Realignment:

Regularly examine and analyze the alignment of the organization with its mission, vision, and values. Monitor changes in the business environment, stakeholder expectations, and internal dynamics that may necessitate modifications. Ensure that the guiding principles stay current and continue to steer the company successfully. Actively solicit comments and input from stakeholders to inform realignment efforts.

8. Lead by Example:

Leaders have a critical role in driving alignment. They must embody the mission, vision, and values and lead by example.

Demonstrate behaviors consistent with the guiding principles, make choices that reflect the shared values, and express the significance of alignment via their actions. Leadership commitment to alignment produces a culture that encourages the desired behaviors and mentality.

By employing these tactics, firms may establish a stronger alignment of mission, vision, and values across the company. This alignment provides consistency, clarity, and a common understanding, eventually pushing joint efforts toward reaching the intended future state and fulfilling the organization's full potential.

a) Define and clarify: Let's take the time to clarify our mission, vision, and values. Are they laser-focused, appealing, and relevant to our target market? If not, it's time for some fine-tuning. We must ensure they represent our objectives and speak clearly to the shifting demands of our consumers.

b) Communicate and Engage: Consistent and effective communication is crucial. We need to guarantee that all stakeholders, from workers to consumers, understand and accept our mission, vision, and values. Regular interaction and open communication build a common understanding, commitment, and buy-in.

c) Integrate into Strategy: Strategic alignment asks us to integrate our mission, vision, and values into the very fabric of our company strategy. Every decision, effort, and action should be reviewed through the prism of our purpose-driven guiding principles. By doing so, we build a unified and effective strategy that strengthens our competitive advantage.

d) Foster a Purposeful Culture: Our workplace culture must mirror our mission and values. We need to develop an atmosphere that supports cooperation, creativity, and accountability. Recognizing and rewarding actions that line with our guiding principles strengthens our purposeful culture and attracts top people who are enthusiastic about our objective.

Inspiring Leadership

Inspiring leadership refers to the capacity of leaders to encourage, empower, and guide people toward a shared goal or vision. It entails encouraging people and teams to realize their greatest potential, promoting a happy and productive work environment, and driving significant change inside the business.

Here are essential features that show the relevance and qualities of inspirational leadership:

1. Visionary Communication:
Inspiring leaders successfully convey a compelling vision and purpose. They define a clear and compelling direction that connects with their team members, linking their efforts toward a common objective. Through passionate and effective communication, they explain the vision's significance, relevance, and potential influence, pushing people to take action.

2. Leading by Example:
Leaders that inspire others lead by example. They exemplify the beliefs, habits, and work ethic they demand from their team members. By continually exhibiting honesty, determination, and a strong work ethic, they establish a high example and motivate others to follow suit. Leading by example fosters trust, credibility, and respect among team members.

3. Empowering and Developing Others:
Inspiring leaders enable people and teams to take responsibility for their work and improve their talents. They create possibilities for advancement, encourage people to venture out of their comfort zones, and build a culture of continual learning. By cultivating talent, promoting professional growth, and encouraging autonomy, they empower people to attain their greatest potential.

4. Building Relationships and Trust:
Inspiring leaders establish solid connections based on trust and mutual respect. They actively listen to their team members, appreciate their opinions, and create an inclusive and collaborative work atmosphere. By developing trust, leaders create a feeling of psychological safety, enabling open communication and cooperation. Trust is important for people to feel motivated, engaged, and inspired to deliver their best.

5. Emotional Intelligence and Empathy:
Inspiring leaders exhibit emotional intelligence and sensitivity. They understand the feelings and needs of their

team members, establishing a supportive and empathic work atmosphere. By displaying empathy, leaders engage with their team on a deeper level, understanding their issues, and offering the appropriate assistance. This sympathetic approach fosters solid connections and provides a feeling of belonging and well-being.

6. Recognition & Appreciation:
Inspiring leaders understand and appreciate the efforts of their team members. They give real praise and acknowledgment for individual and team successes, promoting a healthy and stimulating work culture. Celebrating victories and emphasizing the significance of each team member's contributions boosts morale, motivation, and a feeling of pride in their job.

7. Resilience and Positive Mindset:
Inspiring leaders display resilience and keep a positive perspective, even in trying situations. They embrace difficulties and failures as chances for development and learning. By exhibiting optimism, problem-solving abilities, and flexibility, they empower their team members to approach obstacles with confidence and inventiveness.

8. Continuous Improvement and Innovation:
Inspiring leaders foster a culture of constant development and innovation. They stimulate innovative thinking, accept new ideas, and empower their team to question the existing quo. By building an environment that encourages experimenting

and learning from mistakes, they create a growth mentality and drive innovation throughout the firm.

Stakeholder Engagement

Stakeholder engagement refers to the practice of actively engaging and creating relationships with people or groups that have a vested interest or are impacted by the operations and consequences of a company or organization. Effective stakeholder engagement entails knowing their views, needs, and expectations and actively seeking their opinion and participation.

Here are significant factors that emphasize the relevance and advantages of stakeholder engagement:

1. Understanding Stakeholder Perspectives:
Engaging stakeholders helps companies to obtain a greater grasp of their opinions, issues, and goals. By actively listening and soliciting advice, organizations may unearth significant insights that guide decision-making, strategy formulation, and problem-solving. This knowledge enables firms to adjust to stakeholder demands and expectations, developing trust and fostering productive connections.

2. Building Trust and Relationships:
Stakeholder participation is vital for developing trust and solid partnerships. By including stakeholders in meaningful discourse, companies display respect for their opinions and appreciate their contributions. Transparent and open

communication develops trust, credibility, and long-term connections, building a foundation of support for the organization's efforts.

3. Informed Decision-Making:
Engaging stakeholders offers companies a larger variety of opinions and information for decision-making. By collecting advice and feedback from stakeholders, firms might discover insights that may have been ignored. This inclusive decision-making approach helps ensure that choices are well-informed, relevant, and sensitive to stakeholder interests.

4. Enhancing Reputation and Legitimacy:
Stakeholder involvement aids in developing a favorable reputation and credibility for companies. When firms actively interact with stakeholders, they show their commitment to recognizing and resolving the concerns and interests of individuals touched by their activities. This participation strengthens their social license to function and may boost their reputation as a responsible and trustworthy company.

5. Collaborative Problem-Solving and Innovation:
Stakeholder participation may stimulate cooperation, problem-solving, and innovation. By including stakeholders in talks and decision-making processes, companies may draw their various knowledge and viewpoints. This collaborative approach frequently leads to more imaginative and successful solutions, as stakeholders bring new ideas and insights to the table.

6. Alignment with Stakeholder Expectations:
Engaging stakeholders helps companies connect their actions and strategies with stakeholder expectations. By actively soliciting feedback, companies may better understand the requirements, goals, and values of stakeholders, enabling them to modify their plans and activities appropriately. This alignment boosts stakeholder satisfaction, lowers disputes, and increases support for business objectives.

7. Risk Mitigation:
Engaging stakeholders may help uncover possible risks and difficulties early on, enabling businesses to address them proactively. By integrating stakeholders in risk assessment and management processes, firms may acquire a wider view of possible hazards and devise methods to minimize them. This proactive strategy decreases the possibility of negative repercussions on stakeholders and the company.

CHAPTER 4:NURTURING CREATIVITY

In today's hyper-competitive corporate market, the capacity to produce fresh ideas is a game-changer. Creativity is no longer a luxury; it's a strategic need for keeping ahead of the competition. To achieve long-term success, businesses must develop a culture of creativity that supports the production of breakthrough ideas.

Creating such a culture begins from the top. As company leaders, we must set the tone and emphasize cultivating creativity. We must promote innovation, making it a basic value imprinted in the DNA of our businesses. By building an atmosphere that encourages and celebrates creative thinking, we motivate our employees to push boundaries and think beyond the box.

Collaboration is a crucial driver of creative achievement. By building diverse teams with distinct views, experiences, and skill sets, we can ignite the fires of invention. Encourage cross-functional cooperation and build channels for idea sharing. When employees from multiple departments cooperate and share their skills, they develop a rich tapestry of ideas that leads to innovative solutions.

Investing in the correct resources is crucial for cultivating creativity. Provide cutting-edge tools, technology, and software that allow our employees to unleash their creative potential. By eliminating technology hurdles and providing our employees with the newest innovation-enabling tools, we open the road for transformational ideas to bloom.

A culture of constant learning is a cornerstone of creative thinking. Encourage staff to explore personal and professional development opportunities. By being informed of industry trends, attending conferences, and participating in continuous learning, our staff remains at the forefront of innovation. Incentivize and reward their dedication to continued growth, boosting their enthusiasm for producing fresh ideas.

Building an inclusive and supportive work atmosphere is key to unleashing creativity. Foster a culture where every voice is heard and various ideas are appreciated.

Foster open dialogue, pay attention attentively, and provide constructive criticism. By offering a safe place for speech and courteous arguments, we create an atmosphere where creativity flourishes.

Allocate dedicated time and physical venues for creative thought. Establish designated hours for brainstorming and innovation, away from the stress of everyday deadlines. Create dedicated "innovation labs" or collaborative areas that stimulate creativity. By offering the time and space for unrestrained creative inquiry, we inspire our teams to unleash their imaginations and generate game-changing ideas.

In conclusion, cultivating creativity and producing original ideas are vital for corporate success in today's tough market. As corporate leaders, we must support a culture of creativity, foster collaboration, offer the proper tools, develop an inclusive work environment, and carve out specific time and space for creative thought. By embracing innovation as a major pillar of our business strategy, we position our companies for long-term success and market leadership. So let's stoke the flames of creativity, and watch as our teams transform our industry with their amazing ideas.

In addition to the tactics described before, here are some suggestions to further promote creativity and produce unique ideas inside your business:

Encourage "Out of Office" Inspiration

Encourage workers to experience other surroundings outside the workplace to inspire their creativity. This might involve visiting art exhibits, attending business conferences, or taking part in workshops and seminars. Exposing oneself to different experiences and viewpoints might generate fresh thoughts.

Encouraging "Out of Office" inspiration means actively promoting and supporting activities and experiences outside of the usual office setting to promote creativity and develop unique ideas. This approach understands that creativity and new views sometimes originate from encounters outside the limits of the job.

Here are some crucial elements to consider while fostering "Out of Office" inspiration:

1. Embracing Novel places: Encourage workers to explore other places and situations that are unrelated to their day-to-day job. This might be visiting art galleries, attending

business conferences and trade exhibits, engaging in community activities, or simply enjoying nature walks. By exposing oneself to different environments and circumstances, individuals might receive fresh ideas and inspiration that can be applied to their job.

2. Learning from Other Industries: Encourage workers to investigate and learn from industries beyond their own. By studying how other sectors manage difficulties, embrace new technology, and innovate, workers may obtain useful ideas and apply them in unique ways to their job. This cross-pollination of ideas may lead to novel solutions and methods.

3. Networking and Collaboration: Encourage workers to network and cooperate with individuals from diverse sectors or areas of expertise. This might entail attending networking events, joining professional groups or communities, or engaging in collaborative initiatives outside of their usual job obligations. Interacting with persons from varied backgrounds may expose workers to fresh ideas, viewpoints, and techniques, boosting creativity and producing inventive thinking.

4. continual Learning: Encourage workers to participate in continual learning and self-development activities outside of the job. This might entail attending workshops, seminars, or online courses linked to their hobbies or areas of professional advancement. By investing in their personal growth, workers enhance their knowledge base and skill set, bringing new insights and ideas back to their job.

5. Travel and Cultural Experiences: Encourage workers to discover new cultures, either via personal travel or by interacting with varied populations within their local region. Experiencing diverse cultures broadens minds, exposes people to alternate ways of thinking, and might generate new ideas. Encourage staff to share their travel experiences and cultural learnings with their colleagues, promoting a culture of open-mindedness and inquiry.

6. contemplation and Disconnecting: Encourage workers to take time for contemplation and to unplug from work frequently. This might mean encouraging frequent breaks, supporting vacation time, and fostering a good work-life balance. Providing chances for relaxation and rejuvenation

helps workers to replenish their creative energy and typically leads to greater innovation and new views upon their return.

Embrace Failure as a Learning Opportunity

Create a culture that welcomes failure as a natural part of the creative process. Encourage workers to take measured chances and reward them for their efforts, even if the result is not always successful. By considering failure as a worthwhile learning experience, you build a mentality that fosters experimentation and perseverance.

Embracing failure as a learning opportunity is an attitude and strategy that encourages people and organizations to regard failure not as a setback or cause of shame, but as a beneficial experience from which to learn and develop. By reframing failure in this manner, you create a climate that supports creativity, risk-taking, and resilience.

Here are some crucial elements to consider while accepting failure as a learning opportunity:

1. Cultivating a Growth Mindset: Encourage people to embrace a growth mindset, which is the concept that talents

and intellect can be developed through effort, practice, and learning. This perspective realizes that failure is not an endpoint but rather a stepping stone on the route to success. By creating a growth mentality, people are more inclined to persist, take chances, and regard failure as an opportunity for progress.

2. Normalize Failure: Create a culture that normalizes failure and fosters open dialogues around it. When people feel comfortable and encouraged in expressing their shortcomings, they are more inclined to learn from them and seek constructive comments. By destigmatizing failure, you create a climate where people are ready to take measured chances, experiment, and innovate without fear of criticism or negative repercussions.

3. Extracting Lessons: Encourage individuals and teams to reflect on failures and extract meaningful lessons from them. Facilitate talks or post-mortem meetings where participants may freely discuss what went wrong, what might have been done better, and what insights they got from the experience. Encourage them to develop specific activities and techniques to utilize in future initiatives.

4. Promote Iteration and adaptability: Emphasize the necessity of iteration and adaptability in the face of failure. When a given strategy fails, encourage people to iterate, tweak, and adjust their tactics. By considering setbacks as chances to refine and grow, people gain the resilience and flexibility required to overcome problems and create inventive solutions.

5. Encourage Risk-Taking and Experimentation: Foster a culture that supports measured risk-taking and experimentation. Provide the necessary resources, support, and autonomy for people to explore new ideas and methods. Encourage folks to venture beyond their comfort zones and explore new ideas, even if there is a danger of failure. Celebrate the bravery to take chances and learn from the results, regardless of success or failure.

6. Share Failure experiences: Share experiences of failure and subsequent success inside the company. Highlight cases when failure led to useful insights, course correction, and ultimate breakthroughs. By sharing these tales, you construct a narrative that highlights failure as a normal part of the creative

process and supports the concept that failure may eventually lead to success.

7. Recognize and praise Learning: Acknowledge and praise individuals and teams for their ability to learn from mistakes and apply those lessons successfully. By celebrating the process of learning and progress, you stress the value of accepting failure as a stepping stone toward improvement and innovation.

Foster Interdisciplinary cooperation

Encourage cooperation not just within teams but also between departments and specialties. By bringing together employees from multiple backgrounds, such as marketing, engineering, design, and sales, you may produce a cross-pollination of ideas and build unique solutions that incorporate different viewpoints.

Fostering interdisciplinary cooperation entails encouraging employees from various disciplines, departments, or areas of expertise within your business to come together and work on projects or initiatives. This approach emphasizes that varied viewpoints and skill sets may lead to more imaginative and complete solutions to complicated situations.

Here are some crucial elements to consider while establishing multidisciplinary collaboration:

1. Establish Common Goals: Clearly outline the common goals or objectives that the multidisciplinary team seeks to accomplish. This gives a unifying focus and guarantees that all team members are oriented towards a single objective. Common objectives generate a feeling of coherence and allow cooperation across diverse disciplines.

2.Establish a Collaborative Atmosphere: Cultivate an atmosphere that promotes and facilitates collaboration. Promote open dialogue, trust, and esteem among colleagues. Design physical spaces or digital forums that facilitate the sharing of information, brainstorming, and the exchange of ideas. Urge people to contribute their individual perspectives and attentively listen to the views of others.

3. Break Down Silos: Overcome departmental or disciplinary silos by fostering cross-functional contact and cooperation. Facilitate chances for personnel from various departments or areas of expertise to come together, such as via cross-departmental initiatives, task forces, or working groups.

By breaking down silos, you allow various skills to converge and develop breakthrough ideas.

4. Promote information Sharing: Encourage team members to share their information, experiences, and best practices. Provide chances for learning and skill development across disciplines, such as workshops, training sessions, or knowledge-sharing sessions. This helps people obtain a better grasp of many disciplines and encourages a culture of constant learning and progress.

5. Facilitate Effective Communication: Effective communication is vital for multidisciplinary teamwork. Establish explicit routes and means for communication among team members, such as frequent meetings, project management software, or collaborative platforms. Encourage active listening, empathy, and the capacity to convey ideas across disciplines. By supporting good communication, you promote cooperation and guarantee that everyone's opinions are heard and respected.

6. welcome Diversity of opinion: Recognize and welcome the diversity of opinion and viewpoints within the multidisciplinary team. Different disciplines contribute

distinct skills, perspectives, and ways of thinking to the table. Encourage team members to embrace and exploit this variety to question preconceptions, stimulate creativity, and arrive at more comprehensive and well-rounded solutions.

7. build Mutual Learning: Encourage team members to learn from one another and build a culture of mutual learning. Provide chances for skill-sharing, mentorship, or reverse mentoring, where persons with various degrees of expertise may learn from one another. This encourages a development mentality, develops camaraderie, and boosts teamwork.

8. Facilitate a Shared Language: Interdisciplinary cooperation frequently includes persons from diverse professions with their jargon and terminology. Facilitate the establishment of a shared language or common understanding that facilitates successful communication and information transmission. This might entail building glossaries, providing training workshops on common concepts, or encouraging people to express their ideas in accessible terms.

Implement Idea Management Systems

Establish a method for recording, analyzing, and implementing ideas inside your business. Utilize technological platforms or applications that allow workers to submit and discuss ideas, monitor their development, and acknowledge contributions. This rigorous approach guarantees that no good idea goes ignored or underused.

Implementing idea management systems requires building organized procedures and platforms to collect, assess, and apply ideas inside your firm. These methods give a systematic way to manage ideas, stimulate creativity, and ensure that key insights and proposals are neither neglected nor lost.

Here are some crucial elements to consider while developing concept management systems:

1. Centralized Idea Repository: Establish a centralized repository or platform where workers may contribute their ideas. This may be a digital platform, such as an idea management software or an internal collaboration tool. The repository should be freely available to all workers, enabling them to contribute ideas at any time.

2. Clearly Defined Submission Method: Define a clear and user-friendly method for idea submission. Communicate the parameters, criteria, and expectations for submitting ideas. Make the procedure clear and accessible to promote mass involvement. Provide support and direction to workers who may have issues or require help with the submission process.

3. Evaluation and Selection Criteria: Develop a set of criteria for assessing and choosing ideas. These criteria might include elements such as practicality, impact, alignment with company objectives, resource needs, and possible advantages. Establish a clear review method that assures fairness and consistency in analyzing proposals.

4. Cross-Functional Evaluation Teams: Form cross-functional teams responsible for analyzing and reviewing submitted ideas. Include people from various departments or areas of expertise to contribute varied viewpoints to the review process. These teams may give a full examination of the concepts based on the established criteria.

5. Feedback and Iteration: Provide feedback to those who submit ideas, regardless of whether their ideas are picked or not. Constructive criticism helps workers understand why their ideas were picked or how they might improve their proposals in the future. Encourage people to iterate and modify their ideas based on the feedback received, promoting a culture of continuous improvement.

6. Resource Allocation: Allocate adequate resources, including time, finance, and manpower, to execute chosen ideas. This indicates a commitment to bringing creative ideas to completion and guarantees that viable ideas are given the necessary assistance to succeed. Clearly express the resources available for execution to excite staff and create trust in the idea management process.

7. monitoring and Progress Monitoring: Implement a mechanism for monitoring the progress of chosen concepts. This enables a clear view of the implementation process and assures accountability. Regularly inform participants on the progress and consequences of implemented ideas to reaffirm the importance of their participation.

8. Recognition and Rewards: Establish a framework to recognize and reward workers for their contributions to the idea management process. Celebrate and reward people whose ideas have been adopted and have had a beneficial influence on the company. This acknowledgment stimulates continued engagement and inspires staff to continue developing unique ideas.

Promote a good Work-Life Balance

Recognize that creativity flourishes when people have a good work-life balance. Encourage workers to take breaks, indulge in hobbies, and pursue personal interests outside of work. Providing flexibility and supporting well-being not only promotes creativity but also enhances overall productivity and work happiness.

Promoting a good work-life balance entails developing an organizational culture and adopting procedures that value the well-being and personal lives of workers alongside their professional duties. It emphasizes the significance of maintaining a harmonic integration between work and home life to enhance productivity, contentment, and overall employee well-being.

Here are some crucial elements to consider while creating a good work-life balance:

1. explicit Expectations and Boundaries: Set explicit expectations around work hours, availability, and response times. Encourage workers to set boundaries between work and

personal life, ensuring that they have scheduled time for rest, relaxation, and personal responsibilities. Communicate and emphasize the necessity of respecting these limits.

2. Flexible Work Arrangements: Offer flexible work arrangements, such as flextime, remote work, reduced workweeks, or job sharing. This flexibility enables workers to have greater control over their schedules and tailor their job to their requirements. By adjusting specific situations, workers may better manage their commitments while completing their professional obligations.

3. Urgent Vacation and Time Off: Actively urge workers to take their entitled vacation and time off. Create a supportive atmosphere where workers feel comfortable taking their vacation days without fear of criticism or negative repercussions. Encourage managers to lead by example by taking holidays themselves. Taking frequent breaks and time off increases work-life balance decreases burnout and boosts productivity and creativity upon returning to work.

4. Wellness Programs & Support: Implement wellness programs that encourage physical, mental, and emotional

well-being. Offer services, such as employee assistance programs, mental health initiatives, stress management training, or wellness challenges. Encourage healthy behaviors, self-care routines, and work-life balance education to help workers in preserving their well-being.

5. Respect for Personal Time: Encourage a culture that respects personal time and discourages after-hours work contact unless essential. Encourage managers and team members to be careful of avoiding interrupting or invading others' time unless there is an urgent circumstance. Setting limits around communication outside of business hours fosters a healthy separation between work and personal life.

6. Encourage Hobbies and Interests: Support workers in following their hobbies, interests, and personal passions. Recognize and honor workers' outside accomplishments, like engagement in athletics, creative interests, or community activity. Encouraging workers to participate in activities that offer them pleasure and satisfaction outside of work benefits their overall well-being and work-life balance.

7. Managerial Support and Role Modeling: Train managers to be supportive of work-life balance and lead by example. Managers should encourage their teams to promote work-life balance, model healthy boundaries, and help workers in balancing their personal and professional duties efficiently. Managers that value work-life balance have a beneficial ripple effect across the business.

8. Regular Check-Ins and Feedback: Conduct regular check-ins with workers to measure their work-life balance satisfaction and give help when required. Create an open and trustworthy atmosphere where workers feel comfortable expressing any issues they have in attaining work-life balance. Encourage input on policies and practices to guarantee continual development in fostering work-life balance within the business.

.

Seek External Insights

Seeking external viewpoints includes actively seeking information, thoughts, and comments from persons and organizations outside of your business. It acknowledges the benefits of varied opinions, skills, and experiences in generating innovation, problem-solving, and decision-making.

Here are some crucial elements to consider while obtaining outsider perspectives:

1. Customer Insights: Engage with your customers to obtain a better knowledge of their requirements, preferences, and trouble areas. Conduct consumer surveys, interviews, focus groups, or usability testing sessions to get important feedback. Incorporating the voice of the consumer helps connect your goods, services, and initiatives with their expectations, eventually boosting customer happiness and loyalty.

2. Industry Experts and Thought Leaders: Connect with industry experts, thought leaders, and influencers who possess significant knowledge and expertise in your sector. Attend conferences, seminars, or webinars where these professionals share insights and best practices. Engage in discussions, ask questions, and seek their insights on industry trends, upcoming technology, and novel methods.

3. Advisory Boards and Consultants: Establish an advisory board or engage with external consultants who may give impartial and competent counsel. These people provide new

viewpoints, specific skills, and a better awareness of market trends. They may give insights on strategic decision-making, market analyses, or unique company difficulties, helping you make educated and inventive decisions.

4. Partner and Supplier Collaboration: Collaborate with partners, suppliers, or vendors to acquire their insights on company operations, market trends, or product development. Foster open communication lines and create frequent meetings or joint workshops to exchange ideas, share information, and explore collaboration prospects. This partnership may lead to mutually beneficial ideas and better business results.

5. Cross-Industry Pollination: Look outside your current industry and seek ideas from other sectors or disciplines. Identify analogous difficulties, trends, or creative techniques in other sectors that might be adopted to your own. Attend conferences or gatherings outside of your sector to obtain new insights and find unique methods of problem-solving.

6. User Testing and input: Engage external users or beta testers to gain input on your goods, services, or prototypes.

This user-centric approach helps you to understand how your solutions are viewed, find areas for development, and confirm assumptions. Incorporating external input early in the development process enhances the chance of creating solutions that satisfy consumer expectations.

7. Academic and Research Collaborations: Collaborate with academic institutions, research organizations, or universities to tap into their knowledge and research discoveries. Engaging in collaborative research projects, internships, or knowledge-sharing efforts may give access to cutting-edge research, innovative approaches, and emerging trends in relevant domains. These connections may stimulate innovation and help your business remain at the forefront of knowledge.

8. Networking and Community Involvement: Engage in networking activities and engage in industry or professional communities. Attend networking events, join online forums, or engage in relevant social media groups. Actively seek discussions, ask questions, and contribute your skills. This engagement exposes you to other viewpoints, stimulates

information exchange, and generates chances for cooperation and creativity.

Celebrate and Share Success Stories

Celebrating and sharing success stories requires recognizing and promoting the accomplishments, milestones, and creative triumphs inside your firm. It generates a culture of recognition, inspiration, and learning, while also building a feeling of pride and togetherness among workers.

Here are some crucial factors to consider when celebrating and sharing success stories:

1. Recognition and Appreciation: Recognize and recognize people or teams who have accomplished remarkable accomplishments or milestones. Celebrate their achievements, devotion, and inventive thinking. This acknowledgment may take different forms, such as public acknowledgment at team meetings, company-wide announcements, or individual words of thanks from leaders or peers.

2. Internal Communication Channels: Utilize internal communication channels to communicate success stories

across the business. This may include corporate newsletters, intranet platforms, or specific communication channels like chat groups or forums. Regularly highlight and share success stories to keep staff informed, encouraged, and engaged.

3. Case Studies and Best Practices: Develop case studies or best practice papers that record successful projects, initiatives, or creative solutions. These tools serve as a knowledge-sharing tool and encourage others inside the business. Share these case studies via numerous media, making them available to workers for reference and learning.

4. Peer Recognition and Learning Forums: Establish forums or platforms where workers may acknowledge and learn from one another's accomplishments. Encourage workers to share their success stories, lessons learned, and new ways with their colleagues. This encourages a collaborative and learning-oriented culture, where workers may take inspiration from their colleagues' successes.

5. Cross-Departmental Sharing:
Encourage cross-departmental sharing of success stories to enhance information transfer and stimulate cooperation.

Provide chances for teams or individuals from other departments to communicate their triumphs to others. This not only shows success but also generates a feeling of togetherness and builds a culture of cooperation and learning throughout the business.

6. Awards and Recognition Programs: Establish awards or recognition programs that highlight remarkable contributions, innovations, or accomplishments. These programs might contain categories linked to innovation, consumer impact, collaboration, or individual greatness. Regularly host award ceremonies or events to acknowledge and celebrate the winners, creating enthusiasm and inspiration throughout the workplace.

7. Celebratory Events and Team Activities: Organize celebratory events or team activities to celebrate noteworthy accomplishments or milestones. This might involve team trips, special meals, or company-wide celebrations. Such gatherings give a chance for workers to get together, celebrate collective accomplishments, and improve connections inside the firm.

8. External Recognition: Seek chances to communicate success stories externally, such as via news releases, industry conferences, or awards. External acknowledgment not only increases your organization's image but also stimulates staff by displaying their accomplishments to a larger audience. It may attract talent, prospective partners, and consumers who are inspired by your organization's unique successes.

Provide Mentorship and Coaching

Providing mentoring and coaching entails matching people with more experienced professionals who can advise, assist, and share their knowledge and skills. This mentor-mentee connection supports personal and professional growth, increases skills development, and stimulates creativity inside your firm.

Here are some crucial elements to consider while offering mentoring and coaching:

1. Establish Mentorship Programs: Set up official mentorship programs inside your business. These initiatives might pair experienced personnel with younger or less-experienced persons who would benefit from their instruction and assistance. Provide rules and tools to assist mentors and mentees negotiate their jobs successfully.

2. Identify Suitable Mentors: Identify persons inside your company who have the required skills, experience, and desire to act as mentors. Consider their accomplishments, expertise, and leadership qualities while picking mentors. Ensure that mentors are personable, devoted, and eager to spend time and effort on the growth of their mentees.

3. identify Mentorship aims and Objectives: Identify the aims and objectives of the mentorship program. Ensure that both mentors and mentees have a common knowledge of the targeted objectives and the areas of concentration. This alignment enables mentors to give tailored counsel and aids mentees in reaching their unique development goals.

4. Tailor Mentorship to Individual Needs: Recognize that each mentee has distinct needs and aspirations. Tailor the

mentoring experience to fulfill those unique requirements and connect with the mentee's professional ambitions. This may entail defining specific learning targets, constructing development plans, or prioritizing areas for improvement that are most important to the mentee's growth trajectory.

5. Encourage Regular Interactions: Encourage regular interactions between mentors and mentees. This may take the shape of one-on-one meetings, check-ins, or planned touchpoints. Encourage open and honest communication, enabling mentees to seek assistance, express problems, and receive feedback. Regular encounters establish a supportive and trustworthy connection between mentors and mentees.

6. create Learning Opportunities: Encourage mentors to create learning opportunities for their mentees. This might entail sharing pertinent articles, suggesting books or resources, or enabling access to training programs or seminars. Mentors may also give exposure to diverse projects or experiences that enhance the mentee's skill set and knowledge base.

7. Foster Networking and Professional Connections: Encourage mentees to broaden their professional networks and connect with others who can assist their growth. Mentors might expose mentees to their professional networks, promote industry events or conferences, or make meetings with other professionals. Networking possibilities increase the mentee's progress and provide doors to new prospects.

8. continually examine and offer criticism: Mentors should continually examine the growth and development of their mentees and offer constructive criticism. Regular feedback helps mentees find areas for development, build on their strengths, and make modifications to their learning path. Mentors may give direction, question preconceptions, and promote critical thinking.

9. Encourage Reverse Mentoring: Embrace the notion of reverse mentoring, when mentors also learn from their mentees. Recognize that mentees provide new ideas, information, and expertise that may assist mentors. Encouraging mentees to share their thoughts and new ideas with their mentors develops a reciprocal learning relationship.

10. Monitor and assess mentoring Program: Continuously monitor and assess the mentoring program's success. Collect feedback from mentors and mentees to identify areas for development and make required improvements. Regularly analyze the program's influence on the mentees' development, job happiness, and creative thinking to guarantee its sustained success.

Encourage Diverse Perspectives

Actively seek variety among your staff, not just in terms of demographics but also in terms of cognitive diversity. Embrace people with varied origins, cultures, and ways of thinking. This variety strengthens the creative process and stimulates creativity via the integration of various views.

Encouraging varied viewpoints requires actively soliciting and appreciating input from persons with different origins, experiences, cultures, and ways of thinking. It understands that diversity supports innovation, creativity, and more robust decision-making inside your firm.

Here are some crucial elements to consider while supporting various perspectives:

1. Embrace Inclusive recruiting processes: Ensure that your recruiting processes support diversity and inclusion. Adopt techniques to recruit and hire people from varied origins, cultures, and experiences. This might entail establishing inclusive job descriptions, diverse interview panels, and deliberate outreach to underrepresented groups. By developing a diverse staff, you provide the framework for varied viewpoints to thrive.

2. Cultivate an Inclusive Culture: Foster an inclusive and respectful culture that supports and welcomes varied opinions. Encourage open communication, active listening, and the exchange of ideas across all levels of the company. Promote diversity and inclusion training to strengthen workers' knowledge of unconscious prejudice, cultural differences, and the relevance of varied views.

3. Create Diverse Teams: Form teams that cover a diversity of backgrounds, experiences, and skill sets. Mix employees from various departments, levels, and areas of experience. Diverse teams bring together various viewpoints, which may lead to

more inventive ideas and approaches. Encourage cooperation and communication among team members to capitalize on their various perspectives.

4. Establish Employee Resource Groups: Support the formation of employee resource groups (ERGs) or affinity groups that bring together persons with common qualities or experiences. These organizations may give a forum for minority workers to express their opinions, encourage one another, and advocate for inclusion within the business. ERGs may also help to wider diversity efforts by sharing insights and ideas.

5. Encourage Speaking Up: Foster a culture where people feel comfortable expressing their unique thoughts, questioning assumptions, and presenting diverse opinions. Encourage staff to speak out in meetings, brainstorming sessions, or decision-making processes. Create an atmosphere where various ideas are not only accepted but also respected and considered in defining corporate plans and goals.

6. Seek Feedback and Input: Actively seek feedback and input from workers at all levels of the business. Encourage people to express their thoughts, ideas, and recommendations for change. Establish mechanisms for anonymous feedback to promote honest and transparent participation. Soliciting feedback from varied perspectives guarantees a larger variety of thoughts and helps reveal blind spots that may be ignored otherwise.

CHAPTER 5:MARKET ANALYSIS

In the ever-evolving corporate scene, keeping ahead of the competition is key to success. A detailed market study is the key to uncovering hidden possibilities and detecting possible difficulties. By diving deep into market trends, consumer habits, and rival plans, organizations may develop a competitive advantage that sets them apart. In this article, we discuss how a strategic market study may pave the road for corporate development and maximum profitability.

Understanding the Dynamic Market Landscape

An effective market study starts with knowing the general market landscape. By researching industry trends, market size, and growth estimates, firms may find untapped possibilities. This involves recognizing developing niches, market gaps, or altering customer preferences. Such insights help corporations to change their strategy appropriately, capturing new market sectors before their rivals. By remaining cognizant of market dynamics, organizations may proactively adapt to developments and acquire a first-mover advantage.

The dynamic market landscape refers to the ever-changing and developing circumstances within a certain industry or market. It incorporates numerous elements such as industry trends, market size, growth estimates, customer preferences, technical breakthroughs, and competitive dynamics. To successfully assess and manage this terrain, organizations need to have a comprehensive grasp of its complexity and change their strategy appropriately.

1. Industry Trends & Emerging Markets:
Monitoring industry trends is vital to determining the direction in which the market is moving. This involves spotting developing markets, new consumer requirements, technical developments, and disruptive inventions. By remaining informed of these trends, firms may position themselves as early adopters, grabbing untapped possibilities and earning a competitive edge.

2. Market Size and Growth Projections:
Analyzing the size and growth prospects of a market offers firms crucial insights into its potential. Understanding the market's present size and predicted growth rate assists in analyzing its attractiveness and possibilities for development. This information is vital for making educated choices on market entrance, resource allocation, and long-term planning.

3. Consumer Preferences and Behavior:
One of the main parts of comprehending the changing business environment is collecting insights into customer preferences and behavior. This entails performing market research, evaluating customer data, and following changing consumer trends. By knowing what drives customers, their purchasing patterns, and growing preferences, companies can modify their goods, services, and marketing efforts to fit their demands efficiently.

4. Technology Developments and Disruptions:
Staying up to date with the newest technology is vital for companies to stay competitive in the market. Technologies such as artificial intelligence, blockchain, and virtual reality may have a huge influence on established business strategies and generate new possibilities. Companies that accept and exploit these technologies may get an edge over their rivals and remain ahead of the game.

5. Competitive Dynamics:
Understanding the competitive dynamics inside a market is vital for company success. This comprises examining rivals' plans, strengths, weaknesses, pricing structures, marketing approaches, and product offers. By collecting insights about competitors' activity, firms may find gaps in the market, distinguish their services, and devise plans to surpass their rivals.

6. Regulatory and Legal Factors:
Market analysis should also evaluate the regulatory and legal variables that affect the sector. This involves monitoring changes in rules, compliance requirements, and industry standards. Understanding the legal environment helps firms foresee future issues and change their operations to comply with developing requirements.

Customer-Centric Insights for Targeted Engagement
Deep-diving into customer behavior and preferences is crucial in any market study. By performing rigorous market research

and evaluating consumer data, organizations may acquire significant insights into what inspires their target audience. This information may be utilized to adapt goods, services, and marketing initiatives, leading to successful client interaction. By exploiting these customer-centric insights, firms may develop greater relationships, boost client loyalty, and promote long-term success.

In today's highly competitive business world, knowing consumers and engaging them effectively is crucial to success. Customer-centric insights produced from market research help firms develop a comprehensive knowledge of their target audience, allowing personalized strategies and personalized experiences.

Here's a deeper look at the value of customer-centric information for focused engagement:

1. Market Research and Customer Data Analysis:
Market research serves as the basis for acquiring customer-centric insights. Through numerous research techniques such as surveys, focus groups, and data analysis, companies obtain vital information on client preferences, habits, and pain areas. This data helps identify significant demographic groupings, psychographic profiles, and unique demands within the target market.

2. Tailoring Products and Services:
Customer-centric insights help organizations to design goods and services that connect with their target audience. By

knowing client preferences, pain spots, and wishes, firms may build services that fulfill particular requirements successfully. This personalized strategy not only boosts client happiness but also enhances brand loyalty and generates repeat business.

3. Personalized Marketing Campaigns:
With customer-centric information, firms may design highly focused marketing strategies. By knowing consumers' motivations, attitudes, and preferences, firms can develop messages that appeal to their target audience on a personal level. Personalized marketing initiatives generate a feeling of relevance and connection, enhancing engagement and conversion rates.

4. Enhancing Customer Experiences:
A customer-centric strategy focuses on creating outstanding experiences at every touchpoint. By evaluating customer data and comments, organizations may discover pain areas in the customer journey and proactively fix them. This might entail simplifying operations, increasing customer service, or developing user-friendly interfaces. By increasing the total customer experience, organizations may build client loyalty and advocacy.

5. Building Stronger Relationships:
Customer-centric insights help firms to create closer connections with their consumers. By knowing client preferences, organizations may participate in tailored communication, delivering appropriate offers, suggestions, and assistance. This develops a feeling of trust and loyalty,

enhancing client retention and generating long-term company success.

6. Iterative Improvement and Innovation:
Customer-centric insights enable a feedback loop for continual development and innovation. By monitoring client comments, preferences, and behavior, organizations may find areas for development and change their services appropriately. This iterative approach helps organizations keep ahead of changing client wants and preferences, ensuring their goods and services remain relevant in a dynamic market.

7. Anticipating Future Trends:
Analyzing customer-centric information may also help organizations forecast future trends and remain ahead of the competition. By recognizing growing client requirements and behaviors, organizations may proactively change their strategy, create new goods or services, and position themselves as market leaders. Anticipating trends offers organizations a competitive advantage and helps them capitalize on new possibilities.

Competitive Analysis for Strategic Positioning

Understanding the competition is vital for building an efficient company strategy. A complete competition study gives insights into your rivals' strengths, weaknesses, and tactics. By finding gaps in the market and analyzing your unique value offer, you can effectively position your organization as the better alternative. Moreover, regularly monitoring rivals' pricing, marketing methods, and product advancements lets you remain one step ahead, adjust swiftly, and establish uniqueness in the industry.

In a highly competitive business world, recognizing your rivals is vital for building successful strategies and positioning your organization for success. Competitive analysis entails examining your rivals' strengths, weaknesses, plans, and market positioning to generate important insights that guide your own strategic choices.

Here's a deeper look at the relevance of competition analysis for strategic positioning:

1. Identifying Competitor Strategies:
Competitive analysis helps you acquire insights into your rivals' strategies. By attentively evaluating their marketing techniques, pricing patterns, product offers, distribution networks, and customer interaction strategies, you can learn how they position themselves in the market. This knowledge helps you to analyze their strengths and shortcomings, find opportunities for distinction, and design tactics that set your organization apart.

2. Understanding Competitor Strengths and Weaknesses:
Gaining an insight into your competition is vital for success. By examining their key skills, unique selling features, and advantages, you may acquire insight into what makes companies effective. Additionally, by analyzing their deficiencies, such as poor product offers, bad customer

service, or inefficient procedures, you may discover strategies to outdo them and establish a competitive advantage.

3. Assessing Market Share and Customer Perception:
The competitive analysis gives insights into your rivals' market share and consumer perception. By examining their market presence, client loyalty, and brand reputation, you may measure how well they are positioned within the industry. This information helps you find areas where you may challenge their market share, distinguish your solutions, and attract their consumers by giving higher value or solving unmet requirements.

4. Identifying Market Gaps and Untapped Opportunities:
By evaluating your competition, you may find market gaps and unexplored possibilities. This entails assessing areas where rivals may be underserving or disregarding consumer categories or failing to satisfy particular customer demands. By spotting these gaps, you can position your firm to fill them, delivering distinctive and inventive solutions that attract clients and generate a competitive edge.

5. Adapting and Differentiating Your Offerings:
Competitive analysis helps you modify and distinguish your services. By researching your rivals' product characteristics, prices, and marketing techniques, you may uncover chances for difference. This might entail delivering extra features, providing improved customer service, or creating creative marketing initiatives. By differentiating yourself distinct from

your competition, you may attract clients who appreciate the unique value proposition you provide.

6. Anticipating Competitive Responses:
Analyzing your competition helps you to predict their reactions to your strategic initiatives. By analyzing their expected responses to your market activities, price adjustments, or new product releases, you may better prepare and establish contingency plans. This proactive strategy guarantees that you can handle any competition issues while keeping your strategic positioning and market advantage.

7. Continuous Improvement and Innovation:
Competitive analysis encourages a culture of constant development and innovation. By watching your rivals' activity, you may uncover new market trends, technical developments, or changes in client preferences. This information helps you to change your tactics, invest in innovation, and remain ahead of the competition. By consistently developing and inventing, you can retain a competitive position in the market and fulfill the shifting demands of your clients.

Identifying and Addressing Potential Challenges

A thorough market study involves a full evaluation of prospective problems. By anticipating hurdles such as legislative changes, economic volatility, or technology developments, organizations may proactively prepare contingency plans. Identifying possible issues early helps organizations to reduce risks, change their strategy, and retain stability during stormy times. Embracing change becomes a competitive advantage when equipped with foresight garnered via diligent market study.

In every commercial activity, it is vital to foresee and solve possible problems to guarantee long-term success. Identifying and resolving these difficulties proactively helps firms to reduce risks, modify their plans, and retain stability in the face of adversity.

Here's a closer look at the relevance of detecting and tackling possible challenges:

1. Regulatory and Legal Challenges:
Businesses operate inside a complicated network of rules and legal frameworks. Identifying possible regulatory and legal difficulties is vital to assure compliance and prevent expensive fines. By remaining current on industry-specific rules, monitoring changes in legislation, and understanding the possible effect on your organization, you can take proactive efforts to manage risks, modify procedures, and maintain conformity to legal standards.

2. Economic Fluctuations and Market Volatility:
Economic changes and market volatility may dramatically affect corporate operations. These obstacles may include changes in consumer buying patterns, inflation, interest rate variations, or economic downturns. By regularly monitoring economic data, assessing market trends, and undertaking scenario planning, firms may better prepare for prospective

economic issues. This could entail diversifying income sources, altering pricing methods, improving resource allocation, or introducing cost-saving initiatives.

3. Technological Advancements and Disruptions:
Technological improvements may both generate possibilities and bring obstacles for enterprises. The fast rate of technology innovation implies that firms must continually review and adjust to be competitive. Identifying possible technology disruptions in your sector helps you to proactively adopt new technologies, improve systems and processes, and innovate to preserve a competitive advantage. By embracing digital transformation and investing in appropriate technology, organizations may position themselves for success in an ever-evolving world.

4. Changing Customer Preferences and Demands:
Customer tastes and needs are susceptible to change, driven by numerous variables such as social trends, cultural changes, or developing technology. Identifying possible adjustments in client preferences helps firms to predict changes in demand and alter their offers appropriately. This could entail performing market research, assessing client feedback, and remaining involved with target audiences via frequent contact channels.
By adjusting goods, services, and marketing methods to match growing client requirements, firms may remain relevant and preserve a competitive edge.

5. Supply Chain Disruptions and Operational Risks:
Supply chain interruptions, natural catastrophes, geopolitical upheavals, or unanticipated operational hazards may dramatically influence corporate operations. Identifying possible risks and weaknesses in the supply chain, logistics, or operations helps firms to design contingency plans and implement risk mitigation measures. This may require diversifying suppliers, adopting backup plans, retaining safety stock, or building effective communication lines with stakeholders to mitigate the impact of any interruptions.

6. Competitive Landscape and New Market Entrants:
The competitive environment is always developing, with new rivals joining the market and old competitors altering their strategies. Identifying possible dangers from new market entrants and monitoring the activity of established rivals helps organizations remain ahead. By doing frequent competition analysis, organizations may discover areas of weakness, distinguish their services, and establish plans to preserve or increase their market position.

7. Changing Industry Trends and Disruptions:
Industries are prone to continual change owing to rising trends, innovative technology, or evolving customer habits. Identifying future market trends and disruptions helps organizations to adjust and remain ahead of the curve. By watching industry journals, attending conferences, and interacting in industry networks, firms may discover emerging

possibilities and threats, allowing them to pivot their strategy and embrace new paths for development.

Data-Driven Decision-Making

A well-executed market study serves as the cornerstone for strategic decision-making. Armed with complete data, firms may make educated decisions regarding product development, market entrance, growth strategies, and resource allocation. This data-driven strategy eliminates guessing and enhances the chance of success. By aligning plans with market realities, firms may streamline their operations, stimulate innovation, and grasp profitable opportunities.

Data-driven decision-making is a method that includes obtaining, evaluating, and interpreting relevant data to inform and steer business choices. It stresses the use of objective, quantitative knowledge rather than depending only on intuition or subjective opinion.

Here's a closer look at the relevance of data-driven decision-making:

1. Gathering and Analyzing Data:
Data-driven decision-making starts with the gathering and analysis of relevant data. This comprises internal data (such as sales numbers, customer feedback, and operational indicators) as well as external data (market research, industry trends, and competition analyses). By carefully obtaining and organizing data, organizations may acquire insights into numerous

elements of their operations, market dynamics, and consumer behavior.

2. Objective and Unbiased Decision-Making:
Data-driven decision-making helps minimize biases and subjectivity that may impact judgments based on human beliefs or gut reactions. By relying on data, organizations may make objective evaluations and lessen the risk of making choices that are based on faulty assumptions or missing facts.

3. Identifying Patterns and Trends:
Data analysis helps firms to detect patterns, trends, and correlations in the data they have acquired. By finding these insights, firms may obtain a deeper grasp of client preferences, market trends, and operational success. This helps people to make judgments based on real-time and historical data, rather than merely relying on prior experiences or intuition.

4. Assessing Performance and ROI:
Data-driven decision-making helps firms to track and analyze performance efficiently. By examining key performance indicators (KPIs) and metrics, organizations may analyze the success and efficacy of their goals and efforts. This enables the identification of areas for improvement and the allocation of resources where they may yield the best return on investment (ROI).

5. Forecasting & Predictive Analytics:
Data-driven decision-making also aids forecasting and predictive analytics. By evaluating historical data and employing predictive modeling approaches, firms may forecast future trends, market demand, and consumer behavior. This helps them to make proactive choices and prepare for any difficulties or opportunities in advance.

6. Agility and Adaptability:
Data-driven decision-making helps firms to be more nimble and adaptive. By regularly monitoring and analyzing data, firms may discover fluctuations in market circumstances, client preferences, or industry trends. This helps businesses swiftly alter their goals and operations to coincide with changing conditions, making them more responsive and competitive in the market.

7. Risk Mitigation:
Data-driven decision-making assists in lowering risks connected with corporate choices. By evaluating data and performing risk assessments, firms may discover possible hazards, analyze their effect, and establish strategies to limit or manage those risks. This helps organizations to make better-informed choices that examine possible ramifications and analyze risk-reward trade-offs.

In the ever-evolving and competitive business world, market analysis has become a vital pillar of success. By doing a comprehensive study, organizations may find hidden possibilities, understand their consumers, outmaneuver rivals, and overcome unforeseen difficulties. Embracing a data-driven and customer-centric strategy lays the road for long-term development and profitability. By unlocking the power of market intelligence, firms can position themselves as industry leaders, flourishing despite ongoing change and volatility.

CHAPTER 6:FROM STRATEGY TO ACTION

In today's intensely competitive corporate market, having a well-defined strategy is important. But it's the successful implementation of that approach that differentiates the winners from the others. To achieve lasting success, businesses must bridge the gap between strategy and execution, translating their objectives into concrete achievements. In this article, we expose the keys to building a results-oriented strategy that takes your company to new heights.

Aligning Vision and Execution

Developing a results-oriented strategy begins with matching your organization's goal with the execution. Every move you do must be based on the larger strategic goals. By ensuring that your whole team knows and accepts the vision, you establish a feeling of purpose and direction that motivates them toward common objectives.

Aligning vision and execution is a vital part of building a results-oriented approach. It entails ensuring that every activity made inside an organization is by its broad strategic goals and long-term vision. When vision and execution are aligned, there is a clear and shared knowledge of the organization's purpose, direction, and objectives among the whole team.

Here are some crucial elements to consider when harmonizing vision and execution:

1. Communicate the Vision: Communicate the organization's vision to all stakeholders, including workers, managers, and executives. The vision should address basic questions such as "What do we aim to achieve?" and "Why do we exist?" Effective communication ensures that everyone knows and accepts the vision, generating a feeling of purpose and togetherness.

2. Cascading Objectives: Once the vision is formed, break it down into particular objectives and goals that apply to various levels and departments inside the business. This ensures that every person and team has a clear grasp of how their work contributes to the overarching goal. By synchronizing goals at several levels, you develop a unified and coordinated approach to execution.

3. Consistent message: Consistency in a message is vital to align vision and execution. All communication, whether via official channels such as company-wide meetings or casual contacts, should promote the organization's vision and strategic goals. Consistent messaging helps build a common understanding and minimizes misunderstanding or competing priorities.

4. Engage and Empower workers: Engage workers by incorporating them in the vision-setting process and asking their opinion. When workers feel a feeling of ownership and

contribution to the vision, they are more likely to be dedicated and inspired to execute the plan. Empower them by giving them the required resources, training, and authority to make choices consistent with the goal.

5. Performance Alignment: Align performance management procedures, such as performance evaluations and goal-setting, with the organization's vision and strategic goals. Link individual and team objectives to the wider strategic goals, providing a clear relationship between performance and the overarching vision. This guarantees that everyone's efforts are focused on delivering outcomes that support the organization's long-term success.

6. Continual Communication and Reinforcement: Aligning vision and execution is an ongoing process that needs continual communication and reinforcement. Regularly convey updates on progress, acknowledge triumphs, and resolve any issues or bottlenecks. This reaffirms the significance of the goal and maintains it at the forefront of everyone's thoughts, building a culture of execution.

7. Lead by Example: Leaders play a crucial role in synchronizing vision and execution. They must display a strong commitment to the vision and regularly behave in ways that match the strategic goals. Leaders should serve as role models, reflecting the intended behaviors and values, and actively interact with workers to ensure their actions are consistent with the vision.

When vision and execution are linked, workers have a clear knowledge of the organization's objectives and how their efforts contribute to its success. This alignment provides a feeling of purpose, motivation, and a common commitment to execute the plan successfully, eventually moving the company toward attaining its targeted goals.

Setting Clear and Measurable Objectives

Ambiguity may be the adversary of progress. To transform strategy into action, it is necessary to create clear and quantifiable goals. By creating precise objectives and key performance indicators (KPIs), you give your team a clear path to success. Objectives should be tough but achievable, encouraging people and teams to strive beyond their limitations while promoting a feeling of success.

Setting clear and quantifiable targets is a critical component of building a results-oriented strategy. Clear goals create a feeling of direction and purpose, while quantifiable objectives enable progress to be recorded and assessed. When goals are well-defined and quantifiable, they serve as a roadmap for action and give a foundation for measuring performance and success.

Here are some crucial factors to consider when developing clear and quantifiable objectives:

1. Specificity: Objectives should be explicit and well-stated. Vague or wide goals make it hard to understand what precisely needs to be accomplished. By explicitly expressing

the intended objective, you create a clear target for people and teams to strive towards.

2. Measurability: Objectives should be quantifiable so that progress can be monitored and judged. Measurable goals are measurable and contain defined criteria for accomplishment. They generally incorporate measurements, key performance indicators (KPIs), or objectives that may be objectively assessed and evaluated.

3. Relevance: Objectives should be relevant to the overarching strategic objectives of the company. They should directly contribute to the achievement of the strategy and fit with the organization's goal. Relevance guarantees that efforts and resources be focused on goals that have a significant influence on the intended results.

4. Attainability: Objectives should be demanding but reachable. Setting targets that are too simple may not push people and teams to exceed their capabilities, while aims that are too unattainable might lead to demotivation and discouragement. Objectives should drive people and teams to strive for greatness while keeping within the range of achievability.

5. Time-Bound: Objectives should have a definite timetable or deadline. Setting a precise timetable promotes a feeling of urgency and helps prioritize efforts. Time-bound goals also allow monitoring progress and enable the business to evaluate performance within a set timetable.

6. Alignment and Cascade: Objectives should be aligned and cascaded across the company. Starting with the broad strategic goals, objectives should be broken down and linked with various departments, teams, and people. This ensures that everyone's objectives contribute to the broader strategy and fit with the organization's aims.

7. Regular Evaluation and Adjustment: Measuring progress and assessing performance versus goals is vital. Regularly examine and analyze the progress achieved towards targets, and make modifications as appropriate. This enables course correction and ensures that activities stay aligned with the anticipated objectives. Use the assessment process to discover strengths, shortcomings, and opportunities for growth.

Setting precise and quantifiable goals gives a path for action, generates a common awareness of expectations, and allows effective performance management. It lets people and teams monitor progress, make data-driven choices, and concentrate their efforts on reaching desired objectives. Clear and quantifiable objectives serve as a guidepost for success, directing the implementation of the plan and ensuring that activities are aligned with strategic goals.

Building a Results-Focused Culture

Culture has a key part in implementing your plan successfully. A results-oriented culture emphasizes responsibility, openness, and ongoing progress. Foster a climate where triumphs are acknowledged, setbacks are regarded as learning opportunities, and everyone is encouraged to take responsibility for their job. By developing a culture that values results, you build an unstoppable force that propels your strategy toward success.

Building a results-focused culture is vital for efficiently executing a strategy and attaining targeted goals. It entails building a climate where every employee inside the business is motivated by a shared commitment to achieve quantifiable outcomes. A results-focused culture encourages responsibility, transparency, continuous improvement, and tireless pursuit of excellence.

Here are crucial aspects to consider while developing a results-focused culture:

1. Clear objectives: Clearly explain performance objectives and the intended outcomes to all personnel. Ensure that everyone knows what is expected of them and how their job contributes to the larger objectives of the business. When expectations are clear, people may coordinate their efforts appropriately.

2. responsibility: Foster a feeling of individual and communal responsibility for outcomes. Encourage workers to take responsibility for their work and achievements. When people are held responsible for their performance, they are more likely to be motivated, proactive, and devoted to producing outcomes.

3. Transparent Communication: Establish a culture of open and transparent communication. Encourage workers to share ideas, problems, and comments without fear of punishment. Transparent communication helps detect bottlenecks, address challenges, and inspire teamwork toward attaining outcomes.

4. ongoing Improvement: Emphasize the need for ongoing improvement and learning. Encourage staff to explore creative solutions, experiment with new ideas, and learn from triumphs and mistakes. Promote a growth mentality that values learning and adapts to changing circumstances to achieve continual progress.

5. Recognition & Rewards: Recognize and recognize individuals and teams for their efforts and accomplishments. Celebrate victories, whether large or little, to create a culture that values outcomes. Rewards might be in the form of incentives, promotions, public recognition, or other significant acknowledgments.

6. Empowerment and Autonomy: Empower workers by giving them the necessary tools, resources, and authority to make choices and take ownership of their job. Foster a feeling of liberty and trust, enabling employees to innovate and take measured risks. When workers feel empowered, they are more likely to be proactive and determined to accomplish outcomes.

7. Collaboration and Teamwork: Encourage collaboration and teamwork across departments and teams. Break down silos

and build a collaborative workplace where people work together towards common objectives. Collaboration harnesses varied views, information, and skills, leading to greater problem-solving and more successful execution.

8. Performance Measurement and Feedback: Establish a strong performance measurement system that records progress and gives timely feedback. Regularly analyze performance against goals and give constructive comments to individuals and teams. Feedback helps people realize their strengths, and areas for growth, and direct their efforts toward attaining better outcomes.

9. Leadership Role Modeling: Leaders play a significant role in building the company culture. Lead by example, exhibit a strong commitment to success, and model the appropriate habits. Leaders should actively assist and empower staff, give direction, and establish a culture that appreciates and prioritizes outcomes.

Establishing Actionable Milestones
Transforming strategy into action involves breaking it down into actionable milestones. These smaller, attainable milestones act as stepping stones toward your ultimate objectives. By separating your strategy into manageable parts, you not only simplify the execution process but also keep your team engaged with frequent successes. Celebrate each milestone attained since they signify progress towards your broader objectives.

Establishing actionable milestones is a vital component of building a results-oriented strategy. Milestones break down the plan into smaller, manageable components and set explicit objectives that need to be reached within a specified period. These milestones act as checkpoints for progress, keep the team engaged, and guarantee that the strategy continues on course toward reaching the anticipated results.

Here are crucial considerations to consider while setting actionable milestones:

1. Breakdown of the Plan: Start by breaking down the overall plan into logical segments or stages. Each phase should represent a substantial step towards reaching the final goals. Breaking down the strategy into digestible components makes it less intimidating and allows for a more focused and methodical approach to implementation.

2. Specificity and Measurability: Like goals, milestones should be explicit and quantifiable. They should reflect concrete results that can be objectively assessed. By providing defined criteria for success, milestones give a concrete aim for people and teams to strive towards, enabling progress to be recorded and analyzed.

3. timeline: Assign a reasonable timeline for each milestone. The schedule should find a balance between giving adequate time for substantial development and keeping a feeling of urgency. Establishing deadlines for milestones generates a feeling of responsibility and helps keep the strategy on track.

4. Sequencing and Dependencies: Consider the logical sequencing of milestones and any dependencies between them. Identify milestones that need to be reached before others may be undertaken. By knowing the dependencies, you can plan and allocate resources properly and maintain a smooth flow of progress throughout the execution process.

5. Assign accountability: Assign explicit ownership and accountability for each milestone. Identify the persons or teams who will be responsible for reaching the goals. Clarify duties and objectives, and equip individuals responsible with the necessary authority and resources to accomplish their jobs efficiently.

6. Celebrate Milestone Achievements: Celebrate and recognize the achievement of milestones. Recognize the efforts and successes of people and teams who have accomplished the milestone, encouraging a culture of advancement and drive. Celebrations create a good and gratifying atmosphere that keeps the team engaged and focused on accomplishing the next milestone.

7. examine and Adjust: Regularly examine the progress towards milestones and evaluate their relevance and achievability. If required, make revisions to the milestones, deadlines, or resource allocation to adapt to changing conditions. A flexible strategy allows for course correction and ensures that the plan stays aligned with the targeted results.

Effective Resource Allocation

Effective resource allocation is a vital part of building a results-oriented strategy. It entails strategically allocating and maximizing the resources available to the firm, including financial capital, human talent, technology, and other assets. Proper resource allocation ensures that the proper resources are assigned at the right time and in the right amounts, optimizing productivity, efficiency, and ultimately, the possibility of obtaining desired objectives.

Here are crucial aspects to consider when it comes to successful resource allocation:

1. Identify Resource Requirements: Start by determining the particular resources necessary to execute the strategy properly. This comprises financial resources, such as budget allocations and money, as well as human resources with the essential skills and knowledge. It may also incorporate technology, equipment, buildings, and any other assets necessary to support the plan's implementation.

2. Prioritize Resources: Assess the significance and urgency of each resource demand. Prioritize resources based on their criticality to attaining the targeted results and the timetable within which they are required. This guarantees that the most critical resources are assigned first, reducing bottlenecks and delays in execution.

3. Optimize Resource Allocation: Allocate resources in a way that optimizes their usage and efficacy. Consider aspects such as the abilities and strengths of people, the availability of resources, and the task allocation among teams and departments. Optimize resource allocation to prevent overburdening specific regions while ensuring that all resources are used effectively towards accomplishing the plan's goals.

4. Flexibility and Adaptability: Remain flexible and adaptive in resource allocation. As the strategy proceeds, review resource requirements and change allocations appropriately. Be open to reallocating resources from areas of minimal effect to those that demand extra attention. Flexibility enables changes to be made when new opportunities or difficulties occur, ensuring that resources are matched with changing conditions.

5. Cross-Functional cooperation: Foster cooperation and cross-functional communication while distributing resources. Involve important stakeholders from multiple departments or teams to ensure a comprehensive picture of resource demands and possible conflicts. Collaborative resource allocation encourages openness, exchange of knowledge, and the optimization of resources throughout the business.

6. Monitoring and Evaluation: Continuously monitor resource use and performance to determine their efficacy. Regularly analyze the effect of resource allocation on the execution of the plan and the accomplishment of intended results. Utilize

data and feedback to identify areas where resource allocation might be improved and make data-driven choices to reallocate resources if required.

7. Invest in Resource Development: Allocate resources not just to urgent demands but also to the development and expansion of resources themselves. This involves investing in training and development programs to expand the skills and capacities of personnel, embracing new technologies and tools that promote efficiency and production, and continually upgrading resource management procedures.

Continuous Monitoring and Adaptation

Continuous monitoring and adaption are key components of building a results-oriented approach. They require routinely monitoring progress, reviewing performance, and making appropriate revisions to ensure that the plan stays aligned with the targeted results and successfully reacts to changing conditions. This iterative method helps firms to remain nimble, maximize performance, and boost the chance of obtaining desired goals.

Here are crucial aspects to consider when it comes to continuous monitoring and adaptation:

1. Define Key Performance Indicators (KPIs): Establish unambiguous KPIs that match the goals of the strategy. KPIs should be quantifiable and closely connected to the targeted goals. These metrics give a quantifiable and objective tool to track development and measure success.

2. Regular Progress Tracking: Continuously monitor progress against the set KPIs. Monitor and record key data and indicators to assess how the strategy is functioning. Regular progress monitoring offers insight into areas of success, reveals bottlenecks or areas of concern, and enables early discovery of deviations from the desired route.

3. Data Analysis and Insights: Analyze the data acquired during progress tracking to get insights into performance trends, patterns, and possible areas for improvement. Use data analysis to discover strengths, weaknesses, opportunities, and threats that may influence decision-making and lead adaptation efforts.

4. input & Stakeholder Engagement: Seek input from stakeholders, including employees, customers, partners, and other relevant parties. Engage in chats, questionnaires, or other feedback channels to acquire insights into their viewpoints and experiences. Stakeholder feedback offers vital input for recognizing gaps, resolving difficulties, and suggesting potential for development.

5. Performance Evaluation and Review: Conduct periodic performance reviews to analyze the overall efficacy of the strategy and its implementation. Evaluate the degree to which the strategy is providing the expected goals, and identify areas for refinement or correction. Regular evaluations assist identify what is functioning well and what needs to be improved, allowing evidence-based decision-making.

6. Adaptation and Course Correction: Based on the insights acquired through progress monitoring, data analysis, stakeholder input, and performance assessments, make required changes and course corrections. This may require revising goals, realigning resource allocation, modifying strategy, or deploying new approaches. Adaptation ensures that the strategy stays adaptable to changing conditions, rising possibilities, or unanticipated problems.

7. continual Learning and development: Embrace a culture of continual learning and development. Encourage the company to learn from both achievements and mistakes, promoting a growth mentality and an atmosphere that supports experimentation and innovation. Apply the insights obtained through monitoring and adaptation to modify plans and boost execution effectiveness.

CHAPTER 7: SETTING CLEAR GOALS

In the ever-evolving world of business, having clear objectives and identifying milestones is the key to keeping ahead of the competition. Successful entrepreneurs and firms recognize that without a strategy to guide their efforts, development may be erratic and success elusive. In this post, we will discuss the significance of defining clear objectives and how creating milestones may push your organization toward unrivaled success. Get ready to unleash your full potential and outperform the opposition!

Defining Your Destination

Every trip starts with a goal in mind. Similarly, creating specific objectives provides your firm with a purpose and direction. When you clearly describe what you want to accomplish, whether it's boosting revenue, gaining market share, or releasing a new product, you give a focus point for your whole team. This shared vision becomes the driving factor that keeps everyone united and motivated, working diligently towards a single aim.

"Defining Your Destination" is a vital component of defining clear objectives and establishing milestones. It entails establishing the final objective or success that you want your organization to attain. By identifying your goal, you give a feeling of purpose, direction, and focus for the whole business.

Here are some crucial elements to consider while determining your destination:

1. Vision and purpose: Start by establishing your organization's vision and purpose. The vision depicts the long-term objectives and intended influence of your organization, while the mission describes the purpose and underlying principles that drive your operations. These core aspects offer a guiding framework for defining objectives and milestones that match your overall mission.

2. Specificity: It is crucial to be precise when establishing your goal. Vague or unclear objectives may lead to uncertainty and lack of direction. Instead, explicitly describe what you intend to accomplish. For example, if you aim to raise sales, provide the desired percentage of growth or the target revenue sum.

3. Relevance: Ensure that your specified destination is relevant to your company and sector. Consider the current market circumstances, client demands, and competition environment. Align your objectives and milestones with the market possibilities and challenges that are most applicable to your firm. This ensures that your efforts are concentrated on areas that have the potential for the greatest effect.

4. timeline: Set a realistic timeline for accomplishing your target. Determine if your objectives are short-term, medium-term, or long-term. This helps you to break down your objectives into small stages and measure progress efficiently.

5. Alignment with Stakeholders: Consider the expectations and ambitions of your stakeholders, including workers, customers, investors, and partners. Engage in open contact and seek feedback to ensure that your stated destination connects with their interests and adds to their pleasure. This alignment increases cooperation and support from all major stakeholders.

6. Stretching Your Limits: While it is crucial to establish realistic objectives, don't be scared to push your limits and strive for ambitious ambitions. Challenging objectives may encourage creativity, development, and remarkable achievement. Strive for a balance between attainability and straining your limitations to release your full potential and surpass your opponents.

Building a Roadmap

Goals without a blueprint are only fantasies. To translate your ideals into reality, break down your big objectives into smaller, practical milestones. These milestones act as indicators of progress, directing you toward your ultimate target. Each milestone completed creates a feeling of success, generating inspiration and momentum.

Building a roadmap is a vital step in identifying clear objectives and establishing milestones. It entails breaking down your overall objectives into smaller, concrete tasks that serve as checkpoints on your route toward accomplishment. Building a plan gives a clear and disciplined approach to reaching your targeted results.

Here's a longer description of the major parts of constructing a roadmap:

1. Break your objectives into milestones: Start by separating your goals into particular milestones or checkpoints along the road. Each milestone symbolizes a noteworthy accomplishment that adds to the ultimate objective. For example, if you aim to introduce a new product, your milestones may involve performing market research, producing a prototype, testing, and eventually, releasing the product.

2. Establish a logical sequence: Arrange your milestones in a logical manner that enables seamless progress toward your target. Consider dependencies and requirements between milestones to establish the most effective order. This sequencing guarantees that each milestone builds upon the work done in previous phases, establishing a unified and efficient roadmap.

3. Set deadlines and timetables: Assign realistic deadlines and timelines to each milestone. This provides a feeling of urgency and helps you remain on track. Be conscious of any

external influences, such as market trends or seasonal swings, that may affect your timeframe. Setting deadlines also helps you to track progress and evaluate if you are accomplishing your objectives within the required period.

4. Define tasks and action steps: Break down each milestone into specific tasks and action steps necessary to accomplish it. Clearly describe what has to be done, who is accountable for each job, and any dependencies or resources required. This degree of detail ensures that everyone involved knows their tasks and can work effectively towards the fulfillment of each milestone.

5. Consider resource allocation: Assess the resources necessary for each milestone, including people resources, money, technology, and equipment. Ensure that you have the proper resources assigned to each milestone to prevent bottlenecks or delays. This resource planning helps you to maximize your efforts and make educated judgments regarding resource allocation across the roadmap.

6. Communicate and share the roadmap: A roadmap is not designed to be a lonely document. Share the plan with your team, stakeholders, and key decision-makers to guarantee alignment and drive cooperation. Transparent communication of the plan fosters responsibility, facilitates effective cooperation, and allows for required modifications along the route.

7. Regularly evaluate and update: Building a roadmap is not a one-time process. It needs frequent assessment and revisions to suit changes in the company environment, market dynamics, or internal issues. Continuously monitor the progress against milestones, alter dates if required, and adapt the action actions as new information becomes available. This flexibility guarantees that your roadmap stays relevant and flexible to the developing demands of your organization.

Measuring Progress

Without milestones, it might be tough to measure progress properly. Establishing quantifiable metrics at each milestone helps you to measure your development objectively. These indicators may include sales data, customer happiness ratings, or project completion rates, depending on the nature of your aims. Regularly monitoring these indicators helps you to spot areas for development and make required modifications, eventually driving you ahead of the competition.

Measuring progress is a vital component of creating clear objectives and establishing milestones. It entails recording and measuring the development toward your targeted results at each milestone along your route. Measuring progress gives vital insights into the success of your tactics, reveals development opportunities, and helps you remain on track toward attaining your objectives.

Here's a longer description of the major factors in assessing progress:

1. identify quantifiable metrics: To properly assess progress, it is vital to identify particular measures that fit with each milestone and contribute to your overall objectives. These indicators might change based on the nature of your aims. For example, if you aim to improve sales, measures such as revenue growth, customer acquisition rates, or conversion rates might be employed. By picking relevant and quantifiable indicators, you may objectively analyze progress and evaluate success.

2. Establish baseline measurements: Before going on your trip, establish baseline measurements for each metric. Baseline measures indicate the beginning point or current performance level. They give a baseline against which you may assess future growth. Baseline measurements assist you understand the extent of change necessary and give a reference point for assessing the efficacy of your methods.

3. Regularly measure and monitor progress: Continuously track and monitor the specified metrics throughout the execution of your plan. This enables you to monitor progress against the defined milestones. Regular monitoring gives real-time information about how well you are doing and if you are on track to reach your objectives within the set period. It also helps you to discover any deviations or locations where more effort may be required.

4. Analyze and evaluate data: As you gather data on your progress, take the time to analyze and interpret it properly. Look for trends, patterns, and correlations within the data that

might give insights into the elements driving your development. Analyzing the data lets you understand what is functioning effectively and what may need change or more attention. It helps you to make educated judgments and optimize your methods as you go ahead.

5. Make required modifications: Based on the insights received from assessing progress, be prepared to make necessary revisions to your roadmap, milestones, or action actions. If you discover that development is slower than expected or particular techniques are not providing the intended outcomes, modify and pivot appropriately. The capacity to make intelligent changes is crucial to keeping momentum and ensuring that you continue on the road toward success.

6. recognize successes and milestones: Measuring progress is not only about finding areas for development; it is also a chance to recognize achievements and milestones along the road. Recognize and praise the efforts and triumphs of your team when you reach major milestones. Celebrations generate a pleasant work atmosphere, increase morale, and reinforce the feeling of success. They also act as an incentive to continue pushing ahead toward the next milestone.

Celebrating Victories

Celebrating milestones along the path is vital for preserving team morale and motivation. When a milestone is accomplished, take the time to appreciate and praise the hard effort that went into obtaining it. Celebrations build a healthy work atmosphere, increase team spirit, and reaffirm the sense that achievement is within grasp. Recognizing milestones not only keeps your staff motivated but also helps retain top personnel, setting your organization apart from the competition.

Celebrating triumphs is an important feature of defining clear objectives and creating milestones. It entails identifying and celebrating the victories and triumphs that occur along the route toward your intended objectives. Celebrations not only raise morale and team spirit but also reaffirm the sense that progress is being made and that success is within grasp.

Here's a fuller explanation of the value of celebrating victories:

1. incentive and morale boost: Celebrating triumphs is a significant source of incentive for your team. It celebrates their hard work, devotion, and efforts toward accomplishing milestones. Recognizing and celebrating successes builds a healthy work atmosphere and increases team morale. It instills a feeling of pride and success, supporting the perception that the team's efforts are having a real difference. This inspiration and morale boost urge your team onward with increased energy and excitement.

2. Reinforces a culture of success: Celebrating accomplishments helps develop a culture of success inside your company. By publicly celebrating successes, you signal that quality and growth are appreciated and rewarded. This

culture of success inspires people and teams to strive for excellence, to go above and beyond, and to consistently push the limits of what is possible. Celebrations serve as reminders that hard effort and devotion lead to real outcomes, fostering an attitude of ongoing development and achievement.

3. Retention of top talent: Recognizing and celebrating accomplishments has a key impact on retaining top talent. Employees who feel valued and acknowledged for their successes are more likely to be engaged and pleased with their job. Celebrations create a feeling of validation and personal satisfaction, helping workers feel appreciated and rewarded for their achievements. This, in turn, promotes employee loyalty and retention, since employees are more willing to remain with a business that honors and celebrates their successes.

4. Inspiration and momentum: Celebrating accomplishments stimulates and motivates others inside the company. When people witness their colleagues being acknowledged and rewarded for their successes, it inspires a feeling of motivation and optimism that they too can succeed. Celebrations build good momentum inside the business, motivating people and teams to strive for their accomplishments. This combined motivation and energy may lead to a ripple effect of success across the whole business.

5. Strengthening connections: Celebrations give a chance to improve ties within your team and between departments. They provide a feeling of kinship, solidarity, and common purpose.

6. Reflecting on progress and learning: Celebrating achievements also allows for reflection on the progress achieved and the lessons gained along the road. It gives a chance to examine what contributed to the achievement, what techniques worked effectively, and what might be improved in the future. This reflection supports a culture of continual learning and progress, ensuring that successes are not merely celebrated but also studied for insights and best practices that may be utilized in future undertakings.

Adapting and Evolving:

Setting defined objectives and creating milestones also helps you to modify and develop your strategy as required. In today's changing corporate market, the capacity to pivot and modify course is a vital advantage. Regularly monitoring your progress against milestones helps you to detect possible barriers, forecast market trends, and make educated choices. By being nimble and responsive, you keep one step ahead of your competitors, ready to capture new opportunities as they occur.

Adapting and changing is a vital component of having clear objectives and creating milestones. It entails the capacity to modify your strategy, tactics, and methods depending on changing conditions, market dynamics, and new possibilities. Adapting and changing guarantees that your firm stays dynamic, responsive, and capable of keeping ahead of the competition.

Here's a fuller explanation of the relevance of adapting and evolving:

1. Embracing change and uncertainty: Adapting and developing needs a mentality that welcomes change and uncertainty. In today's fast-paced and changing business climate, keeping inflexible or averse to change may inhibit development and restrict your capacity to grab new chances. By developing a culture that accepts and embraces change, you position your organization to prosper despite uncertainty and upheaval.

2. Monitoring market trends and changes: Adapting and developing demands a thorough understanding of market trends and movements. Keep a constant watch on industry advancements, client preferences, developing technology, and competitive environment. Regularly examine market data, consumer input, and industry insights to discover possible opportunities or risks that may affect your objectives and milestones. This information supplies you with the knowledge required to change your tactics and methods properly.

3. Regularly monitoring progress against milestones: As you work towards your milestones, regularly examine your performance and determine if you are on pace to reach your objectives. This review process helps you to discover any gaps, problems, or variations from the initial plan. By assessing your progress, you may decide whether changes or course corrections are required. This flexibility and readiness to make adjustments guarantee that you are continually aligned with the developing demands of your organization and market.

4. Leveraging feedback and insights: Gather input from stakeholders, customers, and team members to acquire useful insights into your development and performance. This input gives a new perspective and reveals areas that may need improvement or alteration. Actively listen to input, analyze its validity, and utilize it as a foundation for making educated choices. By integrating feedback and insights into your adaptation process, you may adjust your methods and approaches for better outcomes.

5. promoting innovation and experimentation: Adaptation typically entails welcoming innovation and promoting experimentation. Foster a culture that supports innovation, out-of-the-box thinking, and measured risk-taking. Encourage your team to explore new ideas, try novel ways, and question the current quo. By establishing an atmosphere where experimentation is encouraged, you generate a potential for breakthroughs and discoveries that may provide you with a competitive edge.

6. Agility in decision-making and execution: Adapting and changing demands agility in decision-making and execution. Be prepared to make timely and educated judgments depending on changing conditions. Empower your team to act swiftly and decisively, allowing them to react to new opportunities or obstacles rapidly. Agile decision-making and execution enable you to capitalize on favorable market circumstances and promptly remove any impediments that may occur.

7. Continuous learning and development: Adapting and developing is a continual process of continuous learning and improvement. Encourage a culture of learning inside your firm, where people and teams are encouraged to gain new skills, information, and insights. Embrace a growth attitude that values learning from both accomplishments and setbacks. By always striving to learn and develop, you position your firm to adapt to new market conditions and remain ahead of the competition.

By adopting the process of adapting and developing, you position your firm to stay adaptable, competitive, and responsive in a continuously changing business world. It helps you to grasp fresh chances, overcome problems, and continually enhance your performance. Through regular monitoring, feedback, innovation, and a dedication to continuous learning, you can change your plans and tactics to correspond with the ever-evolving requirements and expectations of your customers and stakeholders.

CHAPTER 8:BUILDING A STRATEGIC FRAMEWORK

In today's fast-paced and competitive business scene, attaining success involves more than simply hard work and drive. It needs a well-defined strategic framework that acts as a roadmap to steer your firm toward its objectives. Building a strategic framework helps you to handle the obstacles and complexity of the industry, placing your organization as a forerunner and helping you to exceed your rivals. In this post, we will uncover the critical measures to establish a competitive strategic framework that will pave the road for unmatched performance.

Identifying Clear Goals

To develop a successful strategic framework, you must begin by identifying clear and quantifiable goals. These goals operate as lighthouses, directing your business toward its ultimate vision. By establishing your goals with clarity, you create a clear direction for your team, ensuring everyone is aligned and working towards a single purpose. When your goals are crystal clear, your firm wins a competitive advantage by simplifying its operations and concentrating its resources on what counts.

Setting defined goals is the cornerstone of a strategy framework and plays a crucial role in obtaining a competitive advantage. When you create precise goals, you specify the intended outcomes or accomplishments that your firm seeks to attain within a particular period.

Here's a more extensive discussion of the necessity and advantages of defining explicit objectives:

1. Alignment and Focus: Clear goals guarantee that everyone in your business is aligned and working towards a single purpose. When goals are well stated, workers have a clear idea of what they need to accomplish, which eliminates confusion and boosts concentration. This alignment of efforts helps increase productivity and eliminates wasted resources on tasks that do not contribute to the overall objectives.

2. Direction and Guidance: Setting explicit goals offers a blueprint for your organization's strategic decision-making process. Objectives act as guideposts, letting you make educated decisions regarding resource allocation, project prioritization, and operational strategies. When presented with multiple alternatives or possibilities, you may assess them based on their alignment with your goals, ensuring that every action taken takes you closer to your final vision.

3. Measurement and Accountability: Clear goals give a framework for monitoring progress and holding people and teams responsible. When objectives are explicit and quantifiable, it becomes easy to assess performance and decide whether you are on pace to meet your goals. This measuring feature helps you to discover areas of growth,

acknowledge accomplishments, and make educated revisions to your tactics if required.

4. Motivation and Engagement: Well-defined goals generate a feeling of purpose and motivation among your personnel. When people understand how their work contributes to the attainment of bigger goals, they experience a sense of significance and are more likely to be engaged and motivated. Clear goals also help you to recognize and reward workers' accomplishments, promoting a healthy work culture and reinforcing desirable behaviors.

5. Adaptability and Agility: Clear goals give a framework for analyzing and adjusting to changing market circumstances. In a changing corporate environment, goals operate as anchors, helping you negotiate uncertainty and make strategic changes. By frequently analyzing and reassessing goals, you can guarantee that they stay relevant and responsive to market developments, technology improvements, and client requests.

6. Differentiation and Competitive Edge: Clear goals help you to distinguish your firm from rivals. When your goals are explicit and suited to your particular capabilities and market positioning, you can present a compelling value offer to your target audience. This uniqueness helps you stand out in a congested marketplace and promotes your firm as a preferred option among clients.

To successfully define clear goals, it is vital to ensure that they are specified, measurable, attainable, relevant, and time-bound (SMART). This SMART method gives clarity and structure, helping you to establish goals that are executable and connected with your broader strategic vision.

Conducting Thorough Market Analysis

No strategy framework is complete without a full grasp of the market. Conducting a detailed market study helps you to discover your competitors, analyze industry trends, and find unexplored possibilities. By keeping ahead of the curve and collecting insights into client preferences, you can modify your plans to match the growing needs of the market. Armed with this information, your firm obtains a competitive advantage, allowing you to position your solutions as the go-to option for clients.

Conducting detailed market research is a vital stage in establishing a strategy framework that leads to competitive advantage. Market analysis entails acquiring and evaluating information about the market in which your firm works. It delivers significant insights into customer behavior, industry trends, competitive landscape, and prospective possibilities.

Here's a more extended explanation of the significance and advantages of undertaking rigorous market analysis:

1. grasp Customer requirements and Preferences: Market study helps you obtain a thorough grasp of your target customers' requirements, preferences, and problem areas. By gathering data via surveys, focus groups, interviews, or evaluating market research studies, you may determine consumer expectations, purchasing behavior, and trends. This

insight helps you to connect your goods, services, and marketing activities with client wants, strengthening your competitive advantage.

2. Identifying Market possibilities: Market research helps you uncover untapped or growing possibilities within your sector. By researching industry trends, customer behavior, and technical improvements, you might find gaps in the market that your firm can benefit from. Identifying these chances early on helps you to position your services in a unique and inventive manner, providing you with a competitive advantage and opportunity for development.

3. Assessing Competitive Landscape: Understanding the competitive landscape is vital for getting a competitive edge. Market analysis lets you analyze your competition, its strengths, weaknesses, strategy, and market share. By evaluating their price, positioning, marketing strategies, and consumer perception, you may uncover areas where you can distinguish yourself and give unique value to customers. This information helps you to build plans that outmaneuver rivals and grab market share.

4. Monitoring market Trends and Disruptions: Market analysis helps you to keep updated about market trends, innovations, and disruptions. By monitoring variations in customer behavior, technical breakthroughs, legislative changes, or market dynamics, you may forecast future developments and alter your tactics appropriately. This proactive strategy helps you remain ahead of the curve,

exploit opportunities, and manage risks, so strengthening your competitive edge.

5. Evaluating Market Size and Potential: Market analysis helps you analyze the size and potential of your target market. By studying market demographics, growth rates, and consumer segmentation, you may determine the market's attractiveness and potential for expansion. This information helps you to make educated choices regarding resource allocation, market entrance tactics, and target audience selection, ensuring that your efforts are concentrated on markets with significant growth potential.

6. Mitigating Risks and Uncertainties: Market analysis helps you to discover and analyze possible risks and uncertainties that may damage your firm. By doing a detailed examination of market trends, consumer behavior, and competition dynamics, you may predict future issues and establish contingency plans. This risk reduction method boosts your capacity to handle uncertainties, adapt to disruptions, and sustain a competitive edge.

7. Supporting facts-Driven Decision Making: Market analysis offers facts and insights that help data-driven decision-making. It helps you obtain objective information, analyze possibilities, and estimate the probable consequences of strategic decisions. By relying on data and market information, you may make educated judgments, decrease biases, and raise the probability of success.

Identifying Strengths and Weaknesses

To surpass your competition, it is vital to comprehend your organization's internal environment. Conducting a comprehensive examination of your strengths and shortcomings helps uncover areas where you thrive and those that need work. Leveraging your abilities helps you to distinguish yourself and profit on your unique selling propositions. Addressing vulnerabilities proactively helps you to increase your skills and narrow the gaps in your competitive arsenal, making your business more robust and flexible.

Identifying strengths and weaknesses is a vital component of establishing a strategy framework for competitive advantage. It entails doing an internal examination of your company to find areas where you excel (strengths) and areas that need development (weaknesses).

CHAPTER 9:RESOURCE ALLOCATION

In the dynamic and ever-evolving business environment, resource allocation plays a vital role in deciding the success or failure of enterprises. Efficient and efficient resource allocation is vital for increasing production, eliminating waste, and obtaining a competitive advantage in the marketplace. In this article, we investigate the necessity of optimizing resource allocation and provide numerous ways that might boost efficiency and effectiveness.

Maximizing Efficiency(Doing More with Less)

Efficiency sits at the foundation of resource allocation optimization. Businesses must seek to increase efficiency by using resources to their greatest capacity while eliminating waste and needless costs. Streamlining processes, reducing redundancies, and introducing lean methods may greatly boost efficiency, enabling firms to accomplish more with fewer resources.

In today's corporate environment, when resources are frequently limited and competition is severe, firms confront the continuing challenge of doing more with fewer resources. Maximizing efficiency in resource allocation is a significant way to overcome this difficulty. It entails maximizing the usage of existing resources, avoiding waste, and decreasing needless costs, all to do more with fewer resources.

Here's a deeper look at the notion of optimizing efficiency and how it might help businesses:

1. Streamlining Processes: By examining and reevaluating business processes, firms may find areas of inefficiency and streamline them. This entails reducing redundant or superfluous stages, automating repetitive operations, and using lean concepts to eliminate waste and enhance efficiency. Streamlining procedures allows firms to execute tasks more promptly and efficiently, minimizing the pressure on resources.

2.Identifying and Removing Waste: Waste can take many forms, such as excessive inventory, overstaffing, unnecessary equipment, or inefficient use of time. Companies can reduce wasteful expenses and optimize resource utilization by conducting thorough analyses and implementing waste reduction strategies like Just-in-Time (JIT) inventory management. This will result in improved operational efficiency and cost savings.

3. Optimizing Resource Allocation: Efficient resource allocation includes carefully allocating resources to projects or activities that provide the best possible return on investment. It involves a complete awareness of corporate goals and objectives, as well as a clear appraisal of the effect and relevance of each resource. By aligning resource allocation with strategic goals, businesses may concentrate their efforts on areas that provide the greatest value, allowing them to accomplish more with their limited resources.

4. Embracing Technology and Automation: Technology plays a significant role in optimizing efficiency. Automation technologies, sophisticated analytics, and digital platforms help speed operations, boost accuracy, and decrease human mistakes. By embracing technology, firms may automate tedious operations, enhance data analysis, and get important insights to optimize resource allocation choices. This helps organizations to deploy resources more accurately and efficiently, reducing wasteful behaviors.

5. Continuous Improvement: Maximizing efficiency is a continual activity that demands a culture of continuous improvement. Businesses should encourage workers to discover areas of inefficiency, provide remedies, and engage in process improvement activities. By cultivating a culture of continuous improvement, firms may continually refine their resource allocation techniques, adapt to changing conditions, and enhance efficiency over time.

Benefits of Maximizing Efficiency:

a. Cost Savings: By eliminating waste, minimizing needless spending, and improving resource allocation, firms may realize considerable cost savings. This enables for more efficient use of financial resources, freeing up funds for other strategic projects or investments.

b. Enhanced Productivity: Maximizing efficiency helps firms to do more within the same period, raising productivity levels.

With simplified procedures and optimal resource allocation, staff can concentrate on value-adding activities and provide higher-quality outputs.

c. Improved Customer Satisfaction: Efficient resource allocation helps firms to offer goods or services in a timely way, satisfying customer expectations and boosting satisfaction levels. This may lead to enhanced client loyalty, favorable word-of-mouth recommendations, and eventually, a competitive edge in the industry.

d. Competitive advantage: Organizations that optimize efficiency have a competitive advantage over their opponents. They may operate with fewer budgets, invest in innovation, and react more rapidly to market changes. By deploying their resources more efficiently, these organizations may react promptly to new opportunities, outperform rivals, and prosper in adverse business conditions.

Effective Resource Prioritization(Focus on High-Impact Areas)

Effective resource allocation entails strategic prioritizing based on the value and possible effect of each resource. By properly understanding company goals and objectives, firms may identify vital resources and deploy them to activities that correspond closely with strategic priorities. This technique guarantees that resources are allocated to high-impact areas, supporting development and retaining a competitive edge.

Resource allocation, it's not only about spreading resources fairly among diverse projects or efforts. Effective resource prioritizing requires deliberately allocating resources to high-impact areas that correspond closely with business goals and objectives. By concentrating resources on projects that provide the greatest potential for success and value generation, firms may maximize their results and achieve a competitive edge.

Let's go more into the topic of effective resource prioritization:

1. Alignment with Strategic goals: Effective resource prioritizing starts with a clear knowledge of the organization's strategic goals. By aligning resource allocation choices with these goals, organizations guarantee that their resources are focused on activities that directly contribute to the overall purpose and vision of the firm. This alignment helps allocate resources in a manner that optimizes their influence on important strategic objectives.

2. Evaluation of Potential effect: Resource prioritizing includes examining the potential effect of each project or effort on the organization's objectives. This review entails analyzing elements such as revenue creation, cost reduction, market share growth, customer happiness, and long-term sustainability. By completing a detailed study of the possible effect, firms may identify high-impact areas that warrant more resource allocation.

3. Risk vs. Reward Assessment: Resource prioritizing also entails analyzing the risks involved with each project or

endeavor. High-impact regions may entail higher degrees of risk, but they also provide bigger potential benefits. By carefully examining the risks and benefits of various projects, organizations may make educated judgments on how to use their resources efficiently. This guarantees that resources are given to initiatives with a balanced risk-reward profile and favorable prospects of success.

4. ROI and Value Analysis: Effective resource prioritizing entails examining the return on investment (ROI) and value potential of various projects or efforts. By examining the projected financial returns, strategic value, and long-term advantages of each choice, firms may allocate resources appropriately. This study helps identify projects that provide the highest ROI and value, allowing firms to focus resources on efforts with the most potential for achieving concrete outcomes.

5. Continuous Evaluation and Adjustments: Resource prioritizing is not a one-time choice; it's a continuing process. Businesses should regularly analyze the success of programs and initiatives, documenting their progress and results. By monitoring the outcomes and comparing them to the original resource allocation choices, businesses may make modifications as required. This iterative strategy guarantees that resources are constantly allocated to high-impact sectors, allowing rapid decision-making and resource optimization.

Benefits of Effective Resource Prioritization:

a. Enhanced concentration and Efficiency: By allocating resources to high-impact areas, firms may concentrate their efforts on activities that correspond with strategic goals. This concentration of resources promotes efficiency, as teams can concentrate their time and skills on initiatives that have the highest potential for success. It avoids spreading resources too thin across several efforts, resulting in better results and enhanced overall performance.

b. Optimal Resource Allocation: Effective resource prioritizing helps businesses to distribute resources effectively, ensuring that they are focused on where they will have the most significant impact. By minimizing resource allocation to low-priority or low-impact initiatives, organizations may improve resource usage, decrease waste, and maximize the return on their expenditures.

c. Strategic Decision-Making: Prioritizing resources effectively enhances strategic decision-making. By aligning resource allocation decisions with strategic goals, companies may make educated choices about where to spend their resources for long-term success. This helps firms allocate resources in a manner that supports their entire company plan, promoting growth and competitive advantage.

d. Risk Mitigation: Prioritizing resources based on possible effects and risk assessment helps companies minimize risks. By allocating resources to efforts with a balanced risk-reward profile, firms may decrease the likelihood of resource wasting on high-risk ventures that may not generate desired results. This risk-aware strategy promotes decision-making and preserves the organization's overall financial stability.

Agility and Adaptability(Responding to Changing Demands)

In today's fast-paced and dynamic business world, firms confront ongoing changes in market demands, client preferences, technical breakthroughs, and industry trends. To flourish in such an environment, organizations need to be nimble and adaptive in their resource allocation techniques. Agility and adaptability entail the capacity to react fast and efficiently to changing needs, ensuring that resources are directed to the correct places at the right time.

Let's study the topic of agility and flexibility in resource allocation:

1. Flexibility in Resource Allocation: Agile businesses have the flexibility to alter their resource allocation rapidly and effectively in response to changing conditions. This requires having a flexible attitude and mechanisms in place that enable for reallocation of resources as required. By being able to reallocate resources swiftly, firms may capture new opportunities, react to abrupt market adjustments, and minimize risks efficiently.

2. Swift Decision-Making: Agility and flexibility in resource allocation demand simplified decision-making procedures.

Organizations must be able to make choices swiftly, based on up-to-date information and insights. This may entail empowering decision-makers at different levels within the company, allowing them to make educated decisions about resource allocation. Swift decision-making helps guarantee that resources are deployed promptly to capitalize on market opportunities and solve shifting obstacles.

3. Resource Redeployment: Agile businesses can redeploy resources from underperforming or less strategic areas to those with greater potential or urgent requirements. This may require reallocating financial resources, human capital, technology, or other assets to various projects or initiatives. By successfully redeploying resources, firms may improve resource use, eliminate waste, and adjust to changing needs in a timely way.

4. Cross-Functional cooperation: Agility and flexibility in resource allocation necessitate efficient cross-functional cooperation within the company. This cooperation entails breaking down silos and developing a culture of information sharing, teamwork, and knowledge exchange. By bringing together varied viewpoints and experiences from multiple departments or teams, firms may make better-informed choices regarding resource allocation, considering a larger variety of considerations and possible repercussions.

5. Continuous Monitoring and Evaluation: Agile businesses continually monitor and assess the performance of projects, initiatives, and resource allocation choices. This entails

recording key performance indicators (KPIs), assessing results, and getting feedback from stakeholders. By routinely analyzing resource allocation effectiveness, firms may discover areas for improvement, make required modifications, and maintain continued alignment with developing needs and strategic goals.

Benefits of Agility and Adaptability in Resource Allocation:

a. Competitive Advantage: Agile and adaptive resource allocation offers firms a competitive advantage by allowing them to react promptly to market developments, consumer needs, and new possibilities. By distributing resources in an agile way, organizations may exploit competitive advantages, adjust their plans, and remain ahead of their competition.

b. Increased Responsiveness: Agile resource allocation helps firms to adapt quickly and effectively to changes in the business environment. By being able to reallocate resources immediately, firms may alter their strategy, improve operations, and meet new issues or opportunities as they occur. This responsiveness helps organizations match consumer expectations, capitalize on industry developments, and retain a solid market position.

c. Risk Mitigation: Agility and adaptation in resource allocation help firms reduce risks. By monitoring market circumstances and making appropriate modifications to resource allocation, organizations may proactively react to possible hazards or market downturns. This risk-aware strategy helps maintain the organization's financial stability and resiliency.

d. Resource Optimization: Agile companies optimize resource usage by ensuring that resources are allocated to areas with the best potential for success. By regularly analyzing resource allocation choices, firms may detect inefficiencies, remove inefficient practices, and shift resources to projects or initiatives with higher prospects. This improvement enhances overall performance and cost-efficiency.

Technology-Driven Optimization(Harnessing Data and
Automation)

In today's digital world, technology plays a transformational role in improving resource allocation. With the amount of data and powerful automation technologies available, organizations may harness technology to make data-driven choices and automate resource allocation procedures. Technology-driven optimization includes utilizing data and automation to better the accuracy, efficiency, and effectiveness of resource allocation.

Let's go more into this concept:

1. Data-Driven Decision Making: Technology helps firms to gather, analyze, and understand huge volumes of data linked to resource allocation. By employing sophisticated analytics and data visualization technologies, companies may get significant insights into resource use patterns, past performance, and future trends. These insights allow

data-driven decision-making, helping firms to deploy resources more precisely and efficiently based on objective analysis rather than subjective assumptions.

2. Resource consumption Analysis: Technology allows firms to monitor and evaluate resource consumption in real time. With the use of digital platforms and software programs, companies may monitor the allocation and consumption of resources, such as money, human capital, equipment, or inventories. This research helps uncover unused or overutilized resources, enabling firms to improve their allocation techniques and resolve any imbalances that may emerge.

3. Predictive Analytics: Technology allows utilizing predictive analytics algorithms that can foresee future resource demands and results. By examining historical data and applying machine learning algorithms, firms may estimate resource needs, foresee future bottlenecks, and improve their allocation choices. Predictive analytics provides proactive resource allocation, ensuring that the relevant resources are accessible at the right moment to meet business goals and objectives.

4. Automation of Resource Allocation Processes: Technology-driven optimization entails automating resource allocation processes via the use of digital tools, algorithms, and workflows. Automation removes manual and time-consuming processes involved with resource allocation, such as data input, computations, and repeated decision-making. By automating these procedures, firms may

speed up resource allocation, decrease human error, and deploy resources more effectively.

5. Resource Allocation Simulation: Technology allows firms to model multiple resource allocation scenarios. Through simulation tools, companies may simulate alternative resource allocation techniques and analyze their prospective results. This helps firms to experiment with numerous scenarios, assess the effect of changes, and determine the most optimum resource allocation approach before adopting it. Simulation helps decrease risks and uncertainty involved with resource allocation choices.

6. Integration with business Systems: Technology-driven optimization entails integrating resource allocation procedures with other business systems, such as project management software, customer relationship management (CRM) systems, and financial management systems. The integration enables smooth data flow, real-time updates, and increased insight into resource allocation across multiple functional areas. This connection helps firms make more informed resource allocation choices and guarantees alignment with larger corporate processes.

Benefits of Technology-Driven Optimization:

a. Improved Accuracy: Technology-driven optimization minimizes the dependence on manual procedures and human judgment, decreasing mistakes and biases in resource allocation choices. By exploiting data and employing modern analytics, firms may make more accurate forecasts and allocate resources based on objective analysis, leading to better results and enhanced resource usage.

b. Increased Efficiency: Automation of resource allocation procedures removes time-consuming manual operations, allowing firms to distribute resources more effectively. By optimizing processes and lowering administrative load, firms may free up important time and concentrate on strategic decision-making and value-added operations.

c. Enhanced Resource use: Technology helps firms to acquire insights into resource use trends, detect inefficiencies, and enhance allocation tactics. By knowing how resources are being used, companies may make educated choices to enhance resource usage, decrease waste, and remove bottlenecks.

d. capacity and Adaptability: Technology-driven optimization offers firms the capacity to adjust swiftly to changing needs. Real-time data, predictive analytics, and simulation capabilities enable firms to modify their resource allocation plans immediately and proactively, ensuring that resources are matched with developing demands and market dynamics.

Collaboration and Communication(Enhancing Decision-Making)

Efficient and efficient resource allocation depends on teamwork and communication inside a company. Establishing open lines of communication and establishing a collaborative culture encourages cross-functional collaboration and information exchange. When teams work together, they can align objectives, use varied viewpoints, and collaboratively make educated choices regarding resource allocation. This collaborative approach guarantees that resources are directed to programs and activities that have the greatest potential for success.

Collaboration and communication are essential aspects of maximizing resource allocation within businesses. Effective cooperation and communication promote the interchange of information, alignment of objectives, and group decision-making processes. By cultivating a collaborative culture and providing clear communication channels, firms may strengthen decision-making related to resource allocation.

Let's investigate this topic further:

1. Cross-Functional Collaboration: Collaboration entails bringing together personnel from diverse functional areas within the company to collaboratively make choices regarding resource allocation. By incorporating stakeholders from other areas, such as finance, operations, marketing, and human resources, firms may use varied viewpoints and experiences. Cross-functional cooperation offers a comprehensive perspective of resource allocation demands, considers multiple opinions, and fosters improved decision-making.

2. information exchange: Collaboration allows the exchange of information and ideas between teams and departments.

When people share their skills, experiences, and best practices, it leads to a greater understanding of resource allocation difficulties and possibilities. This information exchange helps businesses to make better-informed choices, learn from prior experiences, and avoid possible errors in resource allocation.

3. Alignment of Goals: Effective cooperation ensures that all stakeholders are aligned with the organization's goals and objectives. By creating a common understanding of strategic goals, organizations may allocate resources in a way that supports the overall vision and purpose. When teams and people are linked with shared objectives, decision-making related to resource allocation becomes more focused and coherent.

4. Transparent Communication: Clear and transparent communication is vital for better decision-making in resource allocation. Transparent communication guarantees that essential information is provided freely and consistently throughout the company. It provides stakeholders to have a clear view of resource availability, project needs, and possible trade-offs. With transparent communication, decision-makers may make educated decisions regarding resource allocation, considering the demands and restrictions of various projects or initiatives.

5. Stakeholder Engagement: Collaboration and communication include actively involving stakeholders in the decision-making process. This involves obtaining input,

feedback, and buy-in from people or teams affected by resource allocation choices. By including stakeholders throughout the decision-making process, companies may gather useful insights, resolve issues, and build a feeling of ownership and commitment to the resource allocation plan.

6. Decision-Making Processes: Collaboration and communication enhance decision-making processes linked to resource allocation. By building explicit decision-making frameworks, businesses may clarify roles, responsibilities, and decision power. This clarity helps expedite the decision-making process, minimize needless delays or bottlenecks, and guarantee that choices are made in a timely and efficient way.

Benefits of Collaboration and Communication in Resource Allocation:

a. Enhanced Decision Quality: Collaboration and communication contribute to higher-quality choices in resource allocation. By harnessing the combined knowledge and skills of teams, companies may evaluate diverse viewpoints, discover blind spots, and make well-informed choices that reflect the larger effect on the company.

b. Improved Resource Alignment: Collaboration ensures that resources are given to projects and activities that correspond with strategic objectives and priorities. By integrating key stakeholders, firms may better understand the resource demands of various initiatives, evaluate their strategic value, and allocate resources appropriately. This enhances resource alignment and raises the chance of effective results.

c. Increased responsibility: Collaboration and communication generate a feeling of shared responsibility among stakeholders. When people are participating in decision-making processes, they have a higher feeling of ownership and responsibility for the allotted resources. This responsibility encourages efficient resource use, as employees seek to achieve optimum outcomes and show their dedication to the organization's success.

d. Enhanced Adaptability: Collaboration and communication allow businesses to respond swiftly to changing resource allocation demands. When teams cooperate successfully, they may recognize developing resource needs, modify priorities, and reallocate resources appropriately. This flexibility enables firms to adjust to altering market circumstances, consumer needs, and competitive dynamics.

Continuous Evaluation and Improvement (Iterative Resource Allocation)

Resource allocation is not a one-time operation but a continual process. Organizations must frequently analyze and assess the success of their resource allocation methods. By gathering input, monitoring performance, and assessing results, firms may find areas for improvement and enhance their allocation processes. This iterative approach helps firms to adapt to changing conditions, improve resource use, and preserve a competitive edge.

Resource allocation is not a one-time exercise but an ongoing process that needs regular examination and improvement. Organizations that emphasize constant review and improvement in their resource allocation techniques may adapt to changing conditions, maximize resource use, and boost overall performance.

Let's go more into the notion of continual review and improvement in resource allocation:

1. evaluating Performance: Continuous assessment entails evaluating the performance of programs, initiatives, and resource allocation choices. This involves measuring key performance indicators (KPIs), such as project milestones, financial metrics, customer satisfaction, and resource utilization rates. By monitoring performance, companies may analyze the success of their resource allocation methods, identify areas for improvement, and make data-driven choices based on real-time insights.

2. input Collection: Gathering input from stakeholders is vital for analyzing the effect of resource allocation choices. Feedback may come from project teams, department leaders, clients, or other relevant parties. By actively soliciting feedback, companies may receive insights into how effectively resources are being allocated, discover pain areas or bottlenecks, and collect recommendations for change. This feedback-driven method helps businesses make educated improvements to their resource allocation plans.

3. Data Analysis and Insights: Continuous evaluation entails examining data to get insights into resource allocation patterns and results. By employing data analytics tools and methodologies, companies may spot trends, reveal patterns, and assess the success of resource allocation choices. Data analysis helps uncover areas of inefficiency, highlight the potential for improvement, and give a platform for evidence-based decision-making.

4. Iterative Decision-Making: Continuous review and improvement require an iterative approach to decision-making. Organizations should frequently evaluate and revise resource allocation choices, including new information, changing conditions, and lessons gained from past iterations. By adopting an iterative strategy, firms may make incremental changes, learn from their experiences, and modify their resource allocation techniques over time.

5. Process Optimization: Continuous review and improvement can require improving the resource allocation process itself. This involves finding and reducing inefficiencies, optimizing operations, and applying best practices. By consistently improving the resource allocation process, companies may boost efficiency, decrease waste, and establish a more efficient and agile decision-making framework.

6. Learning Culture: Organizations that value continual review and development promote a learning culture among their staff. This entails encouraging workers to share their views, learn from triumphs and errors, and actively engage in

the resource allocation review process. A learning culture supports creativity, cooperation, and the ongoing pursuit of excellence in resource allocation.

Benefits of Continuous Evaluation and Improvement:

a. Adaptability: Continuous review and improvement allow firms to adjust their resource allocation techniques to changing conditions. By frequently monitoring performance, receiving feedback, and analyzing data, companies may make timely changes and reallocate resources to solve growing difficulties or grasp new possibilities.

b. Optimization of Resource usage: Continuous examination and improvement assist optimize resource usage. By identifying areas of inefficiency, obtaining insights from performance data, and implementing process changes, companies may make more efficient use of their resources. This optimization avoids waste, decreases expenses, and maximizes the value created from given resources.

c. Enhanced Decision-Making: Continuous assessment provides businesses with the essential knowledge to make educated choices regarding resource allocation. By evaluating data, gathering feedback, and examining performance, decision-makers may get insights into the success of their resource allocation plans. This leads to enhanced decision-making and the capacity to spend resources more strategically.

d. Continuous development and Innovation: Continuous review and improvement build a culture of development and innovation inside the company. By encouraging workers to engage in the review process, exchange thoughts, and learn from experiences, firms may constantly improve their resource allocation techniques. This culture of development and innovation supports creativity, cooperation, and the pursuit of excellence in resource allocation processes.

Risk Management

In the field of resource allocation, businesses need to include risk management as a crucial component of the decision-making process. Allocating resources with risk considerations includes identifying possible hazards connected with various projects or efforts and strategically allocating resources to manage such risks. By incorporating risk management into resource allocation, firms may protect themselves from unanticipated catastrophes, maximize resource use, and promote long-term sustainability.

Let's go more into the topic of risk management in resource allocation:

1. Risk Assessment: Risk assessment is the first stage in risk management for resource allocation. It entails identifying and analyzing possible risks that may affect the success or consequences of various projects or activities. This evaluation involves detecting both internal and external risks, such as market volatility, regulatory changes, project delays, budget overruns, or technical threats. By analyzing risks, companies

may acquire full knowledge of the possible threats and their potential influence on resource allocation choices.

2. Risk Mitigation Strategies: Once risks are recognized, businesses may build risk mitigation strategies to address and decrease the effect of those risks. Risk mitigation tactics entail allocating resources in a manner that decreases the chance or severity of prospective dangers. This may involve diversifying assets, preserving contingency reserves, creating risk-sharing systems, or employing insurance to shift risks. By proactively considering risk mitigation measures during resource allocation, firms may secure their resources and mitigate the negative implications of prospective hazards.

3. Resource Allocation Trade-offs: Risk management in resource allocation demands careful assessment of trade-offs. While certain projects or efforts may have bigger potential benefits, they may also involve higher dangers. On the other side, lower-risk initiatives may provide greater stability but produce lower profits. By understanding the risk-return trade-offs, businesses may make educated choices regarding resource allocation, considering both the possible advantages and hazards associated with each alternative.

4. Scenario Planning: Scenario planning entails examining numerous risk scenarios and their possible consequences on resource allocation choices. By analyzing numerous hypothetical circumstances, businesses may analyze the durability of their resource allocation processes and discover weaknesses. Scenario planning helps businesses proactively

prepare for multiple risk scenarios, build contingency plans, and allocate resources appropriately.

5. Monitoring and Contingency Planning: Risk management in resource allocation needs constant monitoring and contingency planning. By regularly monitoring projects, analyzing risk indicators, and reviewing the success of risk mitigation techniques, companies may spot early warning signals and take required steps. Contingency planning entails having alternate resource allocation strategies available in case of unanticipated occurrences or changes in risk profiles. This helps firms to adapt fast to reduce risks and distribute resources efficiently in dynamic conditions.

Benefits of Risk Management in Resource Allocation:

a. Risk Mitigation: Integrating risk management in resource allocation helps firms proactively identify and reduce possible hazards. By evaluating risks throughout the allocation process, firms may deploy resources effectively to limit the possibility and impact of undesirable occurrences. This proactive strategy strengthens the organization's capacity to absorb risks and assures the long-term sustainability of resource allocation choices.

b. Improved Decision-Making: Risk management provides decision-makers with a thorough grasp of the hazards connected with resource allocation. By analyzing risks with possible benefits, decision-makers may make better-informed decisions that balance risk and return. This enhances decision-making by examining a larger variety of variables and their implications on resource allocation.

c. Enhanced Resource consumption: Risk management in resource allocation helps maximize resource consumption by addressing risk considerations. By detecting and minimizing risks, firms may limit resource waste resulting from unplanned occurrences or project failures. This optimization optimizes the efficiency and efficacy of resource allocation, ensuring resources are directed to projects with the best potential for success.

d. Financial Stability: Risk management helps firms to safeguard their financial stability by allocating resources responsibly. By assessing risk considerations, companies may avoid devoting excessive resources to high-risk initiatives that may compromise financial stability. This guarantees a balanced distribution of resources that supports the organization's overall financial health and sustainability.

Employee Empowerment

Effective resource allocation requires matching resources with the skills and capabilities of people. By knowing the talents and strengths of their workforce, businesses can deploy resources in a manner that enhances employee productivity and engagement. Assigning duties that fit with workers' competence and giving chances for professional advancement helps maximize resource usage and unleash the full potential of the workforce.

Employee empowerment is a critical part of resource allocation since it includes matching resources with the expertise and abilities of individuals within a business. By identifying and using the unique strengths and knowledge of people, organizations may distribute resources in a manner that enhances employee productivity, engagement, and overall performance.

Let's study the topic of employee empowerment and its relevance in resource allocation:

1. awareness Employee Expertise: Employee empowerment starts with a detailed awareness of the skills and talents of individual workers. By examining their skills, knowledge, experiences, and areas of specialty, companies may receive insights about how best to deploy resources to match their strengths. This insight helps firms to tap into the full potential of their staff.

2. Skill-Based Resource Allocation: Empowering workers includes matching resources with their talents and competencies. By allocating activities, projects, or initiatives that fit with individuals' skills, firms may improve resource use. When workers are engaged in projects that use their talents, they are more likely to perform at their best, leading to more productivity and better results.

3. Professional Development Chances: Employee empowerment also entails offering chances for professional growth and development. By investing in training programs,

skill-building initiatives, and continual learning, firms may boost the skills of their employees. This encourages people to take on increasingly complex tasks or responsibilities, hence maximizing resource allocation by matching resources with developing skill sets.

4. Cross-Functional Collaboration: Empowering workers entails establishing a collaborative culture where cross-functional cooperation is encouraged. By fostering cooperation and enabling communication across teams with various skills and experience, businesses may exploit the aggregate knowledge and talents of their workers. Cross-functional cooperation helps maximize resource allocation by promoting the exchange of ideas, creative problem-solving, and effective usage of existing resources.

5. Autonomy and Decision-Making Authority: Employee empowerment means offering workers a certain amount of autonomy and decision-making authority in resource allocation. By including workers in decision-making processes and allowing them the opportunity to make informed decisions regarding resource allocation within their area, firms tap into their creativity and knowledge. This empowerment generates a feeling of ownership, responsibility, and dedication to the success of resource allocation choices.

6. Performance Recognition and Rewards: Recognizing and rewarding employee performance is a vital aspect of employee empowerment. By recognizing and praising

workers' contributions to resource allocation and overall organizational performance, firms build a happy and motivated work environment. Recognition and prizes not only boost employee engagement and work happiness but also inspire individuals to constantly produce their best, further optimizing resource allocation.

Benefits of Employee Empowerment in Resource Allocation:

a. Optimized Resource Utilization: Aligning resources with the ability and abilities of workers optimizes resource utilization. When resources are assigned to people who possess the relevant knowledge, activities are accomplished more efficiently and effectively. This optimization avoids wasting resources and ensures that they are employed in areas where they may have the most significant effect.

b. Increased Productivity and Performance: Employee empowerment leads to better levels of productivity and performance. When workers are allocated activities that fit with their talents and knowledge, they are more likely to be motivated, engaged, and involved in providing high-quality outcomes. This enhanced productivity significantly influences resource allocation results and overall organizational effectiveness.

c. Employee Satisfaction and Retention: Empowered workers tend to be more happy with their work and have a greater degree of job satisfaction. By matching resources with their abilities and skills, firms create a healthy work environment where workers feel valued and appreciated. This, in turn, increases employee retention rates, minimizes turnover costs, and retains a trained and devoted team.

d. Innovation and Creativity: Employee empowerment stimulates innovation and creativity inside the company. When individuals are enabled to share their unique views and ideas, they may offer new insights into resource allocation choices. This encourages a culture of innovation, where workers feel comfortable offering changes or discovering possibilities for more effective resource use.

Efficient and efficient resource allocation is a critical driver of success in today's competitive company market. By maximizing efficiency, prioritizing resources strategically, embracing agility, leveraging technology, fostering collaboration, continuously improving allocation strategies, considering risk management, and aligning resources with talent and skills, organizations can unlock their competitive advantage. Optimized resource allocation helps firms to manage resources effectively, boost productivity, and position themselves for sustainable development in an ever-changing environment.

CHAPTER 10:BOLD DECISION-MAKING

In today's tough corporate world, fast decision-making is the key to establishing a competitive advantage. Yet, numerous firms suffer from the crippling consequences of analysis paralysis—a condition of overthinking and interminable discussion that stifles development and impedes growth. It's time to break free from the bonds of indecisiveness and embrace the power of courageous decision-making. In this post, we'll dig into the art of beating analysis paralysis and empower you with clever ways to make confident judgments that launch your organization to success.

Tap into the Force of Intuition

While statistics and analysis play a key part in decision-making, never underestimate the influence of intuition. Trust your instincts and harness your experience to drive you towards ambitious decisions. Savvy entrepreneurs and outstanding leaders frequently credit their instinctive inclinations for their exceptional accomplishments. By achieving a balance between logical thinking and intuitive insights, you may make bold judgments that set you apart from your opponents.

When we speak about tapping into the power of intuition, we're talking about the intrinsic potential that every one of us has to make judgments based on instinct, gut emotions, and personal experiences. Intuition is that inner voice that steers us, sometimes unconsciously, towards a given option or path.

In the corporate world, where statistics and analysis rule supreme, intuition can be considered untrustworthy or unscientific. However, great entrepreneurs and leaders recognize that intuition can be a tremendous tool for making daring choices. ***Here's why:***

1. Rapid Decision-Making: Intuition functions at a lightning-fast pace. It may give immediate insights and help you to make swift judgments when time is of importance. While analysis and data are vital, they frequently involve time-consuming methods. Intuition may augment these processes and help you make timely decisions.

2. Pattern Recognition: Over time, via experiences and observations, our subconscious mind develops a capacity to perceive patterns and connections that may not be immediately evident to our conscious mind. Intuition taps into this pattern recognition skill, allowing you to draw upon a plethora of implicit information to influence your judgments.

3. Emotional Intelligence: Intuition is intimately tied to emotional intelligence. By being in touch with your own emotions and the emotions of others, you may acquire vital insights into the underlying dynamics of a situation. This emotional awareness may assist you in making judgments that not only examine the cognitive components but also the human considerations involved.

4. Navigating Uncertainty: In the fast-paced and ever-changing corporate scene, not all choices can be based on clear facts or historical research. Intuition assists you to negotiate difficult and ambiguous circumstances, giving you a feeling of direction when there are no clear-cut solutions accessible.

While intuition is a valuable tool, it's crucial to highlight that it should not be the main foundation for decision-making. It works best when accompanied by data-driven analysis and logical reasoning. By incorporating intuition into your decision-making process, you build a more holistic approach that balances both logic and instinct.

Enhancing and honing your intuition requires self-awareness, practice, and a readiness to rely on your gut feelings. By being attentive to your instincts, reflecting on past decisions and their outcomes, and practicing mindfulness, you can sharpen your intuition and access its potential to make daring choices that make you stand out from the crowd.
Remember, intuition is a talent that can be nurtured and perfected through time. Embrace it as a crucial component of your decision-making toolset and harness it to make confident decisions that move your organization ahead.

Set Crystal-Clear Goals and Prioritize

Analysis paralysis sometimes originates from imprecise objectives and a lack of prioritizing. To combat this, describe your goals with crystal-clear accuracy and divide them down into manageable stages. By zeroing in on what genuinely matters, you can cut through the noise of information overload and make choices based on what matches your fundamental goals. Clarity of purpose will allow you to make bold decisions that deliver concrete consequences.

Setting crystal-clear objectives and prioritizing them efficiently is a vital component of overcoming analysis paralysis and making courageous choices. When your objectives are well-defined and prioritized, you receive clarity on what matters and can concentrate your efforts on obtaining the most meaningful results. ***Here's why this technique is crucial:***

1. Clarity and Focus: Crystal-clear objectives give a clear vision and direction for your decision-making process. They reduce uncertainty and guarantee that everyone involved knows the intended objective. This clarity helps you to filter away distractions and extraneous information, enabling you to focus on the crucial variables that affect your choice.

2. Alignment with Objectives: Clearly defined goals are tightly associated with your bigger company objectives. They act as guiding principles and help you assess solutions based on their ability to contribute to those aims. When decision-making aligns with your objectives, you make decisions that support your larger plan and propel your firm forward.

3. Prioritization: Prioritizing goals is vital since not all objectives possess the same amount of significance or

urgency. By prioritizing, you guarantee that your decision-making efforts are focused on the most crucial areas that have the largest influence on your organization. This technique saves time, avoids indecision, and helps you to spend resources efficiently.

4. Effective Resource Allocation: Clear objectives and priorities help you to deploy your resources—such as time, money, and manpower—efficiently. When you know your top priorities, you can target your resources towards activities that correspond with those goals, improving your odds of success and maximizing the return on your efforts.

5. Decision Evaluation Criteria: Well-defined objectives give a set of evaluation criteria for examining prospective choices. You may define important criteria or benchmarks against which you assess the feasibility and alignment of each alternative. This framework helps you remove alternatives that don't correspond with your objectives, allowing you to make confident selections based on a methodical review process.

To define crystal-clear objectives and prioritize effectively:

1. Be Specific: Define your objectives with accuracy, ensuring that they are obvious, quantifiable, and time-bound. Vague or unclear objectives may lead to uncertainty and unproductive decision-making.

2. Align with Strategy: Ensure that your objectives are linked with your broader company strategy and vision. They should contribute directly to the success of your business.

3. Consider effect: Evaluate the possible effect of each objective on your company and prioritize them based on their relevance and urgency. Focus on targets that will produce the most meaningful outcomes.

4. Communicate and Involve Stakeholders: Engage relevant stakeholders in the goal-setting and prioritizing process. Collaboration and open communication help develop an agreement and guarantee that everyone is working towards the same goals.

5. Regularly Review and Update: Goals and priorities may shift over time as market circumstances change or new opportunities emerge. Regularly examine and update your objectives to ensure they stay current and connected with your business's requirements.

Cultivate an Experiment-Friendly Culture

Conquering analysis paralysis rests on building a culture that thrives on innovation inside your firm. Encourage your team members to explore unexplored territory, take measured risks, and extract vital lessons from failures. By adopting a mentality that supports experimentation, you create an atmosphere that fosters daring decision-making. Remember, the greatest discoveries frequently result from courageous jumps into the unknown.

Cultivating an experiment-friendly culture inside your firm is a strong method to overcome analytical paralysis and support during decision-making. This culture enables your team members to explore new ideas, take measured chances, and learn from setbacks. ***Here's why building such a culture is crucial:***

1. stimulates Innovation: An experiment-friendly culture develops an atmosphere that welcomes innovation and stimulates creative thinking. It allows workers to think outside the box, seek unusual ideas, and question the current quo. By cultivating an attitude of inquiry and experimentation, you offer possibilities for new ideas to emerge.

2. Promotes Risk-Taking: Analysis paralysis typically arises from a fear of making errors or taking chances. However, in an experiment-friendly culture, measured risks are considered as chances for development and learning. It encourages people to move out of their comfort zones, explore unfamiliar territory, and try new ideas. This approach switches the emphasis from avoiding failure to accepting it as a stepping stone toward achievement.

3. Rapid Learning and Adaptation: In a continuously changing corporate world, the capacity to learn fast and adapt is vital. An experiment-friendly culture develops a philosophy of constant learning and growth. It fosters an iterative approach, where choices are made, experiments are undertaken, and insights are obtained. This cycle of learning and adaptation

helps your firm to be nimble and react successfully to shifting market circumstances.

4. ignites Creativity and cooperation: When workers are encouraged to explore and share ideas, it ignites creativity and cooperation. Different viewpoints and various skill sets come together to solve challenges and produce new solutions. This collaborative atmosphere generates a feeling of ownership and participation among your team members, leading to enhanced motivation and productivity.

5. Reduces Analysis Paralysis: Analysis paralysis sometimes happens when decision-makers feel overwhelmed by the number of possibilities and possible consequences. By building an experiment-friendly culture, you enable folks to take action rather than being trapped in a loop of overthinking. The focus on experimenting fosters a predisposition towards action, helping to overcome analytical paralysis and push development.

To build an experiment-friendly culture:

1. Lead by Example: Leaders should exemplify the qualities of exploration and risk-taking. Encourage and encourage your team members' efforts to explore new ways. Demonstrate your openness to new ideas and appreciate both achievements and setbacks as chances for development.

2. Provide Resources and Support: Create an atmosphere that offers essential resources, such as time, money, and tools, for

workers to experiment and explore new ideas. Offer assistance and direction to help people navigate through problems and learn from their experiences.

3. Create a Positive Environment: Establish an atmosphere where individuals feel secure taking risks, expressing their thoughts, and making mistakes without dread of severe criticism or negative consequences. Promote open communication, attentive listening, and constructive criticism.

4. appreciate Learning and adaptability: Recognize and appreciate the significance of learning and adaptability. Encourage people to share their thoughts and lessons learned from their experiments, establishing a culture of continual development and information sharing.

5. Provide Learning Opportunities: Invest in training programs, seminars, and knowledge-sharing platforms that develop skills, foster creativity, and encourage a growth mentality. Encourage staff to seek personal growth and explore new areas of knowledge.

By establishing an experiment-friendly culture, you enable your business to embrace innovation, take measured risks, and make bold choices. This culture produces a dynamic and adaptable atmosphere that stimulates development, moves your firm ahead, and sets you apart from the competition.

Surround Yourself with Diverse Perspectives

When presented with challenging choices, the knowledge of many viewpoints may be useful. Embrace cooperation and aggressively seek opinions from workers, advisers, or industry experts. By requesting a diversity of opinions, you improve your knowledge of the problem and unleash new ideas. This variety of opinions will inspire you to make confident choices that rocket your firm ahead of the competition.

Surrounding oneself with varied opinions is a vital approach for overcoming analysis paralysis and making courageous judgments in the corporate environment. By soliciting feedback from people with various backgrounds, experiences, and skills, you have access to a greater variety of thoughts and ideas. ***Here's why adopting varied ideas is essential:***

1. Expanded Understanding: When you connect with individuals from varied backgrounds, you have access to a range of ideas and ways of thinking. Each individual provides a unique collection of expertise, cultural influences, and problem-solving skills. This variety broadens your comprehension of a situation, helping you to contemplate a larger range of alternatives and possible consequences.

2. Challenge preconceptions: Interacting with folks who have diverse opinions challenges your preconceptions and prejudices. It challenges you to examine your previous assumptions and seek alternate views. By breaking away from limiting thinking, you open yourself up to discoveries and inventive solutions.

3. Improved Decision-Making: Diverse viewpoints contribute to more robust decision-making. When you receive information from people with varying experiences and backgrounds, you may balance different viewpoints and insights. This technique helps you detect blind spots, expose possible hazards, and analyze a more broad variety of aspects before making a choice.

4. Creative Problem Solving: Diversity inspires creativity and develops inventive problem-solving. When you bring together people with varied backgrounds and viewpoints, they provide fresh ideas and techniques to handle difficulties. Collaborative problem-solving sessions that incorporate multiple viewpoints frequently result in breakthrough ideas and creative methods that set you apart from the competition.

5. Enhancing flexibility: In a continually changing corporate environment, flexibility is vital. Surrounding oneself with varied ideas cultivates adaptation by exposing you to a diversity of opinions and tactics. This exposure helps you to adjust swiftly to changing conditions, utilize emerging trends, and remain ahead of the curve.

To surround oneself with varied perspectives:
1. Build a Diverse Team: Foster diversity within your team by hiring people from diverse backgrounds, cultures, and areas of expertise. Embrace variety not just in terms of demographics but also in terms of experiences, abilities, and thinking styles.

2. Seek External Input: Engage with external advisers, consultants, or industry experts who contribute new views and ideas. Their different experiences and specialized skills may give vital insight when making key choices.

3. Encourage Open discussion: Create a culture that supports open discussion and courteous sharing of opinions. Establish forums for open conversations, brainstorming sessions, or regular feedback routes where varied opinions may be expressed and considered.

4. Embrace cooperation: Encourage cooperation and teamwork across all departments and levels within your business. Foster an atmosphere where employees feel comfortable discussing their thoughts and engaging with colleagues who offer varied viewpoints.

5. continual Learning: Foster a culture of continual learning and professional growth. Encourage workers to widen their views, acquire exposure to various sectors or specialties, and participate in activities that improve their knowledge and perspectives.

Implement a Battle-Tested Decision-Making Framework

To negotiate the difficult terrain of decision-making, develop a battle-tested decision-making framework inside your business. This framework should incorporate clear principles, well-defined criteria, and a systematic method for assessing solutions. By applying a consistent methodology, you expedite decision-making, relieve analytical paralysis, and guarantee that bold judgments are taken swiftly and successfully.

Implementing a battle-tested decision-making framework is a strategic strategy to overcome analysis paralysis and make bold judgments with confidence. This framework offers an organized and methodical procedure for assessing choices, avoiding ambiguity, and assuring consistent decision-making. *Here's why establishing such a framework is essential:*

1. uniformity and Efficiency: A decision-making framework adds uniformity to the decision-making process. It offers an organized strategy that helps simplify decision-making, particularly in complicated or high-pressure circumstances. By following a predetermined structure, you save time and guarantee that choices are made swiftly and effectively.

2. Clear principles and Criteria: A battle-tested decision-making framework gives clear principles and criteria for assessing possibilities. It explains the essential considerations, measurements, or goals that should be considered while making choices. These rules serve as a reference point and guarantee that choices comply with the general aims and strategic direction of the company.

3. Minimizes Bias and Emotional effect: When choices are made in the heat of the moment or under the effect of personal prejudices, they may not be optimum. A decision-making framework helps limit the effect of subjective biases and

emotional factors. It fosters a more objective appraisal of possibilities based on established criteria, leading to more reasoned and data-driven conclusions.

4. Mitigates Analysis Paralysis: Analysis paralysis frequently originates from an excessive quantity of information or a lack of understanding of how to assess possibilities. A decision-making framework offers an organized procedure that helps reduce analysis paralysis. It breaks down the decision into manageable stages, discovers important facts and information, and directs the decision-maker toward a well-considered option.

5. Facilitates Communication and cooperation: A decision-making framework increases communication and cooperation within teams. When everyone knows the framework and the assessment standards, talks become more focused and productive. It helps people to synchronize their ideas and participate in the decision-making process effectively.

To develop a battle-tested decision-making framework:

1. identify the aims: Identify the aims and goals that the decision-making framework should serve. These goals should be connected with the overall company plan and represent the organization's priorities.

2. Identify essential Decision Factors: Determine the essential factors or criteria that should be considered while assessing

choices. These elements might include financial considerations, market circumstances, client demands, risk assessment, and any other important characteristics related to your sector or company.

3. Establish Evaluation techniques: Determine the evaluation techniques or tools that will be used to examine the choices against the defined criteria. This may involve quantitative analyses, qualitative evaluations, scoring systems, or other relevant methodologies.

4. convey and Train: Convey the decision-making framework to all parties involved. Provide training and assistance on how to utilize the framework successfully, ensuring that everyone knows the process, criteria, and expected results.

5. Monitor and Refine: Regularly examine the efficacy of the decision-making framework and make modifications as appropriate. Seek input from stakeholders and analyze the effect of choices made using the framework. Continuous improvement ensures that the framework stays current and aligned with the developing demands of the company.

In the constant quest for success amidst harsh competition, courageous decision-making is the hidden weapon that sets firms apart. Conquering analysis paralysis needs a mentality change, an unflinching dedication to clarity, and a willingness to take measured risks. By harnessing the power of intuition, setting crystal-clear goals, fostering an experiment-friendly culture, embracing diverse perspectives, and implementing a battle-tested decision-making framework, you can shatter the shackles of indecisiveness and steer your business toward extraordinary accomplishments. So, grasp the occasion, release your boldness, and exceed your opponent with firm and courageous deeds.

CHAPTER 11: EMBRACING RISK

In the dynamic and intensely competitive corporate scene, playing things safe is no longer an option for those aspiring to achieve success. To dominate the market and outperform the competition, firms must become daring risk-takers and make deliberate decisions that offer them an irrefutable advantage. This essay goes into the art of accepting risk and demonstrates how smart risk-taking may unleash unparalleled growth, profitability, and success.

In a world where change is relentless and consumer expectations are ever-evolving, organizations need to break free from old thinking and embrace risk as a strategic necessity. The status quo no longer assures success; instead, it hampers growth and restricts potential. Embracing risk involves traveling into unexplored places, defying conventional knowledge, and pushing the limits of what's possible.

By accepting risk, firms not only become agents of innovation but also obtain the capacity to alter industries and reinterpret market standards. Calculated decisions that embrace risk help organizations disrupt old markets, develop new client groups, and deliver revolutionary goods or services. In this age of fast technology breakthroughs and altering customer habits, firms that embrace risk have the opportunity to overtake their rivals and establish themselves as industry leaders.

Moreover, embracing risk is not a reckless bet; it is a deliberate strategy underpinned by thorough research, market insights, and a deep grasp of consumers' growing requirements and preferences. By weighing the prospective benefits versus the potential dangers, firms may make deliberate movements that have a high possibility of success. This purposeful attitude to risk-taking distinguishes apart visionary leaders who recognize that avoiding risk completely is the riskiest move of all.

Seizing Opportunities

Innovation and danger go hand in hand. Industry giants have proved that taking bold risks frequently leads to innovative ideas. By aggressively accepting risk, organizations build a culture of inventiveness, discovery, and pioneering. Calculated risks push the limits, enabling organizations to pioneer the impossible and earn a significant competitive edge.

In the ever-evolving corporate world, opportunities come and go at a quick pace. Successful firms recognize that exploiting these chances is vital for gaining a competitive edge and generating long-term success. Embracing risk is a vital component of grabbing opportunities since it involves a proactive and forward-thinking mentality that helps firms to capitalize on opportune moments.

Let's investigate this notion further.

1. Identifying Market Trends and Gaps:Seizing possibilities begins with a sharp eye for market trends and recognizing holes in the current environment. By regularly watching

industry trends, consumer behavior, and future technology, firms might detect untapped opportunities, unfulfilled requirements, or new customer preferences. Embracing risk implies having the initiative to act upon these insights, even when the results are unknown. By doing so, firms put themselves ahead of the competition and become pioneers in addressing rising wants.

2. Acting Swiftly and Decisively:
Opportunities seldom linger for long, and procrastination might result in squandered possibilities. Seizing chances demands a feeling of urgency and the capacity to make choices fast and decisively. Embracing risk is being willing to take action, especially in the face of uncertainty. It includes planned steps that help enterprises to position themselves first in the market, create a footing, and establish themselves as leaders before others can catch up. By responding swiftly, organizations may seize opportunities and acquire a competitive advantage.

3. Embracing Disruption and Innovation:
Many chances originate from disruptive forces that transform industries. Embracing risk requires being open to change and actively pursuing methods to innovate and adapt. By questioning traditional knowledge and embracing new ideas, companies put themselves at the forefront of change, rather than being left behind. This approach enables the production of disruptive goods, services, or business strategies that may transform markets and attract people seeking new alternatives.

4. Leveraging Strategic Alliances:

Seizing opportunities might also include building strategic alliances or collaborations with related firms. By merging forces, organizations may access extra resources, knowledge, and client bases, allowing them to capitalize on possibilities that may be beyond their grasp. Embracing risk involves taking the leap of faith to cooperate with others, harnessing their talents to generate mutually beneficial results, and enhancing the effect of grabbing possibilities.

5. Continuous Learning and Adaptation:

Seizing possibilities is not a one-time activity; it takes ongoing learning and adaptability. Embracing risk implies being nimble and adaptive in the face of shifting market conditions. It entails assessing the success of tactics, receiving feedback, and making appropriate improvements. By keeping watchful and receptive to feedback and market signals, firms may embrace new opportunities as they occur and stay ahead of the competition.

Mastering Uncertainty

In the unpredictable sphere of business, uncertainty is a frequent companion. From market swings and shifting customer tastes to technology breakthroughs and unanticipated upheavals, organizations confront a plethora of difficulties that may either paralyze or drive them ahead. Mastering uncertainty is the skill of handling these problems and transforming them into chances for success and competitive advantage. *Let's go further into this subject:*

1. Analyzing Market Trends and Consumer Behavior:
To handle uncertainty, firms must first obtain a comprehensive grasp of market trends and customer behavior. This takes meticulous study, data analysis, and being attentive to the pulse of the business. By monitoring and understanding market signals, firms may spot developing trends, forecast adjustments in customer preferences, and remain ahead of the curve. Embracing risk implies proactively modifying plans based on these findings, rather than submitting to uncertainty.

2. Embracing a Culture of Agility and Adaptability:
Mastering unpredictability necessitates a culture that promotes agility and adaptation. Businesses must be willing to pivot fast, modify strategy, and react successfully to changing conditions. Embracing risk entails breaking away from inflexible structures and hierarchies, and building a culture that supports creativity, innovation, and continual development. By creating a fluid attitude and enabling staff to accept change, organizations can convert uncertainty into fuel for development and success.

3. Embracing Emerging Technologies:
Uncertainty typically develops from disruptive technologies that transform industries. Rather than shying away from technological breakthroughs, organizations that embrace risk grab the chance to exploit evolving technology to their advantage. This entails investing in research and development, investigating new digital technologies, and implementing creative solutions that correspond with company objectives. By accepting risk and implementing new

technology wisely, firms may outrun rivals and acquire a considerable competitive advantage.

4. Diversifying Revenue Streams:
Mastering uncertainty necessitates diversifying income sources to avoid risks associated with market changes or changing customer expectations. Embracing risk includes exploring new company strategies, expanding into adjacent areas, or diversifying product and service offerings. By diversifying revenue sources, organizations may minimize dependence on a single source of income and increase resilience, ensuring they stay profitable even in the face of volatility.

5. Building Strategic Partnerships:
Collaboration is a strong technique for mastering uncertainty. By developing strategic alliances with other firms or industry specialists, corporations may pool resources, exchange information, and harness collective skills to negotiate unpredictable terrain. Embracing risk entails creating relationships that produce synergies, expand market reach, and minimize individual vulnerabilities. Strategic relationships may give access to new markets, distribution channels, or specialized expertise, enhancing the potential to transform uncertainties into victory.

6. Continuous Learning and Risk Assessment:
To master uncertainty, firms must adopt a culture of continual learning and risk assessment. This entails examining the

prospective risks and benefits of numerous choices and making educated judgments based on calculated analysis. Embracing risk requires learning from both triumphs and mistakes, iterating techniques, and improving approaches in response to changing conditions. By adopting a philosophy of continuous improvement and risk appraisal, firms can proactively handle uncertainty and convert obstacles into victories.

Forge Powerful Alliances

In the extremely competitive corporate world, going it alone is typically a bad choice. To develop influence and achieve sustainable success, firms must build strong partnerships that enhance their skills, reach, and effect. By carefully cooperating with other groups, firms may tap into extra resources, experience, and networks that would be tough to acquire separately.

Let's discuss the topic of creating strong relationships and how it may greatly enhance your impact.

1. Accessing New Markets and Customer Segments:
One of the primary advantages of creating partnerships is the potential to reach new markets and consumer groups. By working with organizations that have a presence in various geographic locations or serve diverse client groups, firms may broaden their reach and tap into unexplored markets. Embracing risk involves stepping outside familiar terrain, engaging with complementary partners, and utilizing their

industry expertise and customer contacts to increase impact and grab new possibilities.

2. Leveraging Complementary Strengths and Resources:
Every company contains distinct capabilities and resources. By building successful partnerships, organizations may exploit the complementary strengths of their partners. This might include access to specialist expertise, technology, distribution networks, or production capabilities. Embracing risk includes choosing partners who possess characteristics that match your own, so building synergistic connections that create innovation, operational efficiency, and competitive advantage.

3. Enhancing Competitive Positioning:
Strategic partnerships may be a game-changer when it comes to boosting a competitive stance. By teaming forces with industry leaders or renowned players in the market, firms may boost their reputation and impact. Embracing risk means actively seeking out partnerships that raise your brand image, boost your market position, and separate you from the competition. Collaborating with respected partners may provide a halo effect that enhances consumer trust and loyalty, consolidating your impact in the market.

4. Sharing Costs and Mitigating Risks:
Businesses can incur large expenditures and risks when exploring new projects or entering unknown areas. By creating alliances, these costs and risks may be spread across numerous partners, making them more manageable and less

scary. Embracing risk entails combining resources, sharing financial obligations, and collectively minimizing dangers. By doing so, organizations may explore new markets, engage in innovation, and undertake ambitious initiatives that would be tough or impracticable to pursue separately.

5. Stimulating Innovation and Knowledge Exchange:
Strategic relationships offer a fertile foundation for innovation and information sharing. By partnering with partners who provide varied views and experiences, organizations may tap into new ideas, challenge traditional thinking, and promote a culture of innovation. Embracing risk includes being open to new ideas, embracing collaborative problem-solving, and establishing an atmosphere that supports learning and innovation. These relationships may generate breakthrough inventions and help firms remain ahead of the curve.

6. Expanding Influence and Industry Leadership:
Ultimately, creating effective connections extends your impact and may position your firm as an industry leader. Collaborating with significant partners may open doors to industry events, thought leadership opportunities, and partnerships with other relevant stakeholders. Embracing risk involves actively seeking out connections that boost your industry profile and offer venues for presenting your knowledge. By using the aggregate power of the alliance, firms can make a stronger impact and strengthen their position as leaders in their respective sectors.

Agility and Flexibility

In today's continuously changing business scene, the capacity to adapt fast and remain ahead of the competition is important for long-term success. This demands adopting agility and adaptability as basic concepts in how firms run. By being flexible and sensitive to market conditions, firms may embrace opportunities, handle problems, and retain a competitive advantage. *Let's go further into the notion of agility and flexibility and how they help organizations remain ahead of the pack.*

1. Swift Adaptation to Market Trends:
Agility and flexibility allow firms to rapidly adjust to new market trends. This requires carefully monitoring industry trends, customer preferences, and upcoming technology. By accepting risk, firms may proactively alter their strategy, product offerings, and business models to line with shifting market needs. This helps them to remain current, match client expectations, and capitalize on new possibilities before rivals can respond.

2. Embracing Change as an Opportunity:
Agility and adaptability need firms to perceive change as an opportunity rather than a threat. Instead of opposing or fearing change, effective businesses embrace risk by aggressively searching out new ways to innovate and develop. They establish a culture that supports innovation, learning from failure and constant progress. By accepting risk and being open to change, organizations may transform disruptions into opportunities and position themselves as industry leaders.

3. Streamlined Decision-Making Processes:

Agile organizations have shortened decision-making processes that enable them to adapt fast to market fluctuations. They eliminate bureaucracy, empower workers at all levels to make choices and build a culture of responsibility and ownership. Embracing risk involves trusting people to make educated choices and take calculated risks while providing them with the appropriate support and tools. This helps organizations make quick choices and capture opportunities without being limited by sluggish and complex decision-making systems.

4. Continuous Innovation and Iteration:

Agility and adaptability go hand in hand with ongoing invention and iteration. Embracing risk includes aggressively searching out new ideas, supporting creativity, and developing a culture of innovation. Agile firms continuously question the status quo, experiment with new ways, and iterate on their products, services, and procedures. By accepting risk, organizations can adjust swiftly to changing client demands, solve pain spots, and provide new solutions that set them apart from rivals.

5. Customer-Centric Approach:

Agile organizations promote a customer-centric strategy. They actively listen to customer input, study market information, and make client requirements a major priority in their decision-making. Embracing risk implies being attentive to consumer requests and modifying tactics depending on their growing expectations. By accepting risk and keeping responsive to consumer demands, organizations can create unique experiences, establish client loyalty, and distinguish themselves in the market.

6. Collaborative and Cross-Functional Teams:
Agility and flexibility flourish in an atmosphere that supports cooperation and cross-functional teamwork. By breaking down barriers and enabling cooperation across departments and teams, firms may harness various knowledge, viewpoints, and talents. Embracing risk means allowing teams to work together, exchange ideas, and drive innovation together. This helps firms to adapt swiftly to market changes, utilize internal strengths, and make educated choices that put them ahead of the competition.

Embracing Failure

Failure has long been stigmatized in business, typically considered as something to be avoided at all costs. However, forward-thinking firms recognize that failure is an integral part of the route to success. By accepting failure, organizations may develop a culture of learning, creativity, and continual progress.

Let's discuss the topic of accepting failure and how it leads to development and success via learning and iteration.

1. Shifting the Perception of Failure:
Embracing failure entails altering the view of failure from being a bad consequence to a useful learning experience.

Rather than viewing failure as a clear ending, successful firms perceive it as a stepping stone on the route to success. Embracing risk involves reframing failure as a source of useful insights, learning, and feedback that may shape future choices and tactics. By welcoming failure, organizations create an atmosphere where innovation and learning are rewarded and where people are empowered to take reasonable risks.

2. Learning from Failures:
Embracing failure entails actively seeking chances to learn from errors and setbacks. After suffering a loss, firms should do detailed studies to determine what went wrong and why. This comprises identifying the fundamental reasons, examining the decision-making process, and evaluating the success of plans and actions. Embracing risk includes encouraging open and honest dialogues about mistakes, building a blame-free culture, and supporting the sharing of insights and learnings throughout the business. By learning from failures, firms may find useful insights that influence future decision-making and avoid similar errors in the future.

3. Iterating and Refining Strategies:
Embracing failure also requires leveraging the lessons learned to iterate and develop solutions. Instead of getting disheartened by failures, firms can harness the information obtained to make informed changes and improvements. Embracing risk means being nimble and adaptable, enabling organizations to react swiftly to changing market circumstances. By continually revising plans based on

feedback and insights obtained from failures, organizations may strengthen their competitive edge and raise the chance of success in following efforts.

4. Fostering Innovation and Creativity:
Failure may act as a stimulus for invention and creativity. Embracing risk involves fostering a climate that encourages people to think outside the box, take measured chances, and explore new ideas. When failure is welcomed, people are more eager to experiment, question the current quo, and provide creative solutions. By accepting failure as an inherent part of the innovation process, organizations may develop a culture of continuous improvement, where new ideas are embraced, tried, and modified based on feedback and learnings from failures.

5. Building Resilience and Adaptability:
Embracing failure develops resilience and adaptation within businesses. When organizations regard failure as a learning opportunity, they become more resilient in the face of obstacles and setbacks. Embracing risk implies acquiring the capacity to bounce back from setbacks, swiftly regroup and rethink plans, and adapt to changing conditions. By accepting failure and cultivating resilience, firms are better positioned to negotiate uncertainty, overcome hurdles, and retain a competitive advantage.

In conclusion, accepting failure is not about praising errors but about recognizing their potential for development and learning. By reframing the image of failure, learning from mistakes, iterating and refining strategies, stimulating innovation and creativity, and creating resilience, firms may convert failures into important stepping stones toward success. Embracing risk involves developing a culture that supports measured risk-taking, where failure is considered a chance to learn, iterate, and eventually grow. By embracing failure, organizations may build a culture of continual improvement and generate long-term success.

CHAPTER 12: MAKING TOUGH CHOICES

In the ruthless world of business, making harsh decisions is an unavoidable part of the route to success. Every day, entrepreneurs, business executives, and decision-makers are presented with several alternatives that may dramatically affect the course of their enterprises. These options vary from strategic expenditures and resource allocations to product development and market growth. The capacity to analyze these possibilities and prioritize them properly becomes a vital skill for sustaining a competitive advantage.

Evaluating possibilities needs a detailed consideration of numerous elements, including risks, benefits, market trends, client wants, and resource availability. It goes beyond surface-level evaluations, pushing people to explore deep and unearth hidden jewels that may not be immediately visible. By performing extensive assessments, decision-makers receive insights that help them to make educated and calculated decisions.

Prioritization is equally crucial in the decision-making process. Not all solutions carry the same potential for success or connect with the organization's aims and objectives. Prioritizing options based on considerations including profitability, market demand, resource allocation, and strategy alignment ensures that limited resources are focused toward the most effective decisions. By concentrating on high-priority alternatives, firms may maximize their chances of attaining sustained development and surpassing their competition.

The present corporate environment is more data-driven, and decision-makers must adapt to this paradigm. Gut sensations and intuition alone are no longer adequate. By utilizing market research, consumer insights, industry analytics, and new technologies, such as artificial intelligence and machine learning, decision-makers may make decisions anchored in data-driven insights. This method lowers biases and boosts the chance of making good choices that connect with consumers and seize market possibilities.

However, decision-making in the corporate world is not a static process. It must account for the ever-changing nature of the market, client preferences, and technology improvements. Flexibility and flexibility are key skills for decision-makers, enabling them to pivot fast when circumstances require it. By adopting agility and innovation, firms may proactively adapt to problems and exploit new opportunities, keeping their competitive edge in a changing environment.

To expedite the decision-making process, decision-makers might leverage existing frameworks and technologies. These frameworks, such as SWOT analysis, cost-benefit analysis, and decision matrices, give an organized way to analyze choices and define priorities. Customizing these tools to meet the particular context of the company boosts the efficacy of the decision-making process, minimizing biases and improving the chance of making smart decisions.

The Power of Evaluation

In the world of decision-making, the power of appraisal cannot be emphasized. It goes beyond simply scraping the surface and digs deep into the complexities of each choice. When presented with challenging decisions, taking the time to properly assess the available alternatives might expose hidden gems that may otherwise go overlooked. Here's why the power of assessment is vital in making informed decisions:

1. thorough grasp: Evaluation helps decision-makers to get a thorough grasp of each choice. It requires completing a full examination of numerous issues, including possible risks, benefits, ramifications, and feasibility. By analyzing every part of the possibilities, decision-makers may make better educated and thoughtful judgments.

2. Identifying Opportunities: Delving deep into the review process helps uncover opportunities that may not be immediately evident. It empowers decision-makers to identify hidden possibilities, creative solutions, or unexplored markets. By thoroughly studying each choice, organizations might identify unique selling features, competitive advantages, or emerging trends that can drive success.

3. Risk Mitigation: Thorough examination helps decision-makers to analyze and minimize risks associated with each option. By anticipating possible downsides and

problems, firms may establish contingency plans, identify essential resources, and design tactics to reduce risks. This proactive strategy raises the chance of effective results, especially in unpredictable circumstances.

4.Informed Decision-Making:
Evaluation helps decision-makers to make decisions based on solid evidence rather than assumptions or guesswork. By gathering and evaluating relevant data, market insights, customer feedback, and industry trends, decision-makers may make well-informed choices that are aligned with market realities and consumer demands.

5. Competitive Advantage: The power of assessment offers firms a competitive advantage. By going the additional mile in examining choices, decision-makers might find unique value propositions, market niches, or innovative methods that set them apart from the competition. This comprehensive examination might result in a more unique product, better positioning, and improved market share.

6. Resource Optimization: Evaluation helps decision-makers optimize resource allocation. By examining criteria such as cost-effectiveness, resource needs, and prospective returns, organizations may use their limited resources intelligently. This guarantees that resources are directed toward solutions with the best potential for success, resulting in greater efficiency and optimal returns on investment.

7. Long-Term Perspective: Evaluation urges decision-makers to evaluate the long-term ramifications of their actions. It goes beyond short-term advantages and focuses on sustainable development and durability. By examining choices from a holistic viewpoint, organizations may make decisions that correspond with their long-term vision and objectives, establishing them on a road to continuous success.

Prioritization

When presented with a variety of possibilities, prioritizing becomes a key ability for decision-makers. It includes the skill of assessing which possibilities demand urgent attention and resources, and which may be postponed or deprioritized. Prioritization plays a critical part in focused decision-making and may considerably affect the performance of a company. *Here are some fundamental reasons why prioritizing is essential:*

1. Strategic Alignment: Prioritization ensures that selections are aligned with the overarching strategic goals and objectives of the firm. It helps decision-makers to concentrate their attention on solutions that contribute the most to the long-term vision and goal. By aligning options with strategic goals, organizations may make decisions that move them closer to their targeted results.

2. Resource Optimization: Prioritization helps decision-makers to deploy their scarce resources, such as time, money, and staff, most effectively and efficiently. By giving precedence to solutions with the greatest potential for

success, organizations may maximize resource use and avoid spreading themselves too thin. This focused allocation boosts productivity, lowers waste, and optimizes the return on investment.

3. Risk Mitigation: Prioritization entails analyzing and prioritizing choices based on their associated risks. It helps decision-makers to detect and handle high-risk options early on, limiting possible negative outcomes. By devoting attention to risk mitigation, firms may proactively handle possible risks and difficulties, boosting their chances of success while minimizing the possibility of expensive setbacks.

4. Market Demand: Prioritization takes into consideration the existing and future market demand for various solutions. It examines elements like client preferences, trends, and competitive dynamics. By giving precedence to alternatives that fit with market demand, firms may position themselves strategically to satisfy consumer wants and achieve a competitive advantage. This customer-centric strategy boosts the chances of success in the marketplace.

5. Opportunity Cost: Prioritization entails realizing that picking one choice over another incurs an opportunity cost—the potential advantages lost by not selecting an alternative option. By evaluating the opportunity cost of each option, decision-makers may analyze the trade-offs and make educated choices that optimize the value created for the organization. This helps eliminate lost opportunities and

ensures that resources are directed to choices with the best potential for returns.

6. Time Management: Prioritization helps decision-makers manage their time successfully. By selecting and concentrating on high-priority alternatives, organizations may spend their time and attention on activities that have the most substantial influence on their objectives. This avoids important time from being squandered on low-value or non-essential activities, ensuring that efforts are directed where they matter the most.

7. Adaptability: Prioritization helps decision-makers to be fluid and adaptive in a changing corporate environment. It understands that priorities may need to be altered or reprioritized when circumstances change. By preserving flexibility and continuously reassessing objectives, organizations may adapt promptly to new opportunities or obstacles, remaining ahead of the competition and successfully handling uncertainty.

Data-Driven Decision-Making

Data-driven decision-making is an approach that depends on the study of relevant data to inform and guide the decision-making process. In today's digital age, when massive volumes of data are accessible, harnessing data to drive choices has become a vital competitive edge.

Here's why data-driven decision-making is essential:

1. Objective Insights: Data-driven decision-making eliminates subjective biases and guesswork from the equation. Instead of depending exclusively on intuition or views, decision-makers may rely on factual facts and objective insights gained from data analysis. This technique helps guarantee that judgments are based on facts rather than personal prejudices, resulting in more accurate and informed choices.

2. Identifying Patterns and Trends: Data analysis helps decision-makers to find patterns, trends, and correlations that may not be obvious from observation alone. By reviewing historical data, market trends, consumer behavior, or performance measures, decision-makers might unearth useful insights that assist forecast future outcomes. This helps firms to make proactive choices that fit with market expectations and capitalize on new possibilities.

3. insight client requirements: Data-driven decision-making gives a thorough insight into client requirements, preferences, and behavior. By examining customer data, such as purchase history, demographic information, or feedback, organizations may get insights into what drives customer happiness, loyalty, and engagement. This understanding helps organizations to modify their goods, services, and marketing tactics to meet consumer expectations successfully.

4. Mitigating Risks: Data-driven decision-making helps lessen risks by detecting possible traps or problems. By studying

historical data or performing risk assessments, decision-makers may uncover trends that suggest possible dangers and establish proactive measures to manage them. This method decreases the chance of making actions that may result in unfavorable repercussions, ensuring that firms are well-prepared to face any risks.

5. Improving Operational Efficiency: Data-driven decision-making helps firms to improve their operations and resource allocation. By examining operational data, such as production efficiency, supply chain performance, or labor productivity, decision-makers may discover areas for improvement and make data-backed choices to boost operational efficiency. This method leads to cost reductions, simpler operations, and enhanced overall performance.

6. Real-Time Decision-Making: With developments in technology, firms may access real-time data that enables instant decision-making. Real-time data, like website analytics, sales statistics, or customer feedback, helps decision-makers to react fast to changing market dynamics, consumer wants, or competition threats. This agility and reactivity may provide organizations with a considerable edge in fast-paced sectors.

7. Measuring Success and ROI: Data-driven decision-making helps the evaluation of success and return on investment (ROI). By defining key performance indicators (KPIs) and monitoring important data, firms may measure the success of their actions and investments. This helps decision-makers to

make data-backed modifications and improve their strategy for higher success.

In the world of business, making unpleasant decisions is an intrinsic part of the route to success. By mastering the skill of analyzing possibilities and prioritizing properly, you may achieve a competitive edge that drives your organization ahead. Embrace comprehensive review, prioritize properly, harness data, stay adaptive, and apply decision-making frameworks. With these tactics at your disposal, you'll traverse the complexity of decision-making with confidence, emerging as a genuine champion in your sector. Remember, the decisions you make now will define the direction of your firm tomorrow.

CHAPTER 13:DECISIVE LEADERSHIP

The dynamic nature of the commercial world needs leaders who can make rapid and informed judgments. Decisive leaders possess the clarity of vision and the guts to take measured risks. They recognize that indecision or indecisiveness may delay development and limit success. By exhibiting decisiveness, leaders establish a feeling of trust and confidence among their staff. Employees look up to their leaders as a guiding force, trusting their judgment and competence. This faith in leadership helps firms to simplify processes, manage resources, and adjust swiftly to changing market circumstances, remaining one step ahead of the competition.

Furthermore, decisive leaders have the power to instill confidence among their personnel. They possess a compelling vision and successfully convey it to their personnel. By clearly expressing goals and objectives, leaders establish a feeling of purpose and direction. This shared sense of purpose motivates workers, fuelling their enthusiasm, and inspiring them to achieve their best. When employees trust in their leaders and feel confident in their talents, they are more inclined to take chances, think innovatively, and contribute proactively to the organization's success. This confidence-driven culture encourages cooperation, innovation, and high levels of involvement, offering a competitive advantage in the market.

Accountability is another key part of effective leadership. Leaders who build a culture of accountability establish clear expectations and hold themselves and their teams accountable for their actions and results. By establishing a feeling of ownership, leaders create an atmosphere where employees feel empowered and inspired to achieve to the best of their ability. When workers understand the importance of their contributions and are responsible for their work, they strive for excellence and take proactive efforts to attain corporate objectives. This heightened degree of responsibility leads to better efficiency, fewer mistakes, and a continual push for improvement, boosting the organization's competitive position.

Making Decisive Decisions

In the field of leadership, the capacity to make decisive judgments stands as a distinguishing feature of strong leaders. Decisiveness refers to the power to make rapid, well-informed judgments even under high-pressure and uncertain conditions. This quality is vital in the fast-paced and competitive business climate, where chances must be grasped, difficulties must be conquered, and businesses need to remain ahead of the curve.

Decisive executives possess a clear vision and a strong grasp of their organization's goals and objectives. They have a clear knowledge of the market landscape, industry trends, and the possible ramifications of their judgments. This understanding helps them to analyze risks and benefits promptly, allowing them to make decisions that match the organization's strategic goal.

By making bold choices, leaders generate a feeling of direction and purpose among their employees. Employees turn to their leaders for direction and expect them to deliver clarity among uncertainty. When leaders can make judgments in a timely way, it instills trust in their teams. Employees feel satisfied that their boss has evaluated all the necessary facts and has selected the best course of action. This confidence creates trust, involvement, and commitment among team members.

Decisive choices also help simplify processes and boost efficiency. In a continuously developing corporate world, time is important. Indecisiveness or delay in decision-making may lead to lost opportunities, higher expenses, and lower efficiency. Decisive leaders recognize the necessity of taking action and pushing change. They reduce superfluous contemplation and empower their staff to go ahead, ensuring that projects are performed swiftly and successfully.

Moreover, decisive choices help firms to respond fast to changes in the market. In today's turbulent corporate world, unanticipated difficulties and disruptive forces might surface suddenly. Decisive leaders are nimble and responsive, capable of making course corrections and executing strategy alterations as required. Their capacity to make decisive judgments helps the business navigate through challenges and grab new possibilities, making them competitive and resilient.

It's vital to highlight that making decisive judgments does not entail being impulsive or risky. Decisive leaders thoroughly analyze available information, interact with important stakeholders, and assess the various consequences before making a decision. They are willing to take measured risks, but they also know the need for contingency planning and risk mitigation methods. They establish a balance between speed and deliberation, ensuring that choices are both timely and well-informed.

Inspiring Confidence

Confidence is a major motivator of success in every company. When workers feel confident in their talents and the direction established by their leaders, they are more likely to perform at their best, take risks, and accomplish extraordinary outcomes. Inspiring confidence is a vital feature of decisive leadership since it generates a positive and empowering atmosphere that supports individual and group progress.

Here, we go further into the significance of inspiring confidence and how it leads to a competitive edge in the corporate environment.

1. Clear Communication:
Decisive leaders succeed in expressing their vision, objectives, and expectations to their teams. They have a compelling ability to express their ideas and plans in a manner that connects with personnel. Clear and honest communication fosters trust and ensures that everyone is on the same page, creating confidence in the leader's direction. When workers understand the larger picture and how their job

contributes to the organization's success, they feel a sense of purpose and confidence in their efforts.

2. Leading by Example:
Inspiring confidence goes beyond words—it takes leaders to lead by example. Decisive leaders have a strong work ethic, demonstrate expertise, and show integrity in their activities. They do not shy away from rolling up their sleeves and becoming engaged in day-to-day activities. By showing their knowledge, devotion, and commitment, leaders acquire the respect and admiration of their colleagues, building trust in their leadership skills.

3. Empowering and Delegating:
Decisive leaders empower their people by empowering them with authority and responsibility. They give duties and decision-making power, enabling people to demonstrate their abilities and take responsibility for their work. This empowerment develops confidence as workers feel trusted and respected, and they have the opportunity to develop and progress professionally. When people are enabled to make choices and share their unique viewpoints, it enhances their self-assurance and confidence in their talents.

4. Recognition and Feedback:
Acknowledging and praising employee efforts is a critical component of encouraging confidence. Decisive leaders actively acknowledge and celebrate individual and team successes. They give constructive remarks, giving suggestions for progress while noting positives. This feedback loop instills

confidence in workers by confirming their worth and demonstrating that their efforts are noticed and appreciated. Regular recognition and feedback contribute to a pleasant work environment where workers feel encouraged and inspired to thrive.

5. Creating a Safe and Supportive Environment:
Inspiring confidence demands building a secure and supportive work atmosphere where people feel encouraged to take chances, speak their thoughts, and share their ideas freely. Decisive leaders develop a culture that honors multiple ideas and promotes cooperation. They support innovation and creativity, welcoming new ideas and questioning the current quo. When workers feel secure to express themselves without fear of criticism or retaliation, their confidence surges, resulting in improved engagement and productivity.

6. Professional Development and Growth Opportunities:
Investing in the professional development and evolution of workers is a critical component of inspiring confidence. Decisive leaders give learning opportunities, training programs, and mentorship activities that allow people to better their talents and increase their knowledge. By encouraging workers' progress, leaders display a conviction in their potential and promote a culture of continual learning. This emphasis on growth instills trust in workers, as they know that their leaders are involved in their success.

Fostering Accountability

Accountability is a fundamental factor in corporate performance. It refers to the culture and procedures that hold people accountable for their actions, choices, and consequences. Decisive leaders recognize the value of establishing responsibility within their teams and organizations, as it generates a feeling of ownership, integrity, and quality.

Here, we investigate the value of encouraging accountability and how it leads to a competitive edge in the corporate environment.

1. Setting Clear Expectations:
Decisive leaders create clear expectations for their teams and people. They establish roles, duties, and performance criteria, ensuring that everyone knows what is expected of them. Clear expectations offer a framework within which people may be held responsible for their work. When workers have a clear grasp of their roles and performance goals, they are more likely to take ownership of their tasks and strive for greatness.

2. Leading by Example:
Leaders that create accountability lead by example. They display a strong work ethic, honesty, and dedication to achieving their duties. By demonstrating responsible conduct, leaders set the tone for their employees and establish a culture of responsibility. When workers see their leaders take responsibility seriously, they are more willing to follow suit and hold themselves responsible for their actions and results.

3. Encouraging Transparency:
Transparency is vital for creating accountability. Decisive leaders establish an atmosphere where people feel comfortable being candid about their work, issues, and progress. They promote open and honest communication, giving a secure area for people to seek assistance, exchange criticism, and accept responsibility for their actions. Transparent communication helps leaders to address concerns swiftly, give direction, and hold employees responsible as required.

4. Establishing Performance Metrics and Tracking Progress:
Decisive leaders develop clear performance criteria and systems for measuring success. They create quantifiable objectives and milestones, allowing people to measure their performance and growth. Regular check-ins and performance evaluations allow chances to evaluate successes, identify areas for development, and resolve any gaps in responsibility. By continuously reviewing progress, leaders can guarantee that people remain on track and are held responsible for their promises.

5. Providing Timely Feedback and Recognition:
Feedback and acknowledgment play a critical role in establishing responsibility. Decisive leaders offer timely and constructive feedback to people, stressing areas of growth and appreciating strengths. They acknowledge and celebrate successes, maintaining a culture that values responsibility and performance. Feedback and recognition drive employees to

always strive for improved performance and take responsibility for their job.

6. Cultivating a Learning Culture:
Leaders that cultivate accountability build a learning culture that supports development and ongoing progress. They consider errors and failures as chances for learning rather than causes for blaming. By developing a growth mindset, leaders inspire people to take chances, learn from their experiences, and change their approach. This culture of learning encourages responsibility, as people feel empowered to reflect on their actions, make appropriate modifications, and hold themselves responsible for their growth and development.

Nurturing Growth and Development

In today's competitive business market, firms must emphasize the growth and development of their people. Decisive leaders know that cultivating talent and promoting continual learning is vital for long-term success. By investing in the growth and development of their teams, leaders build a culture of excellence, flexibility, and creativity.

Here, we look into the significance of fostering growth and development and how it leads to a competitive edge in the corporate world.

1. Providing Learning Opportunities:
Decisive leaders give learning opportunities that allow people to gain new skills, improve their knowledge, and develop their capacities. This might include training programs, seminars, conferences, online courses, and mentoring efforts. By

creating options for advancement, leaders demonstrate their commitment to the professional development of their people. Nurturing development via learning opportunities not only develops individual abilities but also enriches the collective knowledge base of the enterprise.

2. Encouraging Skill Enhancement:
Leaders that inspire growth and development push their people to consistently enhance their abilities. They identify areas where people might benefit from additional development and give tools and assistance to enable skill advancement. This may entail giving hard projects, offering stretch tasks, or enabling opportunities to work in cross-functional teams. By fostering skill upgrading, leaders encourage people to attain their greatest potential, creating new prospects for personal and professional success.

3. Embracing Mentoring and Coaching:
Mentoring and coaching programs play a critical role in encouraging growth and development. Decisive leaders build mentorship relationships where experienced personnel assist and encourage their less-experienced peers. These partnerships give crucial direction, feedback, and knowledge transfer. Through coaching, leaders assist people recognize their strengths, areas for development, and growth possibilities. By embracing mentoring and coaching, leaders establish a culture of continual learning and create an atmosphere where people may flourish.

4. Offering Career Development Support:
Leaders that promote growth and development give career development assistance to their staff. They work closely with people to determine their professional ambitions, skills, and opportunities for improvement. This may entail designing individualized development plans, giving chances for progression or lateral transfers, and offering help in gaining relevant skills and experiences. By encouraging workers' professional objectives, leaders develop a feeling of loyalty and dedication while providing a pipeline of talent for future organizational demands.

5. Fostering a Culture of Innovation:
Nurturing growth and development goes hand in hand with cultivating a culture of creativity. Decisive leaders inspire innovation, risk-taking, and a willingness to question the status quo. They create an atmosphere where workers feel empowered to produce and execute new ideas. By offering the opportunity to experiment and learn from mistakes, leaders establish a culture that celebrates innovation and supports continual progress. This culture of innovation fosters growth, keeps firms adaptable, and positions them as leaders in their sectors.

6. Recognizing and Rewarding Growth:
Leaders that encourage growth and development acknowledge and celebrate the accomplishments and successes of their people. They celebrate milestones, recognize skill growth, and provide promotions or new opportunities as appropriate. This recognition and incentives system supports the significance of

growth and development, pushing employees to continue investing in their progress while generating a feeling of success and loyalty inside the firm.

Embracing Change and Innovation

In today's quickly developing business market, change, and innovation have become critical for firms to prosper and retain a competitive advantage. Decisive leaders recognize the necessity of embracing change and promoting innovation within their teams and companies. They know that change is inevitable and regard it as an opportunity for progress rather than a threat.

Here, we discuss the necessity of accepting change and innovation and how it leads to a competitive edge.

1. Adaptability to Market Dynamics:

The business environment is always developing owing to reasons such as technical breakthroughs, shifting client preferences, and rising market trends. Decisive leaders embrace change and urge their employees to be adaptive in response to these dynamics. They stay watchful, continually monitoring the external world, and proactively discover possibilities and obstacles. By embracing change, executives position their firms to swiftly adjust to market upheavals, remain ahead of rivals, and capitalize on new possibilities.

2. Encouraging a Culture of Innovation:

Innovation is a fuel for growth and distinctiveness. Decisive leaders build a culture of innovation by pushing their staff to think creatively, question the status quo, and explore fresh solutions. They build an atmosphere that supports and rewards creative thinking, where people feel empowered to experiment, take measured risks, and learn from setbacks. By embracing innovation, leaders motivate their staff to generate innovative ideas, products, and services, providing their firm with a competitive edge.

3. Promoting Continuous Improvement:
Decisive leaders recognize that standing still is not an option in today's corporate climate. They inspire ongoing progress by creating an attitude of learning and growth. They push their teams to frequently analyze procedures, find inefficiencies, and make improvements to boost productivity and performance. By encouraging a culture of continuous improvement, executives guarantee their firms are continually changing, becoming more efficient, and offering better value to consumers.

4. Driving Change Management Efforts:
Change may be disruptive and greeted with opposition. Decisive executives play a vital role in driving change management initiatives inside their businesses. They clarify the logic behind changes, answer concerns, and give support to workers throughout the transition. By skillfully managing change, leaders minimize disturbance, preserve staff morale, and guarantee seamless implementation of new ideas. Their capacity to handle change effectively prepares the company for development and success.

5. Collaboration and Cross-Functional Integration:
Embracing change and innovation typically demands cooperation across teams and departments. Decisive leaders develop a culture of cooperation and encourage cross-functional integration. They break down silos, foster information exchange, and offer opportunities for divergent viewpoints to converge. By bringing together people with varied experiences and backgrounds, leaders create synergies and stimulate creative thinking that leads to breakthrough ideas and solutions.

6. Embracing Digital Transformation:
In today's digital world, embracing change and innovation typically requires digital transformation. Decisive leaders appreciate the potential of technology and aggressively seek chances to harness it for success. They embrace new technology, invest in digital capabilities, and lead digital transformation programs inside their enterprises. By adopting digital innovation, leaders may optimize operations, improve customer experiences, and achieve a competitive edge in the digital economy.

Decisive leadership is a critical factor for establishing success and keeping a competitive advantage in the corporate world. By making bold judgments, inspiring confidence, and creating accountability, leaders can take their businesses to new heights. Embracing change, supporting development, and building a climate that supports innovation are critical components of good leadership.

As organizations navigate through the ever-changing environment, determined leaders will be the driving force behind their success, encouraging their staff to flourish and accomplish amazing achievements.

CHAPTER14:EXECUTION EXCELLENCE

In today's intensely competitive business market, firms continuously explore strategies to create a competitive advantage and achieve long-term success. While new ideas may flow easily, it is the capacity to properly execute those ideas that set great firms apart. This is when Execution Excellence comes into play.

Execution Excellence is the skill of translating ideas into action with accuracy and efficacy. It goes beyond simple ideation and planning, stressing the rigorous execution of ideas and projects. By understanding the concepts of Execution Excellence, companies may unleash their full potential and achieve sustained development.

In the business world, ideas are aplenty, but execution is the defining feature that differentiates successful organizations from others. Without good implementation, even the most brilliant ideas remain simply notions on paper, having no actual value or impact.

Execution Excellence serves as the cornerstone of success, giving a disciplined methodology that guarantees ideas are transformed into tangible actions. It bridges the gap between conception and execution, translating abstract notions into real strategies. By embracing Execution Excellence as a key value, organizations may limit the risks of idea stagnation or failure, ensuring that initiatives move ahead and generate demonstrable outcomes.

Furthermore, Execution Excellence needs a results-oriented attitude. It redirects the attention from the procedure itself to the outputs and objectives to be reached. By creating clear, quantifiable targets and establishing key performance indicators, organizations can measure progress, encourage responsibility, and build a culture of ownership.

To thrive in execution, firms must also invest in establishing strong execution skills. Effective project management, resource allocation, risk assessment, and ongoing review are all key components of Execution Excellence. By improving these qualities, firms may boost their operational efficiency, flexibility, and agility, allowing them to traverse the ever-changing business environment with ease.

Execution Excellence is not just the job of top-level management. It demands the active engagement and empowerment of every member of the company. By building a collaborative atmosphere and providing workers with the appropriate tools and resources, organizations can harness the aggregate potential of their workforce and develop a culture of execution excellence.

Finally, Execution Excellence is a continuing path of constant progress. Successful firms realize the need of examining prior execution processes, learning from successes and mistakes, and applying corrective actions. By adopting a philosophy of continuous improvement, firms can fine-tune their execution methods, optimize their processes, and remain ahead of the competition.

The Foundation of Success

Execution Excellence serves as the primary basis for attaining success in every commercial effort. It comprises a disciplined methodology that ensures ideas are converted into real actions with accuracy and efficacy. Without a solid foundation of execution, even the most creative ideas and tactics may fall flat and fail to provide the intended objectives.

To grasp the relevance of Execution Excellence as the cornerstone of success, let's investigate its major elements:

1. Driving Productivity: Execution Excellence develops a culture of productivity inside a business. It stresses the optimal usage of resources, good time management, and simplified procedures. By concentrating on execution, firms may reduce inefficiencies, streamline processes, and enhance productivity at all levels.

2. Fostering Innovation: While ideation is vital, implementation is what transforms ideas into reality. Execution Excellence guarantees that creative ideas are not allowed to collect dust, but are actively pursued and brought to life. By building an atmosphere that recognizes and supports the implementation of new ideas, organizations may develop a culture of continuous improvement and remain ahead of the competition.

3. Maximizing Competitive edge: In today's extremely competitive market, establishing a competitive edge is important for sustained success. Execution Excellence helps firms to distinguish themselves by efficiently executing their objectives and projects. It guarantees that ideas are executed fast and effectively, providing firms a head start over rivals who may struggle with execution.

4. Minimizing Risks: Execution Excellence helps firms avoid risks involved with implementing innovative ideas or moving into unfamiliar territory. By employing a disciplined approach to execution, companies may anticipate possible risks and establish contingency plans to handle them successfully. This proactive risk management technique decreases the possibility of expensive errors and helps firms to traverse difficult terrain with confidence.

5. providing concrete outcomes: Ultimately, the cornerstone of success depends on providing concrete outcomes. Execution Excellence ensures that programs and initiatives transcend beyond the planning stage and materialize into quantifiable achievements. It emphasizes attaining objectives, reaching targets, and delivering actual value for consumers and stakeholders.

6. Enhancing responsibility: Execution Excellence develops a culture of responsibility inside the company. By defining clear objectives, creating key performance indicators, and monitoring progress, organizations can hold people and teams

responsible for their responsibilities in executing plans and achieving outcomes. This accountability generates a feeling of ownership and duty, encouraging people to perform at their best.

Bridging the Gap

One of the main issues firms confront is bridging the gap between conception and execution. All too often, excellent ideas are conceived, strategies are established, and plans are formed, but when it comes to implementing those concepts, companies stumble. This is where Execution Excellence plays a critical role in bridging the gap and ensuring that ideas are translated into practical outcomes.

To appreciate the necessity of bridging the gap, let's analyze the essential characteristics of Execution Excellence:

1. Moving from Concept to Action: Execution Excellence is all about taking ideas from the conceptual stage and transforming them into real activities. It emphasizes translating abstract ideas, tactics and plans into real procedures that may be performed efficiently. By bridging this gap, companies may bring their ideas to life and achieve the intended consequences.

2. Overcoming Analysis Paralysis: Many businesses fall prey to "analysis paralysis," when extensive planning and discussion inhibit growth. Execution Excellence helps overcome this by highlighting the necessity of taking action. It promotes firms to establish a balance between extensive

preparation and timely execution, allowing them to grab opportunities and react to changing market circumstances.

3. Managing Change and Uncertainty: In today's fast-paced corporate climate, change and uncertainty are constants. Bridging the gap between conception and execution demands firms to be nimble and adaptive. Execution Excellence offers organizations the skills and techniques required to navigate through uncertainty, alter their plans when necessary, and execute with confidence.

4. Aligning Strategy with Execution: Bridging the gap ensures that strategic goals are matched with execution plans. It guarantees that every activity made contributes to the broader plan and gets the company closer to its objectives. By connecting strategy with execution, firms may avoid the typical issue of having unconnected strategies that fail to produce the expected outcomes.

5. Overcoming Implementation constraints: Execution Excellence tackles the constraints and problems that typically inhibit implementation. It helps identify and overcome possible hurdles such as resource restrictions, resistance to change, lack of communication, or insufficient skills and competencies. By proactively addressing these hurdles, firms may smoothen the execution process and boost the chance of success.

6. Ensuring Consistency and Follow-through: Bridging the gap demands constant effort and follow-through. Execution

Excellence highlights the necessity of being dedicated to the execution process from start to end. It guarantees that activities are not abandoned halfway or lose momentum owing to distractions or conflicting commitments. By maintaining consistency and follow-through, firms may generate sustained success.

Embracing a Results-Oriented Mindset

Execution Excellence necessitates a change in perspective, putting a strong focus on outcomes and results. It goes beyond merely going through the motions of accomplishing activities and instead focuses on producing meaningful and verifiable outcomes. Embracing a results-oriented approach is vital for firms aiming to accomplish their objectives and succeed in execution.

Let's go into crucial features of this mindset:

1. creating Clear, quantifiable objectives: A results-oriented attitude starts with creating clear, detailed, and quantifiable objectives. These objectives should be connected with the organization's overall strategy and give a clear direction for implementation. By creating targets that can be measured, organizations may monitor progress and analyze their performance in reaching intended results.

2. Establishing Key Performance Indicators (KPIs): In addition to creating objectives, companies need to create Key Performance Indicators (KPIs) that serve as standards for performance. KPIs are quantitative indicators that measure

performance and give insights into progress toward objectives. Embracing a results-oriented mentality includes setting appropriate KPIs for each program or project and constantly evaluating them to ensure progress fits with goals.

3. Driving responsibility: A results-oriented attitude develops a culture of responsibility inside the business. It ensures that people and teams take responsibility for their duties and are dedicated to producing outcomes. By holding individuals responsible for their performance and results, firms may generate a feeling of responsibility and promote performance improvement.

4. Focusing on Delivering Value: A results-oriented approach puts a heavy emphasis on delivering value to customers, stakeholders, and the business itself. It moves the emphasis from just executing activities to understanding the effect and value such efforts produce. By connecting execution efforts with the ultimate aim of generating value, organizations can guarantee that their activities have a meaningful effect and drive success.

5. Recognizing Success and Learning from Failure: Embracing a results-oriented attitude means recognizing milestones and victories along the road. Recognizing and recognizing progress and successes promotes morale, motivation, and involvement within the workplace. However, it also entails learning from mistakes and setbacks. By seeing failures as learning opportunities rather than permanent losses, companies may discover areas for development, make

required modifications, and constantly strive for improved outcomes.

6. continual Improvement and Innovation: A results-oriented attitude comprises a dedication to continual improvement and innovation. It pushes firms to regularly analyze their execution processes, find areas for development, and explore novel techniques to achieve better outcomes. By developing a culture of continuous improvement, firms may remain ahead of the competition and achieve sustained success.

Building Strong Execution Capabilities

Execution Excellence depends on the development of strong execution skills inside a company. It entails creating the required skills, procedures, and institutions to successfully convert ideas into action. By investing in and developing execution skills, firms may increase their operational efficiency, flexibility, and agility.

Let's study crucial factors of establishing excellent execution capabilities:

1. Effective Project Management: Strong execution skills demand effective project management methods. This entails defining project scopes, creating explicit goals, establishing timetables, assigning resources, and monitoring progress. By employing comprehensive project management processes, firms can guarantee that projects are completed quickly, risks are controlled effectively, and intended objectives are accomplished.

2. Resource Allocation and Optimization: Building great execution skills entails improving resource allocation. It requires companies to identify and deploy resources such as money, personnel, technology, and equipment efficiently. By carefully aligning resources with the execution of critical goals, firms may increase efficiency, decrease waste, and achieve superior outcomes.

3. Risk Assessment and Mitigation: Execution skills include the capacity to detect and minimize hazards. Businesses need to analyze the risks involved with executing projects and establish ways to mitigate them. This entails doing extensive risk assessments, adopting risk mitigation measures, and building contingency plans. By proactively managing risks, companies may reduce possible interruptions and enhance the chance of successful execution.

4. ongoing assessment and Learning: Building great execution skills demands a commitment to ongoing assessment and learning. Organizations should frequently examine the performance of their execution procedures and find opportunities for improvement. This entails gathering feedback, reviewing performance measures, and applying lessons gained to future endeavors. By developing a culture of constant review and learning, firms may optimize their execution tactics and promote continual development.

5. Communication and cooperation: Effective communication and cooperation are crucial for great execution skills.

Organizations should develop open lines of communication, promote transparency, and foster cooperation across teams and stakeholders. By encouraging open and efficient communication, organizations can guarantee that everyone is aligned, informed, and working together towards a single objective.

6. Agile and flexible mentality: Building excellent execution skills demands an agile and flexible mentality. It entails the capacity to react swiftly to developments, alter plans as required, and embrace unexpected possibilities. Organizations should embrace flexibility, foster inventive thinking, and be open to altering tactics as the business environment develops. By creating an agile and flexible attitude, firms may boost their execution skills and remain ahead of the curve.

Empowering Your Team

Empowering your team is a vital part of Execution Excellence. It entails building an atmosphere where employees are empowered to contribute their skills, knowledge, and expertise toward the implementation of company plans and activities. By empowering your team, you establish a feeling of ownership, engagement, and responsibility, which are critical for driving effective execution.

Let's review crucial areas of empowering your team:

1. Encouraging Decision-Making and Autonomy: Empowerment starts with allowing people the authority and

autonomy to make choices within their areas of responsibility. By trusting your team members to make educated choices, you build a feeling of ownership and responsibility. This helps people to take initiative, be proactive, and contribute to the execution process more successfully.

2. Providing Clear Duties and Responsibilities: Empowerment entails clearly outlining duties and responsibilities for each team member. When people understand their unique contributions and how they match with the larger objectives, they can take ownership of their responsibilities and execute them with more concentration and devotion. Clear roles and duties also enhance cooperation and coordination among team members.

3. Offering Skill Development and Training: Empowering your team requires giving chances for skill development and training. By investing in your workers' growth and development, you provide them with the skills and knowledge required to flourish in their positions. This boosts their competencies and confidence, allowing them to participate more effectively in the execution process.

4. Encouraging Collaboration and Communication: Empowerment flourishes in an atmosphere that supports collaboration and open communication. Encourage your team members to contribute ideas, offer criticism, and participate in productive dialogues. This encourages a culture of cooperation, where varied ideas are appreciated, and novel solutions may be created. Effective communication ensures

that everyone is aligned, informed, and can offer their best to the execution efforts.

5. Providing Resources and Support: Empowerment includes providing your team with the appropriate resources, tools, and support to perform their jobs efficiently. This includes access to technology, knowledge, mentoring, and a supportive work environment. By eliminating obstacles and providing the necessary tools, you empower your team members to concentrate on execution and provide their best work.

6. Recognizing and applauding successes: Empowerment requires recognizing and applauding the successes and efforts of your team members. Acknowledge their triumphs, offer frequent feedback, and publicly acknowledge their work. Celebrating successes promotes morale, motivation, and a feeling of accomplishment, maintaining a culture of empowerment and motivating continuing involvement.

7. Promoting Growth and Advancement Opportunities: Empowerment extends beyond the immediate execution process. It entails giving development and progression possibilities for your team members. Support their professional growth, give mentoring, and establish a career path that matches their ambitions. By displaying a commitment to their progress, you generate loyalty, drive, and long-term involvement.

Embracing Continuous Improvement

Continuous improvement is a fundamental part of Execution Excellence. It incorporates a proactive approach to developing processes, strategies, and execution skills over time. By adopting continuous improvement, firms may remain nimble, adapt to changing conditions, and maximize their execution efforts.

Let's review the crucial factors of accepting continuous improvement:

1. Learning from achievements and Failures: Continuous improvement needs businesses to assess both achievements and failures. By studying successful execution processes, firms may find best practices and duplicate them in future endeavors. Similarly, examining failures helps discover areas for improvement and adopt remedial steps. This learning process helps firms to modify their execution tactics and boost overall performance.

2. Collecting and Analyzing input: Gathering input from stakeholders, consumers, and workers is vital for ongoing development. Feedback gives vital insights into the success of execution efforts, indicates areas of development, and reveals prospective possibilities. By actively soliciting feedback and evaluating it, businesses may make educated choices, resolve problems, and change their execution tactics appropriately.

3. creating Performance Metrics and Objectives: Embracing continuous improvement entails creating performance metrics

and objectives that drive execution efforts. These indicators may be both qualitative and quantitative, indicating particular areas of attention and intended results. By frequently reviewing performance against these indicators, companies may discover gaps, quantify progress, and drive change.

4. Encouraging Innovation and Creativity: Continuous improvement is fuelled by innovation and creativity. Organizations should develop an atmosphere that encourages employees to think outside the box, question the current quo, and provide novel ideas for increasing execution. By embracing innovation and creativity, firms may find new techniques, simplify operations, and promote continual development.

5. Implementing Process Optimization: Continuous improvement entails improving processes to maximize efficiency and effectiveness. This may be done by studying processes, identifying bottlenecks, and adopting process improvements. By reducing procedures, eliminating superfluous stages, and enhancing efficiency, companies may deliver better execution results.

6. Embracing Technology and Automation: Technology plays a significant role in ongoing development. Organizations should embrace technology improvements that boost execution capabilities. Automation, data analytics, and digital technologies may dramatically increase efficiency, accuracy, and decision-making. By utilizing technology, companies may

optimize their execution processes, decrease mistakes, and promote continuous improvement.

7. Encouraging a Culture of Continuous Learning: Embracing continuous improvement means establishing a culture of continuous learning inside the company. This entails encouraging workers to explore development opportunities, learn new abilities, and keep informed about industry trends. By encouraging a learning culture, firms produce a workforce that is adaptive, inventive, and actively participates in continuous improvement initiatives.

Execution Excellence is the gasoline that puts ideas into action and turns firms into industry leaders. By emphasizing execution, establishing strong skills, empowering employees, and adopting continuous improvement, businesses can unlock their entire potential and achieve lasting success in a highly competitive market. Make Execution Excellence your competitive edge, and watch your ideas materialize into remarkable outcomes.

CHAPTER 15: ACTION PLANNING

The fast-paced nature of the commercial world needs more than simply nebulous ideals. It needs a well-defined path that takes you from where you are to where you want to be. Action planning is the hidden weapon deployed by highly successful people and organizations. It gives a disciplined process that guarantees you remain on track, retain clarity, and make continuous progress toward your goals.

By breaking down your objectives into small stages, action planning instills a feeling of purpose and direction in your activities. Each step becomes a concrete milestone that pushes you closer to your final goal. This feeling of progress not only feeds your enthusiasm but also helps you to enjoy tiny triumphs along the road, boosting your dedication and resolve.

Action planning starts with the essential step of identifying your goal. This entails defining objectives that are precise, measurable, achievable, relevant, and time-bound (SMART). Whether you seek to develop your firm, offer a revolutionary product, or increase your professional abilities, your objectives must be ambitious but practical, motivating yet doable.

Once your objectives are determined, action planning breaks them down into bite-sized, doable stages. It helps you to define critical milestones or big actions that must be done to fulfill each objective. By further breaking those milestones into smaller, achievable stages, you develop a roadmap that directs your activities. This technique not only mitigates overload but also adds a feeling of order and clarity to your pursuits.

To guarantee efficient execution, prioritizing and sequencing play a vital role in action planning. Not all steps bear the same weight concerning your final aim. By prioritizing activities based on their relevance and urgency, you may concentrate your attention and resources on the most important acts. Sequencing the processes rationally guarantees a smooth and progressive flow, avoiding inefficiencies and boosting efficiency.

Setting deadlines and milestones is a vital component of action planning. Deadlines provide a feeling of urgency, discouraging procrastination and cultivating a proactive mentality. Milestones operate as checkpoints that enable you to review your progress, celebrate successes, and readjust if required. These intermediate triumphs give a steady supply of encouragement, moving you ahead toward the next stage.

Action planning is not a one-and-done procedure; it involves constant review and change. As you implement your strategy, it's crucial to assess your progress periodically. Assess what is functioning well and what needed modifications. Flexibility and flexibility are crucial attributes of effective action planners, allowing them to pivot when required and maximize their route to success.

The Power of Action Planning

Action planning is the blueprint that converts your aspirations into concrete accomplishments. It gives structure, clarity, and direction, helping you to remain organized and make progress toward your objectives. By breaking down your objectives into doable chunks, you obtain a clear knowledge of what has to be done, when, and how. This not only raises your chances of success but also boosts your drive, since each tiny step puts you closer to your final goal.

In today's fast-paced and competitive corporate climate, the value of action planning cannot be overlooked. Action planning is a systematic process that helps people and organizations to bring their objectives and ambitions into reality. It goes beyond wishful thinking and gives a real foundation for reaching achievement.

Here are some essential features that demonstrate the great potential of action planning:

1. Structure and Clarity: Action planning gives an organized approach to goal accomplishment. It reduces down abstract aims into tangible, practical measures. This method gives clarity and accuracy to your goals, ensuring that you have a clear idea of what has to be done, when, and how. The framework given by action planning lowers confusion, decreases ambiguity, and keeps you on track.

2. Focus and Direction: With action planning, you develop a laser-like focus on your objectives. By breaking things down

into small stages, you reduce distractions and zero in on the exact tasks necessary for success. This concentrated strategy stops you from being overwhelmed by the enormity of your objectives and helps you retain a clear course throughout your trip.

3. Motivation and Momentum: Action planning increases motivation by offering a feeling of progress and success. Each tiny step achieved puts you closer to your objective, giving you a feeling of success and raising your enthusiasm to continue. The momentum built via constant success keeps you motivated and committed, even when confronted with hurdles along the road.

4. Organization and Efficiency: Action planning promotes organization and efficiency by sketching out the essential actions and resources needed for goal accomplishment. By breaking down your objectives into smaller chunks, you may discover possible bottlenecks or resource limits in advance. This helps you to manage resources efficiently, simplify procedures, and enhance your production.

5. flexibility and Agility: Action planning is a dynamic process that provides flexibility and agility. As you grow, you may face unanticipated conditions or possibilities that demand revisions to your initial strategy. Action planning helps you to analyze and alter your strategy, ensuring that you remain sensitive to changes while keeping your ultimate objectives in sight.

6. Accountability and Evaluation: Action planning improves accountability. By creating deadlines, goals, and checkpoints, you build a structure of responsibility for yourself and your team. Regular review of progress against these markers lets you evaluate your performance, identify areas for growth, and make required course modifications to remain on track.

7. Success and Achievement: Ultimately, action planning is a strong instrument for obtaining success. By breaking down your objectives into achievable stages and taking regular action, you position yourself for success. Action planning helps you overcome barriers, manage risks, and enhance your chances of reaching your targeted goals.

Define Your Vision

One of the core tasks in action planning is to establish your vision. Your vision acts as a guiding light, offering a clear image of what you aim to accomplish. It functions as a compass, guiding your efforts and structuring your action plan. *Here's why articulating your vision is vital in the action-planning process:*

1. Clarity and Focus: Defining your vision offers clarity to your ambitions. It helps you express what you genuinely want to achieve and enables you to imagine the intended result. A well-defined vision gives a clear focus, ensuring that you don't get diverted by distractions or deviate from your planned route. It acts as a continual reminder of your final aim and keeps you motivated and determined.

2. Alignment and Purpose: Your vision acts as a touchstone for alignment and purpose. It helps you link your activities and choices with your long-term objectives. When you have a well-defined vision, it becomes simpler to recognize opportunities that connect with your mission and say no to those that don't. It adds a feeling of purpose and satisfaction to your activities, as every step made is a conscious effort toward your goal.

3. Inspiration and Motivation: A captivating vision inspires and encourages you to take action. When you have a clear vision of what you want to accomplish, it becomes a source of motivation through hard times. Your vision functions as a source of internal drive, pulling you ahead and providing you with the tenacity to face hurdles. It drives your enthusiasm and devotion, ensuring that you remain focused on attaining your objectives.

4. Goal Setting and Direction: Defining your vision gives a foundation for successful goal setting. Your vision helps you define precise, measurable, achievable, relevant, and time-bound (SMART) objectives that connect with the greater picture. It gives guidance by directing your goal-setting process and ensuring that your objectives are in line with your vision. This alignment boosts the efficacy and efficiency of your action plan.

5. Communication and cooperation: A well-defined vision fosters efficient communication and cooperation with others. When you clearly describe your vision, it becomes simpler to

convey your aims and objectives to stakeholders, team members, or partners. It establishes a shared understanding and produces a feeling of oneness, facilitating cooperation towards a single cause. A powerful vision may inspire and mobilize others behind your cause, recruiting the ideal individuals to join your journey.

6. Evaluation and Progress Tracking: Your vision acts as a benchmark for assessing your progress. It helps you to judge if your activities are moving you closer to your targeted result. By periodically reviewing your progress against your vision, you can make improvements to your action plan and ensure that you continue on the correct road. This assessment approach creates a feedback loop that helps you develop and enhance your tactics.

Break It Down
Once you have defined your vision and outlined your objectives, the following stage in action planning is to break them down into doable chunks.

Breaking down your objectives into smaller, attainable activities is vital for various reasons:

1. Overcoming Overwhelm: Large ambitions may sometimes seem daunting, leading to lethargy or a lack of direction. Breaking things down into smaller stages makes them more attainable and less frightening. It helps you to tackle one job at a time, creating momentum and confidence as you make progress.

2. Clarity and Specificity: Breaking down objectives into doable phases gives clarity and specificity to your action plan. Each step becomes a precise action that has to be accomplished, offering a clear grasp of what needs to be done. This reduces ambiguity and ensures that everyone involved understands the specific activities necessary.

3. Logical sequence: Breaking down objectives helps you determine the logical sequence of actions. Some tasks may need to be accomplished before others may be commenced. By breaking down the objectives, you may set a logical sequence for performing the activities, ensuring that you move ahead systematically and efficiently.

4. Resource Allocation: Breaking down objectives into smaller phases facilitates better resource allocation. It helps you to analyze the resources required for each work, such as time, money, talents, or equipment. This helps you manage resources more efficiently and ensure that you have everything necessary to finish each phase successfully.

5. Progress Tracking: Breaking down objectives into digestible segments makes it simpler to measure your progress. Each completed step indicates a milestone attained, offering a feeling of success and drive. It also enables you to measure how far you've gone and how much farther you have to go, offering a feeling of direction and purpose.

6. Flexibility and Adaptability: Breaking down objectives into smaller segments makes your action plan more flexible and adjustable. As you make progress, you may find unanticipated events or fresh knowledge that necessitates revisions. Breaking down objectives helps you to adjust and change your strategy as required, without losing sight of the larger vision.

7. Delegation and cooperation: Breaking down objectives enhances delegation and cooperation. Smaller tasks are frequently more achievable and may be given to various team members or stakeholders depending on their abilities and knowledge. This encourages teamwork and shared accountability, enabling everyone to contribute to the broader aim.

Prioritize and Sequencing

In action planning, prioritizing and ordering the actions and stages needed in accomplishing your objectives is vital for efficient execution. Prioritization ensures that you focus your resources, time, and energy on the most necessary and impactful projects. Sequencing defines the logical sequence in which the tasks should be accomplished.

Here's why prioritizing and sequencing are critical in action planning:

1. concentration and Efficiency: Prioritization helps you keep concentration and operate productively. By selecting the most critical tasks, you focus your attention and resources on the

actions that will have the biggest influence on attaining your objectives. This helps you to make the most of your limited resources and avoid spending time and effort on less important chores.

2. Goal Alignment: Prioritization ensures that your tasks correspond with your overall objectives. By examining each task's relevance to your goals, you may filter out any non-essential or peripheral activity. This alignment helps maintain the strategic direction of your action plan and ensures that every job contributes directly to your targeted goals.

3. Risk Mitigation: Prioritizing tasks lets you discover possible hazards and reduce them proactively. By concentrating on high-priority activities first, you handle essential areas of your strategy that may contain larger risks or uncertainties. This helps you to confront possible issues early on, minimizing the total risk exposure and boosting the probability of success.

4. Resource Optimization: Prioritization helps you to manage your resources effectively. By concentrating on high-priority projects, you guarantee that your resources, such as time, cash, and labor, are spent where they will have the largest effect. This eliminates resource loss and helps you achieve optimum efficiency and effectiveness in your action plan.

5. Sequencing: Sequencing defines the logical order in which actions should be executed. It guarantees that you follow a

step-by-step method that leads to the effective completion of each activity. Sequencing analyzes interdependence between activities, ensuring that requirements are satisfied before going on to following processes. This reduces rework and delays, allowing for a seamless and ongoing movement toward your objectives.

6. Avoiding Bottlenecks: Proper sequencing helps you avoid bottlenecks or blockages that may delay development. By determining the key path—the sequence of actions that must be performed to go forward—you can allocate resources and manage dependencies efficiently. This eliminates delays and guarantees that the flow of work stays unbroken.

7. Time Management: Prioritizing and sequencing jobs helps you manage your time successfully. By concentrating on high-priority activities first and structuring them in a logical order, you may set a realistic schedule for goal accomplishment. This lets you allocate time effectively, establish deadlines, and guarantee that you are making progress according to your chosen timetable.

8. Progress monitoring: Prioritization and sequencing give a framework for monitoring your progress. By following the set sequence, you may monitor the completion of each activity and assess your progress against your action plan. This helps you to analyze whether you are on track and make any required modifications to guarantee timely goal attainment.

Set Deadlines and Milestones

Setting deadlines and milestones is a vital part of action planning. Deadlines give a feeling of urgency and responsibility, while milestones operate as checkpoints along the road to monitor progress.

Here's why defining deadlines and milestones is critical in the action-planning process:

1. responsibility and Focus: Deadlines provide a feeling of responsibility and focus. By providing particular dates or timelines for completing tasks or accomplishing milestones, you build a feeling of urgency and commitment. Deadlines help you prioritize your efforts and minimize procrastination, ensuring that you remain on track and make progress toward your objectives.

2. Time Management: Setting deadlines assists you to manage your time successfully. It gives a structure for assigning time to particular activities, helping you keep organized and ensuring that you have adequate time to accomplish each stage. Effective time management ensures that you employ your resources properly and fulfill your intended timetables.

3. Progress Evaluation: Deadlines serve as reference points for measuring your progress. They help you to check whether you are on track and hitting your specified goals. By evaluating your actual work against the stated dates, you may spot any deviations or possible delays and take remedial steps to get back on pace.

4. Motivation and Momentum: Deadlines provide a feeling of urgency that inspires activity. The coming deadline encourages you to be focused, productive, and devoted to completing activities within the allocated time. Each achieved deadline functions as a mini-success, creating motivation and momentum as you get closer to accomplishing your ultimate objectives.

5. Milestone Celebration: Milestones give opportunity for celebration and appreciation of accomplishments. As you complete each milestone, it symbolizes a huge step forward in your action plan. Celebrating these milestones not only raises morale but also recognizes the progress accomplished and encourages the resolve to continue the path.

6. Progress Visibility: Setting milestones helps you to monitor and see your progress. Each milestone reflects a major step or success in your action plan. By breaking down your objectives into smaller milestones, you receive a better sense of the progress you are making. This exposure helps you keep motivated, focused, and aware of how far you have come.

7. Course Correction: Deadlines and milestones allow you to make course adjustments if required. If you realize that you are going behind schedule or having obstacles, milestones allow an opportunity to review your strategy, make modifications, and reallocate resources as required. They operate as decision points where you may assess the efficacy of your action plan and make educated modifications to guarantee success.

8. Communication and cooperation: Deadlines and milestones enable communication and cooperation with stakeholders or team members. They give a shared reference point for conversations, progress reports, and accountability. Clear deadlines and milestones improve clarity, align expectations, and build cooperation among team members, ensuring everyone is working towards similar goals.

Action planning is the secret sauce that allows you to convert your aspirations into reality. By breaking down your objectives into doable stages, assigning deadlines, and prioritizing work, you construct a roadmap that leads to accomplishment. Remember, action without a plan is only a desire. So, take the first step now and begin on a path of intentional action. Unleash your potential, achieve greatness, and build a future that is beyond your greatest aspirations. The power is in your hands—start preparing, start acting, and start winning!

CHAPTER 16: MOBILIZING RESOURCES

In today's fast-paced and ever-evolving business environment, firms confront fierce rivalry, technology developments, and shifting market dynamics. In such an environment, it is not enough for organizations to merely have access to resources; they must be able to mobilize and employ those resources efficiently to acquire a competitive advantage.

While resources like technology, financing, and infrastructure are vital, it is the human element—the high-performing teams inside organizations—that set companies apart. A high-performing team comprises people who possess not only the requisite skills and competence but also display excellent teamwork, drive, and flexibility.

The capacity to deploy resources efficiently is not restricted to leveraging physical assets or financial capital. It also entails utilizing the combined strengths, expertise, and creativity of a well-functioning team. This essay emphasizes the value of creating a high-performing team and analyzes the methods and practices that may help firms attain competitive excellence.

By focusing on building a solid foundation, establishing clear goals and expectations, promoting open communication and collaboration, encouraging continuous learning and development, recognizing and rewarding excellence, and embracing diversity and inclusion, organizations can create an environment where their teams thrive and maximize their potential.

Ultimately, creating a high-performing workforce is a strategic strategy to exploit resources to their maximum potential, allowing firms to achieve competitive excellence and remain ahead in the changing business market.

Building a Solid Foundation

Building a strong foundation for a high-performing team is key to its success. It requires carefully choosing personnel who not only possess the requisite skills and expertise but also connect with the organization's values and culture. *Let's study this further:*

1. Defining the Team's Purpose and Roles:
To develop a firm foundation, it is vital to identify the team's mission and describe each team member's tasks and responsibilities. This offers a clear sense of how their contributions match the team's aims. Clearly express the team's mission, vision, and objectives to establish a feeling of purpose and direction.

2. Selecting the Right Team Members:
Choosing the appropriate folks for your team is crucial. Look for applicants that not only possess the essential technical capabilities but also display attributes such as a development mindset, strong work ethic, and a drive for excellence. Assess

their fit with the team's values and culture to create a cohesive and productive workplace.

3. Fostering Trust and Psychological Safety:
Trust is the cornerstone of every successful team. Encourage open and honest communication, transparency, and mutual respect among team members. Foster an atmosphere where everyone feels secure to voice their views, ask questions, and take cautious risks. Psychological safety allows team members to communicate their opinions without fear of criticism or retaliation, leading to enhanced creativity and problem-solving.

4. Establishing Clear Team Norms and Expectations:
Set explicit standards and develop team norms to build a consistent understanding of conduct, communication, and responsibility. Establish rules for decision-making procedures, dispute resolution, and teamwork. Clearly explain performance objectives and standards to ensure everyone is aligned and working towards a common goal.

5. Encouraging Team Bonding and Relationship Building:
Promote team bonding events and offer opportunities for team members to get to know one another on a personal level. This helps establish trust, builds connections, and creates a healthy team culture. Team-building activities, social gatherings, and shared experiences may go a long way in developing a cohesive and supportive team environment.

6. Providing Adequate Resources and Support:
Ensure that your staff has the required resources, tools, and support to carry out their job efficiently. Address any gaps in training or skills development by providing suitable resources and learning opportunities. Support your team's growth and development with mentoring, coaching, and access to relevant knowledge.

Establishing Clear Goals and Expectations

Establishing clear objectives and expectations is a vital step in creating a high-performing team. When team members have a clear grasp of what they need to do and what is expected of them, it sets the foundation for concentrated efforts and drives success. *Let's study this further:*

1. Specific and Measurable Goals:
Clear objectives are explicit and quantifiable. They give clarity on what has to be completed and allow team members to monitor their progress. Avoid ambiguous aims and instead outline goals that are well-defined and quantitative. For example, instead of presenting a goal as "raise sales," describe it as "grow sales by 10% during the following quarter."

2. Alignment with Organizational Objectives:
Team goals should coincide with the overarching objectives of the company. This guarantees that team activities are oriented toward advancing the organization's success. When team members realize how their particular objectives contribute to the greater picture, they are more motivated and dedicated to attaining them.

3. Challenging yet Attainable Goals:
Goals should be hard enough to encourage and stretch team members, yet practical and achievable. Setting too ambitious objectives might lead to dissatisfaction and demotivation, while relatively feasible goals may not inspire high performance. Strike a balance by establishing objectives that demand work and talent, but are within the team's capabilities.

4. Time-Bound Goals:
Setting time-bound objectives generates a feeling of urgency and helps prioritize work. Assign explicit dates or milestones to objectives, breaking them down into digestible portions if required. This creates accountability and guarantees that progress is routinely monitored and modifications may be made if required.

5. Clear Expectations and Roles:
In addition to creating objectives, it is vital to express clear expectations and identify responsibilities within the team. Clearly describe the targeted results, performance requirements, and duties for each team member. This avoids ambiguity, decreases misunderstandings, and ensures that everyone knows their specific contributions toward attaining the team's objectives.

6. Regular Performance Feedback:
Establish a method for offering frequent feedback and performance reviews. This enables team members to measure their success, identify areas for improvement, and make

required modifications. Feedback should be constructive, timely, and detailed to promote continued learning and growth.

7. Flexibility and Adaptability:
While clear objectives and expectations are vital, it is equally crucial to enable flexibility and adaptation. Business settings are dynamic, and unanticipated issues may occur. Encourage the team to be flexible, sensitive, and imaginative in the face of changing circumstances while keeping the broader objectives in mind.

Promoting Open Communication and Collaboration

Promoting open communication and cooperation is crucial for creating a high-performing team. When team members feel comfortable sharing their ideas, thoughts, and concerns, and when they actively engage with one another, it leads to greater creativity, problem-solving, and overall team performance. ***Let's go more into this aspect:***

1. Creating a Safe and Supportive Environment:
Establish a culture of open communication and psychological safety where team members feel comfortable sharing their opinions and ideas without fear of criticism or retaliation. Encourage a non-hierarchical climate where everyone's participation is recognized and acknowledged. Foster a friendly climate that supports productive discourse and active listening.

2. Regular Team Meetings and Check-Ins:
Organize frequent team meetings to create a forum for open communication and cooperation. These sessions may serve as occasions to share progress, difficulties, and suggestions. Encourage team members to actively engage, give updates, and seek opinions from their colleagues. Additionally, perform frequent check-ins to address specific problems, give feedback, and provide assistance.

3. Establishing Clear Communication Channels:
Ensure that there are clear and effective communication routes throughout the team. Utilize technological solutions such as project management software, instant messaging platforms, and video conferencing technologies to allow smooth communication, particularly for distant or scattered teams. Establish criteria for efficient communication, such as response times, clarity in messaging, and politeness in written and spoken discussions.

4.Foster an environment of active listening within the team: Urge team members to attentively listen to and assess each other's opinions, ideas, and remarks. Create a space where everyone feels heard and comprehended. Stress the importance of providing respectful and constructive feedback, focusing on the concepts and not the individuals. Constructive criticism should be accurate, practical, and aimed at aiding growth and advancement.

5. Team-Building and Collaboration Activities:
Organize team-building events and collaborative projects to enhance connections and increase cooperation. These activities might include brainstorming sessions, workshops, cross-functional initiatives, or team getaways. Encourage team members to work together, exchange expertise, and harness each other's skills to reach shared objectives. Collaboration increases innovation, problem-solving, and the general performance of the team.

6. Embracing Diverse Perspectives:
Value and welcome varied viewpoints within the team. Recognize that diverse team members bring varied backgrounds, skills, and talents to the table. foster the exchange of varied opinions and foster constructive arguments. By including multiple ideas, the team may explore alternate solutions, question preconceptions, and encourage creativity.

7. Documenting and Sharing Information:
Promote the exchange and recording of information within the team. This guarantees that knowledge is available to all members, encourages openness, and eliminates silos of information. Encourage the use of shared documents, knowledge bases, and collaborative technologies to allow quick access to pertinent information.

Encouraging Continuous Learning and Development

Encouraging ongoing learning and growth is a critical component of creating a high-performing team. When team members are supported in their professional progress, given learning opportunities, and empowered to enhance their skills and knowledge, they become more motivated, engaged, and better suited to confront new problems.

Let's study this further:

1. Establishing a Learning Culture:
Create a culture that emphasizes ongoing learning and growth. Encourage team members to adopt a growth mindset, which stresses the concept that talents and intellect can be improved through devotion and hard effort. Foster an atmosphere where learning is perceived as a continual journey, and errors are recognized as chances for development and progress.

2. Providing Training and Development Opportunities:
Offer training programs, workshops, seminars, and conferences to develop the skills and knowledge of team members. Identify particular areas where skill development is required and give tailored training to solve those gaps. This might involve technical skills, leadership development, communication abilities, or industry-specific information. Ensure that the training is relevant, interesting, and corresponds with the team's goals and objectives.

3. Mentorship & Coaching Programs:
Implement mentoring and coaching initiatives inside the team. Pair team members with experienced mentors who can give advice, support, and feedback. Mentors may share their experiences, give guidance, and assist team members manage

their career progress. Coaching programs may also be designed to give individualized development plans and assist team members overcome problems and maximize their potential.

4. Encouraging Knowledge Sharing:
Promote a culture of information sharing among the team. Encourage team members to share their experiences, lessons learned, and best practices with one another. This may be enabled via frequent knowledge-sharing meetings, lunch-and-learn programs, or internal newsletters or blogs. By sharing information, team members benefit from collective expertise and build a collaborative learning environment.

5. Continuous Feedback and Performance Conversations:
Provide frequent feedback and participate in performance dialogues with team members. Offer constructive criticism on their strengths and areas for growth, and find development opportunities matched with their professional ambitions. This input should be continual and focused on development and progress. Encourage self-reflection and the formulation of personal development objectives to encourage team members to take control of their learning path.

6. Learning from Failures and Celebrating Successes:
Create a safe atmosphere where failures are recognized as learning opportunities. Encourage team members to reflect on their experiences, identify lessons gained, and share those ideas with the team. Similarly, recognize victories and recognize accomplishments to encourage a culture of constant

learning and progress. Recognition and incentive systems may be developed to acknowledge team members' achievements and inspire a commitment to progress.

7. Supporting Professional Development Initiatives:
Support team members in pursuing external professional development activities. This might involve attending conferences, acquiring credentials, engaging in industry groups, or pursuing further education. Provide resources, financial assistance, and flexibility to facilitate these activities. By investing in their professional growth, you show a commitment to their development and enable them to bring new information and abilities back to the team.

Recognizing and Rewarding Excellence

Recognizing and rewarding achievement is a great method to create a high-performing team. When people's excellent performance and contributions are recognized and rewarded, it supports a culture of accomplishment, pushes team members to continuously offer their best, and develops a feeling of pride and commitment.
Let's study this further:

1. Establishing Clear Performance Metrics:
Define explicit performance measurements and criteria that match the team's goals and objectives. These indicators might be quantitative (such as hitting sales objectives or project milestones) or qualitative (such as exhibiting great cooperation or problem-solving abilities). Ensure that these

metrics are conveyed to the team so that everyone knows what is anticipated.

2. Timely and Specific Recognition:
Provide timely and personalized appreciation when team members achieve excellence. Acknowledge successes quickly to enhance their effect and significance. Be explicit in identifying the activities, behaviors, or consequences that contributed to the remarkable achievement. This strengthens the relationship between the acknowledged behavior and the intended consequences.

3. Various Forms of Recognition:
Recognition may take numerous forms, depending on the interests and culture of the team. It might be public or private, official or casual. Consider methods like vocal gratitude in team meetings, handwritten notes or emails, certificates or awards, social media shout-outs, or public announcements of successes. Tailor the recognition strategy to the tastes and personalities of team members.

4. Individual and Team-Based Recognition:
Recognize both individual successes and great team contributions. Celebrate individual triumphs to honor the unique contributions of team members. Simultaneously, reward great cooperation, collaboration, or successful project completion to stress the collaborative efforts and reaffirm the value of collaboration within the team.

5. Inclusive and Peer Recognition:
Encourage a culture of peer appreciation where team members may recognize and appreciate one another's successes. This generates a friendly and collaborative atmosphere where everyone feels appreciated and respected. Implement tools, such as peer nomination programs or feedback channels, to enable peer-to-peer recognition.

6. Rewards & Incentives:
Consider incorporating awards and incentives to further inspire and recognize excellent achievement. These may include money incentives, bonuses, promotions, or non-monetary prizes like more paid time off, professional development opportunities, or unique privileges. Ensure that awards are linked with individual and team objectives, and regularly implemented to preserve fairness and transparency.

7. Continuous Feedback and Growth Opportunities:
Combine recognition with constant feedback and development possibilities. Provide comments on areas of improvement and provide development opportunities to assist the continued growth and professional development of team members. This indicates a commitment to their long-term success and pushes them to strive for ongoing progress.

8. Celebration of Milestones and Team Successes:
Celebrate major milestones, project completions, and general team triumphs. This promotes a feeling of achievement, enhances morale, and strengthens team togetherness. Organize team gatherings, trips, or celebrations to honor key moments,

providing team members with a chance to get together and participate in their successes.

Embracing Diversity and Inclusion

Embracing diversity and inclusion is a vital component of developing a high-performing team. When businesses recognize and welcome variety in all its manifestations, including varied origins, experiences, viewpoints, and abilities, it stimulates innovation, creativity, and a larger range of ideas. ***Let's study this further:***

1. Appreciating the Value of Diversity:
Recognize and express the benefits that diversity offers to the team and company. Different origins and viewpoints may contribute to unique ideas, innovative problem-solving, and superior decision-making. Emphasize the advantages of diverse teams, such as enhanced agility, improved customer comprehension, and the capacity to solve a broader variety of difficulties.

2. Building Inclusive Practices:
Create an inclusive atmosphere where everyone feels appreciated, respected, and empowered to participate. Develop and implement inclusive practices and policies that promote equality, justice, and respect. Encourage open communication, active listening, and cooperation among various team members. Address any prejudices or discrimination swiftly and maintain a safe and supportive work environment.

3. Diverse Recruitment and Hiring Practices:
Adopt diverse recruiting and hiring processes to attract a broad variety of skills and viewpoints. Implement techniques to reduce prejudices in the employment process, such as blind resume screening or diverse interview panels. Actively seek out people from underrepresented groups and give equal opportunity for all applications. By expanding the talent pool, you boost the possibility of a high-performing team.

4. Creating a Culture of Belonging:
Foster a culture of belonging where team members feel included, regardless of their origins. Encourage folks to bring their real selves to work and acknowledge their unique contributions. Implement programs like Employee Resource Groups (ERGs) or affinity networks to offer support and networking opportunities for different team members.

5. Leveraging Diverse Perspectives:
Actively seek and exploit varied viewpoints within the team. Encourage team members to contribute their experiences, thoughts, and ideas. Create spaces for open debates and brainstorming sessions where varied opinions are appreciated. By welcoming multiple ideas, you may unearth unique solutions and encourage innovation within the team.

6. Diversity Training and Education:
Invest in diversity training and education for team members. Offer courses or seminars that promote knowledge of unconscious biases, cultural competency, and inclusive leadership. Provide chances for learning and conversation

around diversity and inclusion concerns. This helps team members build empathy, better their awareness of other views, and foster a more inclusive mentality.

7. Mentorship and Sponsorship Programs:
Implement mentoring and sponsorship programs that encourage diversity and inclusion. Pair team members from underrepresented groups with mentors who can give advice, support, and chances for advancement. Sponsors may advocate for the promotion of diverse team members, assist them manage professional hurdles, and offer exposure inside the business.

8. Evaluating and Addressing Bias:
Regularly assess team procedures, decision-making methods, and rules for possible biases. Implement actions to reduce prejudice and guarantee equitable opportunity for all team members. Encourage open communication and feedback to identify and resolve any instances of prejudice or discrimination swiftly.

Mobilizing resources and creating a high-performing team is a process that takes careful planning, nurturing, and ongoing development. By developing a firm foundation, defining clear objectives, supporting open communication, encouraging learning, recognizing success, and accepting diversity, you create an atmosphere where your team can thrive and push your organization toward competitive greatness. Remember, a high-performing team is not an instant feat, but the commitment to establishing one will bring long-term success.

CHAPTER 17: AGILE EXECUTION

The corporate environment is in a perpetual state of upheaval, driven by technology breakthroughs, shifting customer tastes, and global market dynamics. In this fast-developing world, organizations must be nimble in their execution to remain competitive and capture new possibilities. Agile execution is a dynamic methodology that helps firms to react swiftly to change, capitalize on new trends, and generate success in an ever-shifting market.

Traditional company models, with their inflexible structures and extended planning cycles, are ill-equipped to prosper in today's fast-paced environment. They typically struggle to keep up with shifting client needs and fail to take advantage of time-sensitive possibilities. Agile execution, on the other hand, accepts change as an integral part of the business journey and allows teams to adapt fast and decisively.

In an agile company, teams work cooperatively, breaking down complicated projects into simple tasks and iterating fast based on feedback and insights. This iterative method enables continual improvement, allowing firms to learn, adapt, and develop in real time. By implementing agile approaches like Scrum or Kanban, organizations can handle uncertainty with confidence and make data-driven choices that move them ahead of the competition.

Agile execution not only helps organizations adapt to change but also provides them with the skills and mentality to grasp opportunities as they emerge. By remaining sensitive to new trends and market movements, agile firms may proactively position themselves to take advantage of advantageous situations. They are agile and fast to adapt, enabling them to capitalize on time-sensitive opportunities that rivals may overlook.

Another essential feature of agile execution is the emphasis on cooperation and empowered teams. Traditional hierarchical systems may hamper communication and innovation, resulting in delayed decision-making and wasted opportunities. Agile companies encourage a culture of cooperation, breaking down silos and encouraging cross-functional teams to work together. This collaborative atmosphere fosters information sharing, innovation, and group problem-solving, all of which are crucial for recognizing and grabbing opportunities in a continuously developing corporate world.

Furthermore, agile execution emphasizes customer-centricity at the center of its strategy. By actively incorporating consumers throughout the development process, organizations obtain vital insights into their wants, preferences, and problem areas. This customer-centric mentality helps firms to create goods and services that engage with their target audience, creating loyalty and distinctiveness in a crowded market.

Embracing Change

In today's dynamic corporate climate, change is a continual force that cannot be disregarded. The capacity to adjust rapidly and effectively to change is a fundamental part of agile execution. Embracing change is viewing it as an opportunity for development and progress rather than a burden or danger.

Here are some crucial aspects regarding accepting change in the context of agile execution:

1. Agility in Decision-making: Agile firms promote speed and flexibility in their decision-making processes. They recognize that waiting for perfect knowledge or attempting to foresee the future might be unhelpful. Instead, they make judgments based on the existing knowledge and modify their trajectory when new insights arise. This rapid decision-making helps organizations to adapt fast to market fluctuations, client needs, and new trends.

2. Iterative Approach: Agile execution entails breaking down complicated projects or endeavors into smaller, achievable tasks. This iterative method enables teams to achieve small progress while continually modifying and improving their ideas. It helps firms to obtain feedback, learn from errors, and make required improvements along the route. By adopting an iterative attitude, firms may avoid risks associated with large-scale changes and make course corrections more efficiently.

3. Continuous Learning: Agile businesses encourage a culture of continuous learning and progress. They promote innovation, accept failure as a learning opportunity, and seek input from both internal and external stakeholders. By approaching change as a chance to learn and grow, organizations may acquire the resilience and flexibility required to survive in an uncertain business world.

4. Flexibility and Adaptability: Agility needs businesses to be fluid and adaptive in their structures, processes, and mentality. This requires being open to new ideas, questioning old standards, and being prepared to modify techniques as required. Agile businesses enable their people to think creatively, embrace innovation, and explore different ways of problem-solving. By developing an attitude of flexibility, organizations may proactively adjust to change and grab new possibilities.

5. Embracing Technology: Technological breakthroughs are a primary driver of change in today's corporate sector. Agile firms acknowledge the revolutionary power of technology and are eager to adopt new tools, platforms, and digital solutions. They recognize that harnessing technology may improve efficiency, simplify procedures, and enhance consumer experiences. By embracing technological progress, organizations may place themselves at the forefront of their industry and acquire a competitive advantage.

Seizing Opportunities

In the dynamic and competitive corporate world, chances might occur unexpectedly and must be grabbed immediately to obtain a competitive edge. Seizing opportunities is a critical part of agile execution, allowing firms to capitalize on favorable market circumstances, developing trends, and consumer wants. It incorporates a proactive and flexible mentality that helps firms to move rapidly and decisively when opportunities occur.

Here are some crucial aspects regarding exploiting chances in the context of agile execution:

1. Agility in Spotting Opportunities: Agile firms actively scan the market, analyze industry developments, and remain responsive to client demands. They are fast to spot new possibilities and alterations in the business environment. This agility helps firms to notice opportunities early and proactively position themselves to take advantage of them. By remaining informed and exploiting data-driven insights, agile firms are better positioned to discover and analyze prospective possibilities.

2. Rapid Decision-making: Seizing opportunities demands making rapid judgments. Agile execution stresses quick decision-making methods that allow teams to take action rapidly. Instead of long approval hierarchies and bureaucracy, agile companies distribute decision-making power to the right teams or people. This helps organizations respond fast,

capture time-sensitive opportunities, and surpass rivals who may be impeded by sluggish decision-making procedures.

3. Experimentation and Iteration: Agile execution emphasizes experimentation and iteration to test and enhance ideas. When possibilities exist, agile firms are prepared to take calculated risks and explore new ways. They exploit the iterative nature of agile approaches to collect feedback, learn from errors, and modify their plans appropriately. This iterative method helps organizations to develop their offers and maximize their reaction to grasp opportunities successfully.

4. Data-driven Decision-making: Agile firms depend on data and insights to guide their decision-making process. They employ analytics, market research, and consumer input to evaluate prospects and estimate their potential. By making data-driven choices, firms may boost the chance of success when grabbing opportunities. Data gives significant insights into consumer behavior, market trends, and competitive landscapes, helping firms to make educated decisions and enhance their chances of success.

5. Agility in Execution: Seizing opportunities needs agility in execution. Agile businesses have flexible structures and procedures that allow them to adjust rapidly to changing situations. They value speed and agility in implementing their plans, using their cross-functional teams and empowered workforce. Agile execution empowers firms to manage resources effectively, shift priorities, and produce outcomes swiftly when grabbing opportunities.

Collaboration and Empowered Teams

Collaboration and empowered teams are crucial components of agile execution. In an agile company, cooperation is promoted to break down silos, increase information exchange, and utilize the collective intellect of the workforce. Empowered teams, on the other hand, have the autonomy and authority to make choices, take responsibility for their work, and drive innovation.

Here's a further analysis of cooperation and empowered teams in the context of agile execution:

1. Cross-functional cooperation: Agile companies foster cross-functional cooperation, bringing together workers from diverse departments and disciplines to work towards similar objectives. By breaking down barriers and promoting cooperation, organizations may use varied viewpoints, information, and skills. This teamwork provides for greater problem-solving, enhanced creativity, and improved decision-making. Cross-functional cooperation allows teams to work together smoothly, harnessing the capabilities of each team member to create greater outcomes.

2. information exchange: Collaboration within agile teams allows the exchange of information and best practices. Team members have the chance to learn from one another, share ideas, and build upon collective knowledge. This information exchange not only increases individual progress but also boosts the overall skills of the team. Agile companies

generally build mechanisms such as regular meetings, knowledge-sharing sessions, and collaborative technologies to support successful communication and information exchange.

3. Collective Problem-solving: In an agile workplace, empowered teams are encouraged to take responsibility for their work and jointly solve issues. This develops a feeling of shared duty and accountability among the team. When confronted with hurdles or barriers, teams cooperate to discover innovative solutions, using their varied talents and views. By incorporating all team members in problem-solving procedures, agile businesses tap into the collective intellect of the team and build a culture of creativity.

4. Decision-making Autonomy: Empowered teams in agile companies are allowed decision-making autonomy within their areas of responsibility. This liberty allows teams to make timely, informed choices without being hampered by bureaucratic procedures or excessive hierarchical approvals. Empowered teams are more flexible and responsive to change since they can make on-the-spot choices that match the organization's goals and objectives. This empowerment generates a feeling of ownership and commitment, promoting better levels of engagement and motivation among team members.

5. Continuous Improvement: Collaboration and empowered teams lead to a culture of continuous improvement. Agile businesses encourage teams to reflect on current processes, find areas for improvement, and experiment with new ideas.

The feedback loop between teams and their stakeholders allows continual learning and encourages innovation. Empowered teams have the flexibility to explore new methods, learn from mistakes, and modify their strategy in real time. This continuous improvement approach helps agile firms to develop and adapt to changing market situations efficiently.

Customer-Centricity

Customer-centricity is a core tenet of agile execution that puts the customer at the center of corporate strategy, decision-making, and product/service development. It entails recognizing and addressing customer wants, preferences, and expectations to provide value and develop enduring connections.

Here's a further analysis of customer-centricity in the context of agile execution:

1. consumer Insights and Feedback: Agile businesses aggressively seek consumer insights and feedback throughout the product development lifecycle. They engage consumers early and frequently, employing tactics like customer interviews, surveys, usability testing, and analytics to acquire useful insights. By knowing client demands, pain spots, and preferences, organizations can build goods and services that connect with their target audience.

2. Iterative Development with Customer Involvement:
Agile execution adopts an iterative development methodology, where goods or services are built progressively and iteratively. This strategy enables organizations to integrate user input and make improvements along the route. By including clients in the development process, agile companies may confirm assumptions, get input on prototypes or minimal viable products (MVPs), and ensure that the final product fulfills customer expectations.

3. Continuous interaction:
Agile businesses cultivate continuous interaction with customers to create strong connections and get continuing input. This may include consumer advisory boards, user communities, social media engagements, and customer support channels. By having an open channel of contact with consumers, firms can remain attentive to their growing requirements and preferences. This continual involvement allows agile firms to recognize new trends, predict changes in consumer behavior, and alter their plans appropriately.

4. Personalization and Customization:
consumer-centricity entails modifying goods, services, and experiences to fit specific consumer preferences. Agile firms employ consumer data and insights to create personalized experiences, customized features, or targeted marketing initiatives. By knowing consumers on an individual level, firms may boost customer pleasure, loyalty, and advocacy.

5. Anticipating and Exceeding Customer Expectations:
Customer-centric firms go beyond satisfying fundamental customer expectations. They proactively anticipate consumer wants, identify trouble spots, and seek to surpass expectations. By studying consumer behavior, evaluating data, and keeping current with industry trends, agile firms may uncover chances to innovate and give extra value to customers. This proactive strategy helps organizations distinguish themselves and establish a loyal consumer base.

6. Customer Empathy and Empowerment:
Customer-centricity requires empathizing with customers and enabling them to accomplish their objectives. Agile firms put themselves in the shoes of their customers, aiming to understand their difficulties, motivations, and intended results. They give help, resources, and tools that allow clients to succeed. By enabling consumers, companies develop trust, loyalty, and long-term connections.

By emphasizing continual improvement and adaptation, organizations may stay ahead of the curve, remain responsive to client expectations, and grasp new possibilities. Agile execution guarantees that firms are continually learning, changing, and improving their operations. Continuous development and flexibility equip firms to survive in a quickly changing business environment and establish a durable competitive edge.

CHAPTER 18: MAXIMIZING IMPACT

In the face of quickly developing markets, changing consumer expectations, and technology improvements, organizations must regularly analyze their performance and make required modifications to remain ahead of the competition. Monitoring, measuring, and modifying tactics give a framework for businesses to successfully examine their operations, find areas for development, and maximize their overall performance.

By using a data-driven strategy, firms may discover important insights that drive informed decision-making. Monitoring and analyzing key performance indicators (KPIs) help firms to gather and evaluate valuable data about their operations, consumer behavior, and market trends. This data serves as a platform for strategic modifications and helps firms obtain a full picture of their strengths, shortcomings, and opportunities.

The notion of constant improvement is another key part of the increasing effect. By adopting a mentality that welcomes change and stresses constant modifications, firms may guarantee that their plans stay relevant and aligned with market expectations. Regular review of processes, products, and consumer feedback helps firms to adjust fast and remain ahead of developing trends. This drive to continual improvement helps firms to maximize their services, boost customer happiness, and retain a competitive advantage.

To successfully monitor, assess, and adapt plans, firms need to set clear goals and identify appropriate KPIs. These goals offer a path to success, while KPIs operate as quantitative indicators to monitor progress and quantify the effect of strategic activities. Aligning KPIs with strategic objectives ensures that efforts are focused on the areas that matter, helping organizations remain on track and optimize their effect.

Real-time monitoring plays a crucial part in optimizing effect as well. With the use of new technology and analytics tools, organizations may measure performance indicators in real-time. This helps them to make prompt, data-driven choices, exploit opportunities, manage risks, and adapt swiftly to changing market dynamics. Real-time monitoring allows proactive modifications, ensuring that plans stay nimble and successful.

Lastly, obtaining input and interacting with important stakeholders is vital for gathering insights and boosting effect. By regularly listening to consumers, workers, partners, and industry experts, organizations may gather unique views, discover pain issues, and find new trends. This feedback loop supports ongoing development and pushes focused modifications that have a meaningful effect.

Embrace the Power of Data

In today's digital era, data has emerged as a vital tool for organizations. By efficiently monitoring and evaluating key performance indicators (KPIs) and embracing the power of data analytics, firms may get useful insights that drive decision-making and help optimize their impact.

1. Informing Decision-making: Data-driven decision-making is a vital part of optimizing effect. By monitoring and measuring important data, organizations may acquire insights into different elements of their operations, such as sales performance, customer behavior, marketing campaigns, manufacturing processes, and more. These insights allow educated decision-making based on solid information rather than assumptions or conjecture. By exploiting data, organizations may spot trends, patterns, and opportunities that may otherwise go overlooked, leading to more effective strategies and better results.

2. Enhancing Operational Efficiency: Data may play a vital role in increasing operational efficiency. By monitoring and evaluating important data, organizations may find bottlenecks, inefficiencies, and places for improvement within their operations. For example, data analysis may uncover manufacturing inefficiencies, supply chain concerns, or customer service deficiencies that need to be rectified. Armed with this knowledge, firms may make data-driven improvements to optimize processes, cut costs, and boost overall efficiency.

3. Identifying Customer Insights: Understanding customer behavior and preferences is crucial for maximum effect. By employing data analytics, firms may acquire comprehensive insights into client demographics, purchase behaviors, preferences, and satisfaction levels. This information helps organizations to customize their goods, services, and marketing activities to better suit client demands. With data-driven insights, organizations can customize their offers, enhance customer experiences, and develop deeper connections with their target audience.

4. Facilitating Market Analysis: Data gives a plethora of information on the market landscape, industry trends, and competitor activity. By monitoring and analyzing market data, organizations may spot new trends, changes in client preferences, and prospective risks or opportunities. This insight helps firms to change their strategy appropriately, profit from market trends, and distinguish themselves from rivals. With a data-driven strategy, organizations can remain nimble, react to market dynamics, and optimize their effect in a quickly changing environment.

5. Enabling Predictive Analysis: Data analytics may also empower firms with predictive capabilities. By studying past data and trends, organizations may develop forecasts about future market behavior, client preferences, and demand patterns. Predictive analysis helps firms to foresee changes, plan, and proactively adapt their tactics to remain ahead of the competition. By employing data to forecast future events,

organizations can make educated choices that maximize their effect in the long term.

Continuous Improvement

Continuous improvement is a mentality and systematic strategy that focuses on making incremental modifications and additions to processes, products, and strategies over time.

By adopting this approach, firms may remain nimble, adapt to changing market conditions, and optimize their effect in the following ways:

1. Adapting to Market Demands: Markets are dynamic, and client preferences alter over time. Continuous improvement helps firms to stay responsive to these developments. By continually assessing consumer input, industry trends, and competition activity, organizations may detect growing wants and adapt their services appropriately. This may entail improving current goods, introducing new features, or even branching into new markets. The art of adjustment ensures that enterprises remain relevant and fulfill the growing demands of their target audience.

2. Streamlining Processes and Increasing Efficiency: Continuous improvement entails the frequent review and optimization of internal processes. By identifying bottlenecks, inefficiencies, and opportunities for improvement, firms may make gradual improvements to boost operational efficiency. This may require embracing new technology, reengineering procedures, or establishing best practices. The objective is to

remove waste, decrease expenses, and enhance productivity, eventually maximizing the effect of the organization's resources.

3. Embracing Innovation: Continuous improvement creates a culture of innovation inside the firm. It provides an atmosphere where people are encouraged to produce ideas, experiment, and contribute to the growth of goods and processes. By adopting innovation, organizations may remain ahead of the competition, distinguish themselves in the market, and build distinct value propositions. The art of adjustment guarantees that firms are continuously seeking creative solutions and exploring new development opportunities.

4. Responding to Customer Feedback: Customers are an excellent source of information for organizations. By actively collecting and evaluating consumer feedback, firms may discover areas for development and make modifications appropriately. This may entail improving customer service methods, fixing pain spots, or boosting the overall customer experience. By consistently listening to their consumers, organizations can develop closer connections, promote loyalty, and optimize their influence by meeting and surpassing customer expectations.

5. Learning from errors: Continuous improvement promotes a culture of learning from errors and setbacks. Rather than perceiving failures as hurdles, companies perceive them as opportunities for development and progress. By examining

failures and understanding the underlying reasons, businesses may make required modifications to avoid similar difficulties from happening in the future. This iterative learning process helps firms to fine-tune their strategy, products, and processes, eventually maximizing their effect by avoiding repeating errors.

6. Striving for Excellence: Continuous improvement is motivated by a dedication to excellence. It is about continuously lifting the bar and establishing greater expectations. By benchmarking against industry best practices, monitoring key performance indicators, and tracking progress, firms may analyze their performance and make modifications to attain excellence. This pursuit of excellence means that companies are continually pushing the limits and seeking to produce the greatest possible results.

Establishing Clear Objectives and Key Performance Indicators (KPIs)

Establishing clear goals and selecting relevant Key Performance Indicators (KPIs) is a vital step in increasing corporate effectiveness. Clear goals give a clear direction for the business, while KPIs serve as quantitative measurements to monitor progress toward those objectives.

Here's a deeper look at why this technique is essential:

1. Strategic Alignment: Clear objectives guarantee that everyone in the company is aligned and working towards the same goals. They offer a feeling of purpose and direction,

driving decision-making and resource allocation. By defining goals that are tightly related to the organization's purpose and vision, firms may build a cohesive strategy and optimize their influence.

2. Focus on High-effect Areas: Objectives help target efforts and resources on the areas that have the most significant effect. By clearly stating what the company aims to accomplish, firms may focus their energy on the key areas of their operations. This concentration helps them to manage resources effectively and make educated choices that lead to concrete benefits.

3. Measurable Progress: KPIs play a critical role in monitoring and assessing the progress towards targets. They give quantitative indicators that show the performance and efficacy of particular processes, projects, or initiatives. KPIs help firms to measure their performance over time, identify areas for development, and analyze the effect of their strategy. Measuring success against particular KPIs helps firms to make data-driven choices and take prompt action.

4. Motivating and Engaging workers: Clear goals and KPIs give a feeling of purpose and direction to workers. When workers understand how their job contributes to the broader goals and can see progress via quantifiable KPIs, it boosts their motivation and engagement. Having a clear knowledge of what they are working towards and how their efforts are contributing to the organization's success empowers workers and develops a feeling of ownership.

5. Accountability and Performance Management: Clear goals and KPIs allow successful performance management. They give a framework for defining expectations and holding people, teams, and departments responsible for their performance. By matching individual goals with corporate objectives and assessing performance against relevant KPIs, firms may find areas of excellence and areas that need development. This accountability culture supports a results-oriented attitude and pushes continual growth.

6. Agility and Adaptability: Objectives and KPIs should not be fixed in stone. They should be frequently examined and updated to reflect changes in the business environment, market circumstances, or strategic goals. This flexibility guarantees that goals stay relevant and that KPIs continue to deliver valuable information. By routinely reassessing and realigning goals and KPIs, firms may adapt to new conditions and optimize their effect in dynamic marketplaces.

Real-Time Monitoring and Agile Decision-Making

Real-time monitoring and quick decision-making are essential aspects of optimizing business effects. They entail the use of modern technology and analytics tools to continually monitor performance indicators and make fast, data-driven choices.

Here's a deeper look at how real-time monitoring and agile decision-making contribute to corporate success:

1. Timely Insights: Real-time monitoring delivers up-to-date insights into numerous facets of corporate operations. It includes the collection and analysis of data as it is created, providing organizations to have a real-time perspective of their performance. This rapid access to data helps firms to discover patterns, uncover abnormalities, and react promptly to changing situations. Timely insights provide decision-makers with the knowledge required to take action before situations develop or opportunities pass by.

2. Proactive Adjustments: Real-time monitoring helps firms to proactively alter their plans and operations. By measuring key performance indicators (KPIs) in real-time, companies may discover areas that need attention or development. For example, if sales are dropping, real-time monitoring may assist detect the underlying reasons, such as a sudden decline in website traffic or customer complaints. With this information, organizations may immediately change their marketing activities, enhance consumer experiences, or solve operational concerns to prevent negative consequences and capitalize on new possibilities.

3. Agility in Decision-Making: Real-time monitoring facilitates agile decision-making by giving the required facts and insights to make educated decisions swiftly. Instead of depending on past reports or intuition, decision-makers may use real-time data to analyze performance, assess risks, and uncover possibilities. This agility helps organizations to adapt fast to market developments, client requests, or competition threats. Agile decision-making guarantees that firms can grasp

opportunities, handle difficulties, and remain ahead of the competition in a fast-paced commercial environment.

4. fast Problem Resolution: Real-time monitoring allows fast problem resolution by spotting problems as they emerge. By monitoring numerous operational components, such as manufacturing processes, supply chain activities, or customer service indicators, firms may discover and manage issues in their early phases. Real-time alerts or notifications may be set up to identify deviations from targeted performance levels, allowing timely action to minimize the effect on customers, operations, or the bottom line.

5. Optimized Resource Allocation: Real-time monitoring helps improve resource allocation by offering insights into resource consumption and efficiency. By monitoring resource-related variables, such as inventory levels, equipment use, or personnel productivity, companies may make data-driven choices regarding resource allocation. This ensures that resources are distributed properly, reducing waste and optimizing their influence on business objectives.

6. Continuous Performance examination: Real-time monitoring enables continuous examination of performance. By regularly measuring KPIs, organizations may measure the performance of their plans, initiatives, and procedures. This constant review helps businesses to detect trends, patterns, and opportunities for development in real time. By regularly reviewing performance, firms may make incremental

modifications, fine-tune tactics, and optimize their influence over time.

The Importance of Feedback and Stakeholder Engagement

To properly monitor, assess, and adapt strategy, firms must solicit input from important stakeholders. This includes customers, staff, partners, and industry experts. By actively interacting with these stakeholders, firms may gather important insights, uncover pain spots, and grasp new trends. This feedback loop guarantees that modifications are targeted and informed, promoting ongoing development and maximizing the good effect a firm can make.

The Importance of Feedback and Stakeholder Engagement:

Feedback and stakeholder involvement play a significant role in enhancing corporate impact. They entail aggressively soliciting information, ideas, and viewpoints from diverse stakeholders, including customers, employees, partners, and industry experts. Here's a deeper look at why feedback and stakeholder involvement are essential:

1. Customer Insights: Customers are at the core of every organization. Their input gives essential insights into their experiences, preferences, and requirements. By actively soliciting and listening to customer feedback, firms may obtain a better knowledge of their target audience, discover problem issues, and find chances for growth. consumer insights enable organizations to modify their goods, services,

and experiences to better match consumer expectations, eventually boosting customer happiness and loyalty.

2. Employee Engagement: Engaging workers and respecting their opinion is vital for a flourishing firm. Employees are frequently the closest to everyday operations and engage directly with consumers, procedures, and systems. Their views and comments may unearth potential for efficiency improvements, innovation, and increased consumer experiences. By developing a culture that fosters and honors employee input, organizations can tap into the collective intellect of their staff and drive continuous development.

3. Partnership and cooperation: Engaging with partners, suppliers, and other stakeholders develops cooperation and improves relationships. By collecting their opinions and input, organizations may obtain a better grasp of market dynamics, new trends, and industry best practices. This cooperation may lead to strategic partnerships, shared learning, and the capacity to harness pooled skills to maximum effect. Engaging with partners builds a feeling of mutual trust and may open doors to new chances for development.

4. Industry Insights and Expertise: Engaging with industry professionals and thought leaders offers access to outsider viewpoints and insights. By actively engaging in industry forums, attending conferences, or working with experts, organizations may keep updated about the newest trends, emerging technology, and best practices. Industry insights and knowledge help firms assess their performance, discover areas

for growth, and learn from the triumphs and problems of others.

5. Targeted Adjustments: Feedback and stakeholder participation inspire targeted adjustments and improvements. By listening to stakeholders, organizations may discover particular areas that need improvement, such as product features, customer service operations, or marketing tactics. This feedback-driven strategy enables businesses to make educated modifications that directly address stakeholder complaints and preferences, ensuring that efforts are focused on the most relevant areas.

6. Relationship Building and Trust: Engaging with stakeholders promotes better ties and builds trust. Actively soliciting and respecting their comments displays a commitment to knowing their needs and viewpoints. This trust is crucial in creating long-term collaborations, consumer loyalty, and a strong brand reputation. Stakeholder engagement promotes a feeling of participation, teamwork, and shared purpose, leading to greater support and advocacy for the firm.

CHAPTER 19:PERFORMANCE METRICS

In today's highly competitive corporate environment, keeping ahead of the game demands more than simply desire and hard effort. It takes a detailed awareness of your business's performance and the capacity to monitor development efficiently. This is where performance measurements come into play. Performance metrics are strong tools that enable you to measure, evaluate, and monitor important indications of success, delivering significant insights into your organization's performance.

Imagine beginning a trip without a map or any sense of direction. Without performance indicators, your organization functions similarly, missing clarity and a clear route to success. Performance measurements act as a compass, directing you in the correct direction and helping you navigate through the obstacles and uncertainties of the business environment.

By measuring progress and important indicators, you obtain insight into the strengths and weaknesses of your firm. You can determine which techniques are effective and which ones need improvement. Performance metrics help you to make educated choices, manage your operations, and allocate resources effectively.

Furthermore, performance indicators encourage responsibility inside your business. They establish a level of excellence and give a baseline against which progress can be assessed. With performance metrics in place, you can hold yourself and your employees responsible for attaining particular objectives and targets. This responsibility promotes a culture of ownership and guarantees that everyone is aligned toward a single cause.

In addition to responsibility, performance measurements assist you to keep ahead of the competition. They give real-time data on your progress, helping you to analyze patterns, uncover upcoming opportunities, and forecast market movements. By watching crucial indicators, you may alter your plans and make proactive modifications to keep a competitive advantage.

Performance indicators also stimulate continued improvement. They assist you uncover areas of underperformance, bottlenecks, and inefficiencies. Armed with this intelligence, you may adopt focused efforts to streamline operations, boost productivity, and drive growth. Performance metrics operate as a feedback loop, allowing you to assess the efficacy of your improvement efforts and adapt your strategy appropriately.

Lastly, performance metrics empower your team. By defining clear milestones and measuring progress, you offer your staff a feeling of purpose and direction. Performance metrics offer transparency and link individual goals with the organization's objectives. They also help you to recognize and reward excellent achievement, promoting a culture of excellence and pushing your staff to strive for greatness.

Elevate Your Decision-Making

In the ever-evolving business world, making smart judgments is important for the success of your corporation. However, judgments made exclusively based on intuition or gut sensations may be dangerous and may not deliver ideal results. This is where performance measurements play a significant part in upgrading your decision-making process.

Performance metrics give you quantitative data and insights into numerous parts of your company's operations. By measuring vital indicators, you acquire full knowledge of what drives your performance and where changes may be made. This data-driven approach helps you to make educated choices, supported by solid facts and analysis.

When you have access to performance metrics, you may detect patterns, trends, and correlations in your company data. For example, you may learn that a certain marketing effort resulted in a big boost in consumer engagement and sales. Armed with this knowledge, you may make the option to dedicate additional resources to that campaign or reproduce its success in other areas of your organization.

Performance indicators also help you to compare various strategies and projects. By examining the data, you may discover which tactics are providing the expected outcomes and which are falling short. This helps you to make data-driven modifications and improve your plans for optimum effect.

Moreover, performance indicators give vital insights into the efficacy of your resource allocation. You may assess how various departments or teams are employing their resources and discover areas of inefficiency or over utilization. This information helps you to make educated choices regarding resource allocation, ensuring that your investments are aligned with your company objectives and producing the highest potential results.

By integrating performance data into your decision-making process, you may limit risks and prevent making blind judgments. Rather than depending on assumptions or guessing, you have real evidence to guide your decisions. This data-driven strategy not only raises the likelihood of making effective judgments but also strengthens your credibility as a leader.

Furthermore, performance measurements enable you to monitor the effect of your actions over time. By evaluating the results against your original assumptions, you may assess the efficacy of your actions and learn from both triumphs and mistakes. This iterative process of decision-making and assessment generates a continuous improvement cycle, helping you to modify your tactics and make even better judgments in the future.

Unleash the Power of Accountability

When it comes to reaching your company objectives, responsibility is key. Performance metrics help you to hold yourself and your teams responsible by defining clear objectives and evaluating progress. By defining standards and measuring critical indicators, you build a culture of responsibility within your firm. This generates a feeling of ownership and allows employees to take proactive efforts towards accomplishing their goals, boosting overall company success.

Accountability is the cornerstone of organizational success. When people and teams take responsibility for their tasks and are liable for their actions, it generates a culture of high performance and produces excellent results. Performance metrics play a critical part in unlocking the power of responsibility inside your firm.

Performance metrics establish explicit standards and objectives against which success may be assessed. By recording important indicators, you develop tangible objectives that serve as a reference point for assessing success. This clarity helps people and teams to understand their roles and the expectations put upon them.

When performance measurements are communicated properly, everyone in the company knows how individual efforts contribute to the bigger objectives. This common understanding generates a feeling of purpose and drives employees to take responsibility for their positions. Knowing that their performance will be assessed based on precise indicators, workers are more inclined to be proactive, accountable, and dedicated to obtaining goals.

Accountability, facilitated by performance measurements, motivates employees to establish personal goals linked with the organization's objectives. When workers have insight into their development and the influence of their job, they become more self-aware and engaged in their success. This personal responsibility goes beyond merely performing duties; it entails taking ownership of results and striving for excellence.

Performance indicators also promote honest communication and feedback. When people and teams are aware of their development and performance regarding the defined metrics, it offers up possibilities for productive interactions. Regular feedback sessions may concentrate on identifying areas of improvement, celebrating successes, and offering suggestions for professional progress. This feedback loop underscores the significance of responsibility and allows people to make changes and strive for ongoing growth.

Furthermore, performance measurements enable recognition and awards based on objective accomplishments. When people fulfill or surpass their aims, their successes may be recognized and celebrated. This acknowledgment maintains the relationship between performance and responsibility, producing a positive culture that supports persistent high performance.

By leveraging performance metrics to foster accountability, you establish a culture that values transparency, responsibility, and continual progress. Employees feel empowered and engaged since they realize how their efforts contribute to the organization's success. They take responsibility for their tasks, actively explore chances for growth, and interact more effectively with colleagues to reach common objectives.

Importantly, responsibility goes beyond individual individuals. Performance metrics help managers and leaders to analyze their performance in directing their employees. They may examine indicators relating to team performance, identify areas of growth, and give the necessary support and resources to encourage responsibility and drive success.

Stay Ahead of the Curve

In today's dynamic and competitive business market, keeping ahead of the curve is important to remain relevant and succeed. Performance indicators play a key role in helping firms predict market changes, recognize new trends, and proactively position themselves for success.

Performance metrics give real-time data and insights into numerous elements of your company's operations. By measuring important indicators, you acquire a thorough view of your performance and may detect patterns, trends, and possible opportunities before they become publicly known.

With performance metrics, you may monitor market circumstances and consumer behavior. By examining data linked to client preferences, buying habits, and market trends, you may uncover new opportunities or change customer demands. This lets you change your tactics and offers to match growing needs, providing you with a competitive advantage over slower-moving rivals.

Furthermore, performance measurements allow you to evaluate your performance against industry norms and rivals. By comparing your key indicators to those of your colleagues, you might uncover areas where you shine or fall behind. This benchmarking gives useful insights into best practices, industry trends, and development opportunities. Armed with this insight, you can make educated choices to better your goods, services, and customer experience, keeping you ahead of the competition.

Performance metrics also assist you to track and analyze the efficacy of your strategy and activities. By measuring important indicators connected to marketing campaigns, product launches, or operational changes, you may quantify their influence on your company's results. This enables you to develop and adapt your methods based on real-time data, ensuring that you remain on the leading edge and consistently enhance your performance.

Moreover, performance measurements give early warning indications of prospective faults or threats. By regularly monitoring your key indicators, you might spot deviations from anticipated patterns or performance goals. This helps you to take proactive actions to solve emerging difficulties before they grow and influence your organization negatively. By getting ahead of possible difficulties, you can preserve stability, reduce interruptions, and grab opportunities that may come in times of uncertainty.

Performance measurements also assist agility and flexibility. By frequently examining and evaluating your performance data, you may discover areas where modifications or course corrections are essential. This flexibility helps you to adapt swiftly to changing market circumstances, client preferences, or competition challenges. By keeping fluid and adaptive, you can capitalize on new opportunities and overcome problems.

Foster Continuous Improvement

Continuous improvement is a vital element for ongoing success in any company. It incorporates an attitude of continually pushing for better results, improving procedures, and boosting performance. Performance metrics play a critical role in building a culture of continuous improvement inside your firm.

Performance metrics give significant insights into the strengths and shortcomings of your company's operations. By measuring important indicators, you may uncover areas of underperformance, bottlenecks, and inefficiencies. This data-driven approach exposes areas that demand improvement and provides a starting point for launching focused efforts.

Once performance measurements have highlighted areas for improvement, you may proactively take efforts to optimize processes and boost performance. By examining the data and finding core causes, you may make educated judgments about the modifications required to achieve progress. Whether it's simplifying processes, removing redundancies, or investing in training and development, performance metrics lead your improvement initiatives with clarity and purpose.

Performance indicators also serve as a standard against which the success of improvement measures may be judged. By measuring important indicators before and after adopting changes, you can assess the effect of your improvement efforts. This feedback loop enables you to measure the performance of your endeavors, modify methods, and make additional modifications as required.

Additionally, performance measurements allow you to track the success of your improvement efforts over time. By measuring important indicators continuously, you may find trends and patterns that show the efficacy and longevity of your initiatives. This visibility helps you guarantee that the adjustments adopted are creating enduring outcomes and driving continual progress.

A culture of continuous improvement is not simply about making infrequent improvements; it's about cultivating a mentality that encourages learning and progress. Performance metrics support this by giving transparency and data-driven insights. They develop a common vocabulary and understanding of the business, enabling people and teams to actively seek out possibilities for improvement and share their ideas for boosting performance.

Furthermore, performance measurements help you to build a feeling of ownership and responsibility for continual progress. By defining clear objectives and measuring progress, you enable people and teams to take responsibility for their performance and contribute to the overall development efforts. Performance metrics give a framework for identifying and rewarding excellent performance, pushing staff to continually strive for greatness.

Continuous improvement is an iterative process, and performance indicators are vital in driving this cycle. By employing performance measurements successfully, you develop a culture that accepts change, celebrates innovation, and is dedicated to continually boosting performance. This culture of continual improvement not only promotes efficiency and production but also guarantees your firm stays dynamic, adaptive, and well-positioned for long-term success.

Empower Your Team

Performance metrics provide transparency, connecting individual goals with company objectives. Moreover, they allow you to identify and reward excellent achievement, promoting a culture of excellence and pushing your team to strive for greatness.

Empowering your team is a critical component of having a high-performing and motivated staff. Performance metrics play a significant part in this process by giving clarity, openness, and acknowledgment, which all contribute to empowering your team members.

1. Clear aims and Direction: Performance metrics offer clear aims and objectives for people and teams to strive towards. By creating precise objectives and evaluating progress via metrics, you offer your staff a feeling of purpose and direction. They understand what is expected of them and may coordinate their efforts properly. This clarity reduces uncertainty and encourages people to concentrate their attention on creating significant achievements.

2. Transparent Communication: Performance measurements create transparency inside your business. When important indicators and progress are communicated effectively, team members have insight into the overall success of the company and how their efforts contribute to the bigger objectives. This openness builds trust and develops a feeling of ownership. Employees can see the effect of their work, understand how it connects with company goals, and make educated choices appropriately.

3. Data-Driven Decision Making: Performance measurements empower team members to make data-driven choices. When people have access to relevant performance data, they may examine trends, patterns, and consumer insights. This helps students to make educated choices and take charge of their decision-making process. Data-driven decision-making also

minimizes the dependence on subjective judgments and prejudices, leading to more effective and impactful results.

4. Personal and Professional Growth: Performance metrics give feedback on individual and team performance. This feedback allows personal and professional improvement. By measuring important indicators, workers may discover their strengths, places for development, and chances to learn and build new abilities. Performance measurements operate as a compass, leading staff towards continual improvement and creating a development attitude.

5. Recognition and Rewards: Performance metrics allow you to recognize and reward extraordinary performance. When team members meet or exceed their aims, their successes may be recognized and rewarded based on objective data. This award encourages a culture of excellence, pushes individuals to achieve, and allows them to take responsibility for their work. Recognizing individual and team successes based on performance indicators generates a feeling of pride and supports a pleasant, collaborative work environment.

6. cooperation and Teamwork: Performance metrics may enhance cooperation and teamwork inside your firm. When people and teams have access to performance data, they may find possibilities for cooperation, exchange best practices, and help each other in reaching collective objectives. Performance metrics establish a culture of shared responsibility and motivate team members to work together towards similar goals.

In the ever-changing corporate world, success rests on your capacity to evaluate, monitor, and optimize performance. Performance metrics serve as the compass that steers your firm towards its objectives, helping you to make data-driven choices, create accountability, remain ahead of the competition, drive continuous development, and empower your team. By utilizing the power of performance measurements, you unleash the possibility of unprecedented success. Embrace the power of performance metrics now and take your company to new heights.

CHAPTER 20:CONTINUOUS IMPROVEMENT

At its foundation, continuous improvement understands that errors are an intrinsic part of the route toward success. Rather than perceiving them as failures, successful firms perceive errors as precious chances for development and learning. By adopting a mentality that welcomes failures as useful lessons, companies may study the core causes of errors, find areas for growth, and devise methods to avoid such mishaps in the future.

The notion of iteration is a key component of continuous improvement. It entails a constant quest of refining and upgrading goods, services, and internal processes based on consumer input, market data, and new trends. Iteration displays a dedication to offering excellent value to consumers by continually changing and developing. By continuously collecting feedback, tracking market trends, and continually adjusting offers, firms may proactively remain ahead of the competition and surpass consumer expectations.

This essay also underlines the need for an agile problem-solving approach within the scope of continuous improvement. Instead of being overwhelmed by obstacles, firms are urged to take a proactive problem-solving strategy. Agile approaches, such as Scrum, allow firms to break down large challenges into smaller, manageable tasks, promoting fast iteration and continual improvement. This method promotes efficiency, productivity, and the capacity to adapt swiftly to new possibilities or challenges.

Creating a culture of continuous learning and development is another key part of adopting continuous improvement. Encouraging people to discuss ideas, experiment, and take measured risks develops a climate of creativity. Businesses that appreciate constructive criticism and recognize contributions to organizational success tap into the collective intellect of their workforce. By allowing people to actively participate in the development process, companies unleash their full potential and generate a feeling of ownership and engagement.

Furthermore, technology plays a key role in fostering ongoing progress. Digital tools and automation simplify operations, gather and analyze data, and deliver useful insights. Analytics solutions help firms to monitor performance, detect bottlenecks, and make data-driven choices. Embracing developing technologies like artificial intelligence and machine learning provides opportunities for predictive analysis, further streamlining operations and product development processes.

The Art of Learning through Mistakes

Mistakes are unavoidable in every business journey, but it's how we react to them that determines our success. Rather than obsessing over failures, embrace them as wonderful learning opportunities. Encourage a culture where errors are recognized as stepping stones to progress. By examining and understanding the core causes of mistakes, you may discover areas for development and build tactics to avoid such blunders in the future.

However, it is not the errors themselves that determine a company's success but rather how they are managed and converted into learning opportunities. The skill of learning from failures is a fundamental part of continuous development since it helps firms to evolve, adapt, and avoid repeating expensive blunders.

1. Shifting the Perspective:
To properly embrace the skill of learning from failures, it is vital to modify the attitude around failure. Instead of perceiving errors as setbacks or failures, successful firms acknowledge them as vital stepping stones on the way to success. This mentality change helps firms to build a culture that supports risk-taking, experimentation, and innovation.

2. Analyzing Root Causes:
When a mistake happens, it is crucial to go further and discover the underlying reasons. By studying the fundamental causes of errors, firms may find trends, systemic difficulties, or gaps in procedures that led to the error. This study helps firms to address the main problems and create preventative steps to avoid similar errors in the future.

3. Creating a Learning Environment:
Building a learning environment is vital for supporting ongoing progress. It entails developing a culture where errors

are considered opportunities for development and learning rather than sources of blame or punishment. Encourage open and honest communication, so team members feel comfortable sharing their experiences, thoughts, and lessons learned through failures. By establishing a secure and supportive workplace, organizations can uncover the combined knowledge and skills of their workers.

4. Implementing Continuous Feedback Loops:
Feedback loops play a critical part in the art of learning from errors. Regularly solicit input from consumers, workers, and other stakeholders to acquire insights into areas that need improvement. This input may assist detect blind spots, disclose client pain areas, and find innovation potential. By actively integrating feedback into the improvement process, firms may iterate and modify their goods, services, and procedures continually.

5. Documentation and Knowledge Sharing:
Documenting errors, their causes, and the lessons learned is vital for continual growth. By recording this information, firms may develop a store of important insights and best practices. This documentation may be disseminated around the business, ensuring that others can learn from the errors and prevent repeating them. Knowledge sharing allows workers to make educated choices, stimulates teamwork, and speeds the learning process.

6. Iterating and Experimenting:
Learning from failures needs a dedication to repeated exploration. Rather than settling with the status quo, organizations should promote innovation and adopt a philosophy of continual testing and improvement. By iterating on goods, services, and processes, firms may improve and enhance their offerings, fostering innovation and preserving a competitive advantage.

7. Embracing a Growth Mindset:
Finally, having a growth mindset is vital to the skill of learning from errors. A growth mindset understands that intellect, talents, and achievement can be developed through devotion, effort, and continual learning. By creating a growth mentality throughout the company, firms promote resilience, flexibility, and a desire to accept difficulties and learn from setbacks.

Iterating for Excellence

Iteration is a basic tenet of continuous development and a critical component of reaching business excellence. It encompasses the process of refining and upgrading goods, services, and internal processes based on feedback, insights, and increasing consumer demands. By adopting iteration, organizations can aim for perfection, continually improving and offering extraordinary value to their consumers.

Here are some fundamental characteristics of iterating for excellence:

1. Embracing Customer-Centricity:
Iterating for greatness involves a comprehensive grasp of your client's requirements, preferences, and expectations. By regularly listening to consumer input, performing market research, and remaining alert to industry trends, companies may find areas where their solutions can be strengthened. This client-centric strategy creates the basis for iterative improvement, allowing firms to meet and exceed consumer expectations.

2. Gathering and Analyzing Feedback:
Collecting input from consumers, workers, and other stakeholders is critical for successful iteration. This input gives vital insights into areas that need improvement, possible pain spots, and chances for innovation. Utilize surveys, consumer evaluations, focus groups, and other feedback tools to acquire meaningful data. Analyze this input to determine trends, frequent concerns, and places where iterative changes may be made.

3. Rapid Prototyping and Testing:
Iterating for excellence entails quick development and testing of new ideas, products, or functionalities. Instead of waiting for a flawless answer, firms may produce prototypes fast and get real-world input via beta testing or pilot programs. This iterative technique allows for incremental modifications based on user input, leading to a more polished and customer-centric final product.

4. Data-Driven Decision Making:

Data plays a key role in iterating toward excellence. Implement analytics tools and metrics to monitor key performance indicators (KPIs) and analyze the effect of incremental adjustments. Analyzing data gives useful insights into the success of implemented changes, allowing data-driven decision-making. By relying on data, organizations can make educated decisions about which iterations are achieving the expected outcomes and prioritize subsequent upgrades appropriately.

5. Cross-Functional Collaboration:

Iterative improvement frequently needs cross-functional cooperation inside the company. By bringing together varied views, experiences, and talents from multiple teams or departments, organizations may harness collective intelligence to generate greatness. Collaboration supports creativity, encourages creative problem-solving, and ensures that iterations cover all elements of the company, such as product development, operations, marketing, and customer service.

6. Embracing an Agile Mindset:

An agile mentality is necessary for effective iteration. It entails accepting flexibility, adaptability, and response to change. Instead of strictly following preset plans, firms that adopt an agile mentality are open to modifying their path depending on feedback and insights. This approach emphasizes experimentation, risk-taking, and the desire to iterate swiftly in pursuit of perfection.

7. Continuous Monitoring and Evaluation:
Iterating for excellence is a constant process. Businesses should regularly monitor and analyze the effect of their incremental improvements. Regularly analyze the performance of implemented changes, obtain feedback, and measure customer satisfaction to verify that the iterations are generating the intended goals. This continual monitoring and assessment help organizations find areas for additional refinement and fine-tuning.

Agile Problem-Solving

Agile problem-solving is a method that stresses adaptation, cooperation, and quick iteration to handle difficulties and discover successful solutions. It is anchored in the ideas of agile techniques, such as Scrum, and is extensively embraced in numerous sectors as a means to negotiate complicated challenges and promote continuous progress.

Here are the fundamental characteristics of agile problem-solving:

1. Embracing a Collaborative Approach:
Agile problem-solving emphasizes that the collective wisdom and different views of a team are vital for generating new solutions. It encourages cooperation, encouraging persons with varied talents and experience to work together towards a similar objective. By harnessing the collective expertise and talents of the team, firms may attack challenges from different sides, improving the probability of discovering successful solutions.

2. Breaking Down Complex Problems:
Agile problem-solving includes breaking down difficult issues into smaller, achievable tasks or subproblems. By dissecting an issue, organizations may obtain a greater knowledge of its components and identify the most crucial areas to address. This technique simplifies problem-solving, making it more accessible and allowing teams to concentrate on particular areas of the challenge at hand.

3. Rapid Iteration and Feedback:
Agile problem-solving stresses a fast iteration cycle, where solutions are generated and tested rapidly. Instead of spending unnecessary time on elaborate preparation, teams employ an iterative approach, developing small-scale solutions or prototypes and getting feedback early on. This iterative feedback loop helps teams to learn from errors, tweak their ideas, and make incremental changes based on real-world findings.

4. Prioritizing Value and Impact:
Agile problem-solving pushes teams to prioritize the delivery of value and impact. Rather than concentrating on perfection or needless features, teams select the most crucial components that would deliver the most value to consumers or stakeholders. By prioritizing value, firms may address the most essential pain areas or possibilities for development rapidly, ensuring that resources are employed efficiently.

5. Embracing Flexibility and Adaptability:
Agile problem-solving emphasizes flexibility and adaptation in the face of uncertainty. It accepts that solutions may alter as new information arises or circumstances change. Agile teams are empowered to adapt their approach, pivot if required, and identify alternate solutions when early methods prove inadequate. This flexibility helps firms to negotiate complicated and dynamic issue domains with resilience.

6. Continuous Learning and Improvement:
Agile problem-solving encourages a culture of continual learning and progress. It encourages teams to reflect on their experiences, learn from failures, and apply those lessons to future problem-solving efforts. This iterative learning process helps teams to polish their problem-solving abilities, expand their awareness of the business environment, and constantly improve their strategy to meet future difficulties more successfully.

7. Visualizing Progress and Transparency:
Visualizing progress is a crucial component of agile problem-solving. Agile teams commonly employ visual management tools, such as Kanban boards or task boards, to monitor the progress of problem-solving initiatives. These visual representations promote transparency, enabling team members and stakeholders to have a clear perspective of the work being done, the status of tasks, and any barriers that require attention. Visualizing progress develops responsibility, promotes openness, and supports successful cooperation.By embracing agile problem-solving methods, firms may handle

complicated issues more efficiently, adapt to changing conditions, and drive continuous development. The collaborative and iterative nature of agile problem-solving helps teams to create novel solutions, produce value swiftly, and build a culture of learning and progress.

Empowering a Learning Culture

Creating a learning culture inside a business is vital for ongoing development and long-term success. A learning culture supports and fosters continuing growth, information exchange, and innovation. It encourages people to actively seek fresh ideas, learn from experiences, and contribute to the development and progress of the business as a whole. Here are crucial factors in enabling a learning culture:

1. Emphasizing Continuous Learning:
In a learning culture, learning is considered a continuing process rather than a one-time occurrence. Employees are encouraged to participate in continual learning, both officially and informally. This might involve attending training programs, exploring professional development opportunities, participating in workshops or seminars, and engaging in self-directed learning. The company promotes and offers resources for workers to develop their knowledge and learn new skills.

2. Encouraging Curiosity and Experimentation:
A learning culture develops curiosity and encourages people to explore new ideas, techniques, and solutions. It encourages a mentality of experimentation, where people feel empowered

to take measured risks and explore novel ways. This fosters a climate where learning from both triumphs and mistakes is acknowledged, and workers are encouraged to share their learnings with others.

3. Supporting Knowledge Sharing:
Knowledge sharing is a vital feature of a learning culture. Employees are encouraged to share their experiences, ideas, and lessons gained with their colleagues. This may be fostered via formal methods such as mentoring programs, communities of practice, or internal knowledge-sharing platforms. By supporting information sharing, firms tap into the collective intellect of their people and generate chances for cooperation and creativity.

4. Providing Opportunities for Growth:
A learning culture gives possibilities for personal and professional improvement. This might involve sponsoring career development programs, developing avenues for progress, providing demanding tasks, or supporting workers' pursuit of new skills and information. By investing in employee development, firms not only increase individual talents but also build a feeling of engagement, loyalty, and dedication among their workforce.

5. Promoting Feedback and Reflection:
Feedback and reflection are vital to a learning culture. Regular feedback, both from managers and peers, helps people find areas for development and build upon their strengths. Reflection helps people to stop, examine their experiences,

and extract meaningful ideas from their job. By creating a culture of feedback and reflection, businesses allow continual learning and progress at both the individual and organizational levels.

6. Recognizing and Rewarding Learning:
Acknowledging and praising learning successes and contributions to the learning culture promotes its value inside the company. Recognizing workers who actively participate in learning, share information, or contribute to the development of others generates a feeling of worth and gratitude. This appreciation may take numerous forms, such as awards, public recognition, professional progression possibilities, or involvement in special initiatives.

7. Leadership as Role Models:
Leadership plays a critical role in enabling a learning culture. When leaders exemplify a learning mentality and actively engage in learning activities, it sets a tremendous example for the whole business. Leaders may foster learning opportunities, stimulate knowledge exchange, and create a secure and supportive atmosphere where people feel comfortable taking chances and learning from errors.

Leveraging Technology for Continuous Improvement
Technology plays a crucial role in fostering continual development inside enterprises. It helps organizations to simplify operations, acquire data, obtain insights, and make educated choices. By utilizing the power of technology,

companies may improve operations, boost efficiency, and drive innovation.

Here are the major characteristics of harnessing technology for continual improvement:

1. Streamlining Processes:
Technology helps firms to simplify and automate operations, decreasing human effort and enhancing productivity. By using digital tools and software solutions, firms may minimize bottlenecks, streamline operations, and decrease the chance of mistakes. Streamlined procedures guarantee that tasks are finished more quickly, enabling teams to concentrate on value-added activities and manage resources more efficiently.

2. Data Collection and Analysis:
Technology helps the gathering and analysis of data, which is vital for driving continual development. Businesses may employ numerous tools and technology to obtain data on consumer behavior, market trends, operational metrics, and other pertinent elements. This data may be evaluated to uncover patterns, trends, and areas for improvement. Data-driven insights give a strong platform for making educated choices and generating targeted changes.

3. Monitoring Performance:
Technology provides real-time monitoring and tracking of performance measures. Organizations might adopt dashboards, analytics platforms, or business intelligence technologies to display and monitor key performance

indicators (KPIs). Monitoring performance helps firms to discover areas that demand improvement, measure progress, and make data-driven choices. With technology-enabled performance monitoring, firms may immediately discover deviations from objectives and take proactive actions to resolve them.

4. Predictive Analysis and Forecasting:
Advanced technologies like artificial intelligence (AI) and machine learning (ML) allow firms to employ predictive analysis and forecasting. By studying past data and recognizing patterns, businesses may make reliable forecasts about future events or trends. This foresight lets firms proactively prepare and make educated choices, improving operations, resource allocation, and customer interactions.

5. Continuous Feedback and Customer Engagement:
Technology allows continual feedback and client involvement, which are crucial for ongoing development. Businesses may employ digital platforms, such as online surveys, social media monitoring, and customer feedback systems, to gather and evaluate consumer information. This real-time feedback loop helps firms to learn client demands, preferences, and pain areas, enabling incremental adjustments to goods, services, and customer experiences.

6. Automation and Workflow Integration:
Automation technology may simplify operations by automating repetitive activities and minimizing human effort. Robotic Process Automation (RPA) and workflow automation

solutions help firms to minimize human mistakes, enhance productivity, and free up workers' time for more important operations. Integrating processes across systems and departments further boosts efficiency and cooperation, guaranteeing seamless handoffs and eliminating delays.

7. Collaboration and Communication Tools:
Technology offers collaborative platforms and communication technologies that enhance knowledge exchange and cooperation across teams. Cloud-based platforms, project management tools, and virtual collaboration tools offer seamless communication, information sharing, and cooperation across geographies and time zones. These solutions increase cross-functional cooperation, enable rapid problem-solving and speed decision-making processes.

8. Innovation and Experimentation:
Technology may be a stimulus for invention and experimentation. Adopting emerging technologies, such as the Internet of Things (IoT), blockchain, or augmented reality, might bring up new options for product or service innovation. Organizations may utilize technology to build test environments, replicate situations, and experiment with new ideas without compromising actual operations. This helps firms to create, iterate, and optimize solutions depending on consumer input and shifting market demands.

CHAPTER 21: FEEDBACK LOOPS

In today's fast-paced and competitive business world, being ahead of the curve is important for long-term success. To accomplish this, firms must continually change and enhance their strategy, products, and services. One of the most successful methods to promote this continuous improvement is via the development of feedback loops that involve stakeholders at every level of the company. These feedback loops establish a cycle of communication, learning, and action that may push enterprises toward increased outcomes.

input loops are a systematic technique of receiving input from stakeholders, assessing it, and making changes based on the insights acquired. This method helps firms to detect blind spots, find development opportunities, and make educated choices that promote growth. By involving stakeholders in this process, organizations develop a feeling of ownership and cooperation, establishing a culture that values open communication and constant learning.

The effectiveness of feedback loops resides in their capacity to give a forum for stakeholders to communicate their ideas, complaints, and recommendations. This two-way communication channel not only helps enterprises to gain useful insights but also empowers stakeholders by making them active participants in the change process. When stakeholders feel heard and respected, they become more involved in the success of the business and are more inclined to share their knowledge and ideas.

Moreover, feedback loops help firms to adapt to changing market conditions and growing consumer requirements more efficiently. By routinely gathering input from stakeholders, firms may recognize developing trends, notice possible concerns early on, and change their strategy appropriately. This agility and reactivity are crucial in today's continuously developing corporate market.

In this essay, we will investigate the relevance of feedback loops in promoting organizational performance. We will look into ways for engaging stakeholders successfully and illustrate how feedback loops may lead to increased outcomes. By embracing the potential of continuous improvement via feedback loops, organizations may position themselves for sustainable development, competitive advantage, and customer pleasure.

The Power of Feedback Loops

Feedback loops act as a catalyst for change and growth within a company. They build a systematic method of obtaining feedback, interpreting it, and taking action based on the insights garnered.

Here are some fundamental features of the strength of feedback loops:

a. Insightful Decision Making: Feedback loops give firms important insights into their operations, products, and services. By gathering feedback from stakeholders, companies obtain a greater knowledge of their strengths, flaws, and opportunities for progress. This knowledge is the foundation for making educated choices that move the company forward.

b. Identification of Blind Spots: Feedback loops operate as a vital tool for exposing blind spots inside an organization. They assist uncover areas where procedures may be inefficient, consumer demands may not be properly satisfied, or staff issues may go unreported. By casting a light on these blind spots, feedback loops help firms to correct them and boost their overall performance.

c. continual Learning: Feedback loops establish a culture of continual learning inside a business. By actively collecting input from stakeholders, companies stimulate the sharing of information and ideas. This constant learning process helps firms to adapt, develop, and remain ahead of the competition.

d. Stakeholder Engagement and Satisfaction: Engaging stakeholders via feedback loops is crucial for creating strong connections and assuring their satisfaction. When stakeholders are given a voice and their ideas are considered, they feel appreciated and become more involved in the organization's success. This involvement leads to increased levels of stakeholder satisfaction and loyalty.

e. Agility and Adaptability: In today's fast-paced business climate, businesses need to be nimble and adaptive. Feedback loops offer the required systems for monitoring market trends, client preferences, and industry developments. By regularly obtaining input, firms may swiftly modify their strategies and offer to suit growing wants and remain ahead of the competition.

f. Performance Improvement: The ultimate purpose of feedback loops is to drive performance improvement. By examining the comments collected, firms may find areas where they are performing and repeat those results. Simultaneously, they may spot areas that need improvement and design tailored action plans to solve them. This repeated process of development leads to increased outcomes and competitive advantage.

Engaging Stakeholders for Optimal Results

Engaging stakeholders is a vital aspect of the effectiveness of feedback loops. *Here are some techniques to promote active involvement and excellent contributions:*

a. Clear Contact Channels: Establish open lines of contact with stakeholders, ensuring that their perspectives are heard and respected. Utilize numerous methods such as surveys, focus groups, town hall meetings, and internet platforms to obtain input efficiently.

b. Empowerment and Ownership: Foster a feeling of ownership among stakeholders by including them in decision-making processes. Give them the liberty to offer ideas, provide solutions, and take responsibility for their input.

c. Timely Feedback methods: Implement timely feedback methods that give rapid replies and indicate that stakeholders' ideas are taken seriously. Ensure that feedback is heard, and action plans are conveyed, generating a feeling of responsibility.

d. Recognition and Rewards: Celebrate the efforts of stakeholders by appreciating their useful input. Recognize and promote people that actively participate in the feedback process, fostering a culture that appreciates and encourages involvement.

Enhancing Results via Iterative development

Feedback loops create the path for continual development and progress. By examining the input obtained, you may uncover patterns, trends, and areas that need improvement. ***Here's how you can employ feedback loops to better your results:***

a. Data-Driven Decision Making: Utilize the insights collected through feedback loops to make educated judgments. Data-driven decision-making helps you to detect gaps, modify plans, and prioritize projects that line with stakeholder expectations.

a. Course Correction and Innovation: Feedback loops help you to discover areas where your firm may be falling short and make required course corrections. Embrace feedback as a chance to innovate, leading your organization toward competitive advantage and greater results.

c. continual Learning and Growth: Establish a culture of continual learning inside your firm. Encourage stakeholders to share best practices, lessons learned, and success stories, establishing a growth mentality that promotes innovation and flexibility.

Engaging Stakeholders for Optimal Results
Engaging stakeholders is a vital aspect of the effectiveness of feedback loops. When stakeholders are actively engaged and feel appreciated, they become more invested in the organization's objectives and are driven to give their thoughts and knowledge. *Here are some essential ways for engaging stakeholders effectively:*

a. Clear Communication Channels: Establishing open lines of communication is vital for engaging stakeholders. submit multiple avenues via which stakeholders may submit feedback, such as questionnaires, focus groups, suggestion boxes, internet platforms, and frequent meetings. Ensure that these channels are readily accessible, user-friendly, and promote honest and constructive feedback.

b. Empowerment and Ownership: Engage stakeholders by including them in decision-making processes and giving them a feeling of ownership. Encourage their active engagement in brainstorming meetings, problem-solving efforts, and strategy formulation. When stakeholders feel that their ideas and efforts are respected, they are more likely to be involved in the organization's success and actively contribute to its progress.

c. Timely Feedback methods: Implement feedback methods that give timely replies and indicate that stakeholders' ideas are taken seriously. Acknowledge and appreciate the comments received, and communicate honestly about the steps being made based on that feedback. Promptly address any complaints or problems expressed by stakeholders, exhibiting a commitment to continual development.

d. Recognition and Rewards: Recognize and reward stakeholders who actively engage in the feedback process. Highlight their important contributions and publicly appreciate their efforts. This acknowledgment might be in the form of verbal praise, certificates, incentives, or other awards. Celebrating stakeholders' involvement produces a positive feedback loop in itself, promoting continuous engagement and participation.

e. Collaboration and Co-creation: Foster a collaborative climate where stakeholders feel encouraged to work with each other and with the organization. Facilitate opportunities for stakeholders to share their experiences, best practices, and success stories. Encourage cooperation via seminars, forums, and networking activities. By integrating stakeholders in co-creating solutions, companies may tap into their combined expertise and promote innovation.

f. input Integration: Integrate stakeholder input into the decision-making processes and operational operations of the company. Actively share how feedback has informed choices, projects, and changes. This indicates to stakeholders that their feedback is appreciated and has a real influence on the organization's direction.

Feedback loops are a valuable instrument that increases stakeholder involvement and boosts company success. By actively incorporating stakeholders, developing a culture of open communication, and exploiting the insights gathered, you can continually enhance your plans, products, and services. Embrace the feedback loop method as a driver for development and success in today's competitive economy, and watch as your firm achieves new heights via collaborative involvement and iterative improvement.

CHAPTER 22: RISING ABOVE CHALLENGES

In the ever-changing world of business, obstacles, and bottlenecks are certain to occur. However, it is how firms react to these barriers that ultimately define their success. Resilience—the capacity to bounce back, adapt, and prosper in the face of adversity—is a virtue that sets top-performing enterprises different. In this article, we study the art of overcoming hurdles and find ways for creating resilience that will push your business to new heights of accomplishment.

Embracing the Power of Resilience

Resilience is a transforming and powerful attribute that helps enterprises to manage obstacles and hurdles efficiently. When companies embrace the power of resilience, they tap into a spectrum of advantages that push them toward success.

Here's a closer look at the relevance of adopting resilience:

a. Adaptability in a Changing Environment: Resilience offers businesses the ability to adjust and prosper in the face of a constantly developing business environment. It lets firms adapt efficiently to unforeseen shocks, fluctuations in market circumstances, and new trends. Resilient firms embrace change as a chance for progress, proactively modifying their strategy, processes, and services to remain ahead.

b. Determination in the Face of Adversity: Resilience feeds determination and tenacity through hard circumstances. It instills a "never give up" culture throughout the business, pushing people and teams to constantly pursue their objectives despite setbacks. Resilient companies stay focused on their goal, even when confronted with difficulties, setbacks, or temporary failures.

c. Risk Management and Mitigation: Resilience requires proactive risk management and mitigation measures. Resilient companies foresee possible issues and build contingency measures to minimize their effect. By detecting and planning for risks, firms can promptly react and recover from failures, limiting the disruption caused by unforeseen occurrences.

d. Resourceful Problem-Solving: Resilient companies demonstrate resourcefulness in problem-solving. They address difficulties with a creative perspective, finding inventive solutions and investigating alternative ways. Resilience helps teams to think outside the box, exploit given resources efficiently, and discover creative methods to overcome problems. This resourcefulness leads to breakthroughs and possibilities for progress.

e. Emotional Well-being and Team Morale: Resilience is directly connected to emotional well-being and team morale. When people and organizations display resilience, they are better prepared to handle stress, bounce back from setbacks, and keep a positive mentality. This fosters a friendly and positive work atmosphere, enhancing team morale, cooperation, and overall productivity.

f. Learning and development: Resilient companies regard obstacles as opportunities for learning and development. They embrace mistakes and setbacks as useful lessons, utilizing them to refine strategy, improve procedures, and boost performance. Resilience supports a culture of continual learning, where people and teams are encouraged to reflect, adapt, and build new abilities to face future problems successfully.

g. Competitive Advantage: Embracing resilience gives firms a competitive advantage. In an uncertain business world, the capacity to adapt, recover, and grow is crucial. Resilient firms are better positioned to embrace new opportunities, capitalize on market developments, and outperform their rivals. Customers, partners, and stakeholders are drawn to resilient firms that regularly provide outcomes despite adversities.

Shifting Mindset

One crucial part of growing resilience is having a mentality that views setbacks as opportunities for development and progress. When businesses approach difficulties via this perspective, they may convert failures into stepping stones toward success.

Here's a deeper look at the relevance of adjusting the perspective to accept obstacles as opportunities:

1. Cultivating a Growth mentality: Embracing obstacles as opportunities are found in having a growth mentality. This attitude thinks that talents and intellect can be acquired through devotion and hard effort. It promotes people and teams to tackle difficulties with curiosity, a drive to learn, and a notion that failure is not permanent but a stepping stone towards development.

2. Fostering Innovation and Creativity: Seeing obstacles as opportunities drives innovation and creativity. When confronted with challenges, companies are compelled to investigate alternate solutions, think outside the box, and question the status quo. This mentality change allows teams to produce new ideas and innovative methods, leading to breakthrough breakthroughs and competitive advantages.

3. Building Problem-Solving abilities: Embracing obstacles as opportunities promote strong problem-solving abilities. It changes the attention from brooding on problems to actively seeking answers. Resilient companies support a proactive approach to problem-solving, allowing people and teams to uncover core causes, assess diverse viewpoints, and devise successful solutions for resolution. This approach encourages a culture of constant development.

4. Encouraging a Learning Culture: Viewing problems as opportunities encourages a culture of learning inside a company. Instead of fearing errors or defeats, staff are encouraged to evaluate, extract lessons, and apply gained knowledge to future attempts. This fosters an atmosphere

where learning from setbacks is appreciated and embraced, leading to personal and professional progress for people and the company as a whole.

5. Nurturing Agility and Adaptability: Seeing problems as opportunities cultivates agility and adaptability. Organizations grow more comfortable with change and uncertainty, rapidly modifying their plans and procedures to overcome hurdles. This approach produces an agile and responsive culture, helping organizations to prosper in quickly changing market circumstances.

6. Enhancing Resilience and Grit: Shifting the perspective to accept obstacles as opportunities develop resilience and grit. Resilient people and teams are more suited to endure adversity, sustain motivation, and bounce back from setbacks. This mentality feeds motivation and the conviction that setbacks are transitory hurdles that can be overcome with patience and an optimistic perspective.

7. Inspiring a Can-Do Attitude: When obstacles are regarded as opportunities, it generates a can-do attitude inside the business. Employees become more proactive, resourceful, and solution-oriented. They are inspired to take initiative, accept responsibility, and contribute to discovering new solutions. This optimistic mentality seeps across the business, producing a culture of optimism and empowerment.

Agile Planning

In an uncertain corporate climate, flexible planning is a critical component of establishing resilience. It entails the capacity to promptly and efficiently react to unanticipated occurrences, change plans, and handle hurdles. Here's a deeper look at the relevance of agile planning in overcoming roadblocks:

1. Flexibility and adaptation: Agile planning stresses flexibility and adaptation in the face of the unanticipated. It recognizes that conditions might change swiftly, prompting businesses to alter their strategies appropriately. By adopting this approach, firms may proactively adapt to unforeseen events, market upheavals, or emerging trends, ensuring that they stay competitive and capture new possibilities.

2. speedy Decision-Making: Agile planning supports speedy decision-making. When confronted with impediments, companies need to make educated decisions swiftly. Agile planning helps leaders and teams to obtain important information effectively, analyze the situation, and make timely choices to meet the problem at hand. This helps enterprises to reduce the effect of bottlenecks and sustain forward momentum.

3. Iterative method: Agile planning follows an iterative method, which entails continual feedback, assessment, and modification. It understands that original plans may require adjustment when new information becomes available or circumstances change. By routinely monitoring progress,

companies may detect possible bottlenecks early and make required course modifications, averting serious interruptions to their goals.

4. Resource Optimization: Agile planning helps optimize resources by adjusting them to the current circumstances. When bottlenecks develop, businesses may reallocate resources wisely to solve the difficulties successfully. This guarantees that resources are used properly and that the business can traverse bottlenecks while reducing extra strain or wastage.

5. Risk Management and Mitigation: Agile planning involves risk management and mitigation tactics. It entails identifying possible hazards, assessing their potential effect, and devising contingency plans to mitigate them. By proactively analyzing risks and having mitigation measures in place, companies may lessen the negative impacts of bottlenecks and react more effectively when they arise.

6. Embracing Feedback: Agile planning encourages firms to welcome feedback and learn from their experiences. It requires frequently obtaining feedback from stakeholders, analyzing the results of adopted plans, and integrating lessons gained into future planning. By using feedback, companies may enhance their decision-making processes, optimize their strategies, and boost their capacity to handle potential barriers.

7. Emphasizing Continuous Improvement: Agile planning encourages a culture of continuous improvement. It

understands that there is always space for development and encourages organizations to reflect, assess, and learn from their experiences. By continually improving their strategies and procedures, firms become more resilient, flexible, and better positioned to face unanticipated obstacles.

Collaborative Synergy

Collaborative synergy refers to the strength that occurs when people and teams work together towards a similar objective. It stresses the power and effectiveness that may be produced via cooperation, shared knowledge, and group effort.

Here's a deeper look at the relevance of collaborative synergy in overcoming roadblocks:

1. varied viewpoints and knowledge: Collaborative synergy brings together varied viewpoints, experiences, and knowledge. When people from diverse backgrounds and disciplines interact, they bring unique perspectives and ideas to the table. This variety promotes problem-solving ability, as it allows for a full investigation of barriers and the development of novel solutions.

2. Enhanced Creativity and Innovation: Collaboration promotes an atmosphere that inspires creativity and innovation. When teams cooperate, they can combine their skills, develop new ideas, and question traditional thinking. By using group creativity, companies may overcome hurdles by identifying imaginative ideas and solutions that may not have been found via individual efforts.

3. Effective Communication and Knowledge Sharing: Collaborative synergy depends on open and effective communication channels. When people and teams cooperate, they actively exchange knowledge, information, and best practices. This flow of information promotes a greater understanding of bottlenecks, helps to learn from prior experiences, and allows for the application of effective solutions that have been demonstrated elsewhere within the business.

4. Mutual Support and Motivation: Collaboration promotes a feeling of mutual support and motivation among team members. When confronted with difficulties, people may rely upon the knowledge and support of their peers. This support network gives encouragement to continue, creates resilience, and produces a great work atmosphere where everyone feels valued and empowered.

5. Shared Responsibility and Ownership: Collaborative synergy emphasizes shared responsibility and ownership of overcoming hurdles. When people cooperate, they assume the collective responsibility of creating answers and attaining success. This shared responsibility develops a feeling of accountability and dedication, as team members recognize that their efforts directly affect the team's capacity to solve obstacles.

6. Efficient Problem-Solving: Collaborative synergy fosters efficient problem-solving. By harnessing the combined

expertise and abilities of a team, companies may assess bottlenecks from different aspects, explore choices, and arrive at successful solutions more effectively. Collaborative problem-solving decreases the danger of neglecting essential aspects and leads to well-rounded and complete methods to overcome hurdles.

7. Learning and Growth possibilities: Collaborative synergy offers learning and growth possibilities for individuals and teams. Through cooperation, team members may learn from one another's knowledge, share ideas, and obtain fresh insights. This constant learning develops individual abilities, extends knowledge, and fosters personal and professional progress, adding to the overall resilience of the company.

Continuous Learning

Continuous learning is a critical part of establishing resilience within businesses. It entails actively finding chances to extract useful lessons from adversity and employing those lessons to promote progress and growth.

Here's a deeper look at the value of constant learning in overcoming roadblocks:

1. Reflection and Self-Assessment: Continuous learning starts with reflection and self-assessment. When confronted with barriers, companies take the time to examine the issue, identify the causes that led to the difficulty, and reflect on their actions and choices. This introspection allows for a

better knowledge of the blockage and offers a platform for extracting valuable insights.

2. Identifying Areas for development: Adversity shows areas inside the company that may need development. By focusing on the bottleneck and its causes, businesses may identify particular areas, such as procedures, communication, or decision-making, that require adjustment. Continuous learning helps firms to recognize these areas and establish development methods, ensuring that similar bottlenecks may be eliminated or handled more effectively in the future.

3. information Sharing and cooperation: Continuous learning depends on information sharing and cooperation. After hitting a hurdle, businesses encourage team members to share their experiences and thoughts. This cooperation provides for a wider grasp of the situation and helps the discovery of alternate methods or solutions. By pooling collective knowledge, companies may harness the experience of their team members to overcome bottlenecks and boost overall performance.

4. having a Growth mentality: Continuous learning is built-in having a growth mentality. This perspective views setbacks as chances for development and advancement, rather than as insurmountable hurdles. It motivates people and teams to tackle hurdles with curiosity and a drive to learn. By adopting a growth mindset, companies promote an atmosphere that emphasizes resilience, adaptation, and the quest for knowledge.

5. Implementing Feedback Loops: Feedback loops are vital for continual learning. They entail obtaining input from stakeholders, including workers, customers, and partners, on their experiences and viewpoints relating to the barrier. By actively collecting feedback, businesses acquire vital insights that help them understand the effect of the obstacle and suggest areas for improvement. Implementing feedback loops develops a culture of continuous development and ensures that the company stays responsive to the requirements and expectations of stakeholders.

6. Experimentation and Innovation: Continuous learning pushes firms to experiment and develop. After hitting a barrier, firms may investigate new tactics, technology, or strategies to overcome similar obstacles in the future. By adopting a mentality of experimentation, businesses may unearth novel ideas, enhance processes, and establish a culture that encourages creative problem-solving and continual improvement.

7. implementing Lessons learned: The genuine benefit of continual learning resides in implementing the lessons learned through hardship. Organizations aggressively transform the information acquired from barriers into action. They implement the highlighted areas for improvement in their plans, procedures, and decision-making. By using these principles, companies become more resilient, adapt more effectively to new challenges, and achieve continual development and success.

Resource Optimization

Resource efficiency is a vital part of overcoming bottlenecks and establishing resilience within companies. It entails effectively and efficiently using existing resources to overcome hurdles and reach the best results.

Here's a deeper look at the role of resource efficiency in overcoming roadblocks:

1. Strategic Resource Allocation: Resource optimization begins with strategic resource allocation. When confronted with a blockage, companies analyze their available resources, including financial, human, technical, and material assets. They prioritize and distribute these resources carefully, concentrating on areas that directly affect overcoming the blockage and attaining targeted goals. This ensures that resources are used efficiently, maximizing their influence on the organization's capacity to overcome obstacles.

2. Efficient Resource Utilization: Resource optimization strives to use resources efficiently. It entails ensuring that resources are directed to activities and projects that match the organization's goals and have the best potential for overcoming hurdles. By detecting and removing wasteful or duplicate resource allocation, firms simplify their processes, eliminate waste, and boost overall efficiency.

3. Flexibility and Adaptability: Resource efficiency needs companies to be flexible and adaptive in their resource consumption. When confronting bottlenecks, companies may need to reallocate resources or reprioritize their utilization to solve the present difficulties. This flexibility ensures that resources are distributed where they are most required, enabling the organization to react efficiently and adapt to changing conditions.

4. Leveraging Partnerships and Collaborations: Resource efficiency goes beyond internal resources. Organizations may maximize their resources by using partnerships and collaborations with external stakeholders, like suppliers, vendors, or other organizations. By pooling resources, sharing knowledge, and cooperating on solutions, companies may overcome hurdles more efficiently and maximize the potential of existing resources.

5. Innovation and Creativity: Resource optimization stimulates innovation and creativity in resource consumption. When resources are restricted or confined, companies are compelled to think creatively and develop inventive solutions to attain desired results. This may require investigating alternate ways, embracing new technology, or repurposing current resources to overcome hurdles. By promoting a culture of innovation and creative problem-solving, businesses maximize the potential of their resources.

6. continual review and Improvement: Resource optimization is an ongoing activity that involves continual review and

improvement. Organizations frequently examine the efficacy and impact of resource allocation methods, evaluating input, data, and results. Through this examination, companies may discover areas for improvement, enhance resource allocation processes, and adjust to changing demands and situations.

7. Return on Investment (ROI) Focus: Resource optimization is driven by a focus on optimizing the return on investment (ROI) of resources. Organizations carefully analyze the possible advantages and consequences associated with resource allocation choices. By aligning resource allocation with anticipated outcomes and intended results, companies guarantee that resources are allocated towards activities and initiatives that give the highest value in overcoming hurdles and achieving success.

Inspiring Resilient Leadership

Resilience begins at the top, with resilient leaders who inspire and guide their employees through adversities. Resilient leaders display strong commitment, keep a cool manner, and express a clear vision amid times of uncertainty. They enable their staff to embrace resilience, leading by example and promoting a culture of endurance and creativity.
Inspiring Resilient Leadership

Resilient leadership is critical for negotiating hurdles and establishing a culture of resilience inside businesses. Resilient leaders demonstrate certain skills and actions that inspire and guide their teams through adversities.

Here's a deeper look at the value of inspiring resilient leadership:

1. Composure and Emotional Intelligence: Resilient leaders retain composure and emotional intelligence through stressful circumstances. They stay cool, collected, and level-headed, even in the face of hardship. This emotional stability helps them to make sensible judgments, offer support to their employees, and inspire confidence through uncertain or tumultuous circumstances.

2. Clear Vision and Purpose: Resilient leaders have a clear vision and purpose that drives their actions and choices. They successfully convey this vision to their teams, ensuring everyone knows the direction and objectives of the firm. A strong vision offers a feeling of stability and direction through hard times, enabling people to remain focused and determined in conquering hurdles.

3. Effective Communication: Resilient leaders thrive at effective communication. They freely share information, offer frequent updates, and listen to the concerns and suggestions of their team members. Transparent communication promotes confidence, encourages teamwork, and ensures that everyone is aligned and informed, especially during times of uncertainty. Resilient leaders foster open communication and create an atmosphere where people feel comfortable sharing their opinions and concerns.

4. Resilience Role Model: Resilient leaders lead by example. They display resilience in their activities, demonstrating

tenacity, flexibility, and determination in conquering adversities. By exhibiting resilience, leaders motivate their colleagues to adopt the same mentality and approach when confronted with hurdles. Resilient leaders become role models, exhibiting the skills and attitudes essential to overcome adversities.

5. Empowering and Supporting Teams: Resilient leaders empower and assist their teams. They give the essential tools, direction, and autonomy for people to take ownership of their job and overcome hurdles. Resilient leaders create an atmosphere where people feel empowered to make choices, take chances, and learn from their experiences. They give support and encouragement, fostering a feeling of trust and psychological safety inside the team.

6. Strategic Decision-Making: Resilient leaders thrive at strategic decision-making. They acquire pertinent information, examine possible risks and possibilities, and make well-informed choices that consider the long-term repercussions. Resilient leaders adopt a proactive approach to resolving hurdles, discovering alternate options, and altering plans as required. Their strategic decision-making abilities reduce the effect of bottlenecks and keep the business on track toward its objectives.

7. Learning and Growth Orientation: Resilient leaders build a learning and growth-oriented culture. They encourage their staff to learn from obstacles and disappointments, extracting useful lessons that may be implemented in the future.

Resilient leaders facilitate ongoing learning, give chances for skill growth, and promote an attitude of inquiry and progress. By emphasizing learning and development, leaders promote resilience and ongoing progress among their teams.

In the face of hardship, the power of resilience cannot be underestimated. By accepting obstacles as opportunities, implementing agile planning, developing collaborative synergy, continually learning, maximizing resources, and inspiring resilient leadership, businesses may surmount hurdles and reach new levels of success. In a competitive corporate world, it is resilience that sets outstanding businesses apart—the unflinching desire to rise above setbacks, adapt to change and emerge stronger than ever before. Embrace resilience as a key principle, and observe your company fly to unmatched heights.

CHAPTER 23: ANTICIPATING OBSTACLES

In the ever-evolving world of business, where competition is tough and quick changes are the norm, just defining objectives and working towards them is no longer sufficient to assure success. To remain ahead of the curve and surpass your competition, it is necessary to possess the capacity to predict difficulties and effectively traverse them. By proactively recognizing possible impediments before they materialize, you may gain a major competitive edge, allowing you to adapt, develop, and survive in a dynamic business environment.

Anticipating challenges is not about being gloomy or anticipating the worst. Rather, it is a proactive strategy that helps you to predict prospective obstacles, prepare ahead, and design successful solutions to solve them. By aggressively recognizing difficulties in advance, you may limit their influence on your organization, lower the risk of setbacks, and embrace opportunities that others might overlook.

Businesses that fail to foresee barriers sometimes find themselves caught off guard, trying to find answers when presented with unanticipated problems. This reactive strategy may lead to lost resources, missed opportunities, and even the chance for failure. On the other side, firms that embrace the habit of anticipating hurdles are better positioned to tackle adversity head-on, adapt rapidly, and keep their competitive advantage.

Embrace a Forward-Thinking Mindset

To foresee challenges, it is vital to establish a forward-thinking attitude. Encourage your staff to go beyond the immediate objectives and examine possible obstacles that may develop. Foster an atmosphere that supports brainstorming, innovation, and proactive problem-solving. By adopting this technique, you may establish a proactive culture inside your firm.

Embracing a forward-thinking mentality is a vital component of predicting challenges in business. It requires taking a proactive and imaginative attitude that extends beyond current objectives and duties. Instead of just concentrating on the now, a forward-thinking attitude challenges you and your team to examine the future repercussions of your choices and activities.

Here are some crucial aspects to grasp about developing a forward-thinking mindset:

1. Proactive Problem-Solving: Rather than waiting for issues to occur, a forward-thinking perspective drives you to foresee and handle prospective hurdles before they become impediments. It entails actively searching out chances for improvement, innovation, and development, and taking preventative actions to reduce hazards.

2. Future-oriented Planning: A forward-thinking attitude stresses strategic planning and goal-setting with a long-term view. It entails imagining where your firm wants to go in the future and establishing strategies and action plans to attain those objectives. By examining numerous situations and possible impediments, you can better prepare your firm to navigate through uncertainty and remain on course toward its objectives.

3. Embracing Change: In a quickly changing corporate environment, a forward-thinking perspective urges you to welcome change rather than reject it. It includes remaining alert to evolving trends, technology, and market developments, and modifying your plans appropriately. By accepting change and aggressively reacting to it, you may position your firm ahead of the competition and grasp new possibilities.

4. Innovation and Creativity: A forward-thinking mentality develops a culture of innovation and creativity inside your firm. It encourages people to think outside the box, question old ways, and explore new alternatives. By promoting fresh ideas and allowing people to take measured risks, you may unearth creative solutions and identify possible impediments before they become barriers to growth.

5. ongoing Learning: Embracing a forward-thinking mentality entails a commitment to ongoing learning and progress. It demands maintaining current with industry knowledge, market trends, and developing best practices. By investing in

professional development and promoting a learning culture, you and your team may acquire new insights, adapt to changing conditions, and remain ahead of the curve.

Stay Abreast of Industry Trends

Staying current with market trends is a critical component of predicting hurdles in the company. It entails regularly monitoring and assessing the newest developments, movements, and trends within your sector. By remaining updated about market trends, you may get useful insights that help you to recognize possible roadblocks and change your tactics appropriately.

Here are some crucial elements to learn about keeping aware of market trends:

1. Market Dynamics: Industry trends give vital information on changes in the market dynamics, including shifts in consumer tastes, developing technology, new rivals, and shifting regulatory landscapes. By understanding these dynamics, you can predict how they can affect your firm and identify possible difficulties that may occur as a consequence.

2. Competitive Advantage: Monitoring industry trends helps you to keep an eye on your rivals and their plans. By evaluating their activities, product offers, and market positioning, you may find areas where your organization might distinguish itself and acquire a competitive edge. It also helps you foresee any competitive risks or problems that may result from your rivals' efforts.

3. customer Behavior: Industry trends typically mirror changes in customer behavior, such as growing demands, tastes, and expectations. By examining these patterns, you may acquire insights into what your target audience wants and identify possible difficulties that may occur if your firm fails to fulfill its increasing needs. This insight may inform your product development, marketing strategy, and customer experience efforts.

4. technology breakthroughs: Industries are continuously altered by technological breakthroughs and inventions. Staying current on industry trends helps you uncover upcoming technology that might disrupt your business or provide new possibilities. By proactively accepting current technologies and exploiting them to your advantage, you may keep ahead of possible roadblocks and capitalize on new trends.

5. Collaboration and Partnerships: Industry trends might indicate possibilities for collaboration and partnerships with other firms. By remaining informed of these developments, you may spot possible synergies and build strategic relationships that help tackle challenges jointly. Collaborative activities may give access to new markets, pooled resources, and expertise, improving your position in the face of industry disruptions.

6. Future Planning: sector trends give insights into the way your sector is moving. By recognizing these patterns, you may

foresee future difficulties and opportunities, enabling you to align your company strategy and investments appropriately. This forward-looking strategy helps you to position your firm to prosper in the long run while eliminating possible barriers along the road.

Conduct Risk Assessments

Conducting risk assessments is a vital step in identifying possible roadblocks and minimizing hazards in your organization. Risk assessments include carefully assessing many parts of your company operations to discover weaknesses, possible dangers, and places where hurdles may occur. By performing thorough risk assessments, you may proactively identify and solve possible impediments, limiting their influence on your business's performance.

Here are crucial aspects to learn when doing risk assessments:

1. Identify Potential hazards: Risk assessments entail identifying and recording potential hazards that may influence your organization. These risks might vary across numerous domains, such as operational, financial, legal, reputational, or technical. By reviewing each element of your organization in depth, you may find particular risks that might represent impediments to your operations, development, or profitability.

2. Evaluate chance and effect: After identifying possible risks, it is vital to analyze their chance of occurrence and the potential effect they may have on your firm. This assessment

helps you to prioritize risks and spend resources appropriately. Risks with greater probability and large potential implications demand more attention and proactive preparation to reduce their effects.

3. Mitigation methods: Once possible risks are identified and analyzed, the following step is to establish effective mitigation methods. These tactics try to limit the possibility of hazards arising or diminish their effect if they do materialize. Mitigation techniques might involve adopting safeguards, building contingency plans, constructing backup systems, or applying control measures to address recognized risks.

4. Monitoring and Review: Risk assessments should not be a one-time process. It is vital to develop a mechanism for regular monitoring and assessment of identified hazards. Regularly reassessing the success of mitigation techniques and monitoring changes in the business environment helps ensure that your risk management strategy stays up-to-date and effective. This proactive strategy helps you to discover new risks or changing situations that may necessitate revisions to your mitigation methods.

5. Compliance and Legal Factors: Risk assessments should also include factors linked to compliance with relevant laws, regulations, and industry standards. By recognizing and managing compliance risks, you may prevent legal challenges, fines, or brand harm. It is crucial to remain informed with applicable rules and maintain compliance as part of your risk management processes.

6. Employee Involvement: Conducting risk assessments should entail the involvement of workers across all levels and departments of your firm. Employees typically provide significant insights and information regarding possible dangers in their areas of expertise. Encouraging their active engagement in risk assessment procedures not only increases the accuracy and efficacy of risk identification but also promotes a culture of risk awareness and accountability across the business.

Seek Customer Feedback

Seeking consumer feedback is an essential strategy for spotting possible roadblocks and assuring the success of your organization. Customers are a significant source of information since they engage directly with your goods, services, and overall brand experience. By actively seeking and listening to customer feedback, you may develop a greater knowledge of their requirements, preferences, and concerns. This information helps you to foresee prospective problems and make educated choices to handle them successfully.

Here are crucial elements to learn about getting client feedback:

1. Understanding Customer Pain Points: Customer feedback gives insights into the pain points and issues that your customers may be encountering. By requesting feedback via surveys, feedback forms, or even direct chats, you may uncover areas where consumers are encountering challenges,

unhappiness, or hurdles in their interactions with your organization. This information helps you to proactively address those pain areas and eliminate hurdles from your customer journey.

2. Product or Service Improvement: Customer feedback is a significant resource for enhancing your goods or services. Customers may give comments, identify defects, or indicate places where advancements might be made. By actively soliciting and evaluating this input, you may discover possible impediments that may occur due to product or service restrictions, and take actions to improve and iterate upon them. This iterative strategy helps you connect your offers with client expectations and remove possible impediments.

3. Anticipating Changing client demands: Customer feedback is a great tool for remaining responsive to developing client demands and preferences. By routinely requesting feedback, you may discover changes in consumer behavior, developing trends, and shifting expectations. This information helps you to predict possible difficulties that may occur if your firm fails to adapt to growing client requirements. By integrating consumer input into your decision-making processes, you can connect your plans and offers with their shifting wants.

4. Enhancing Customer Experience: Customer feedback gives vital insights into the entire customer experience. By monitoring feedback connected to contacts with your organization, you may uncover possible impediments that may affect client pleasure, loyalty, or retention. This input

might help you reveal areas where changes are required, such as in communication, response times, or support services. By proactively resolving these impediments, you may improve the entire customer experience and develop better customer connections.

5. Building Customer Loyalty: Actively soliciting and adopting customer input displays that you appreciate their ideas and are devoted to addressing their demands. This may create consumer loyalty and advocacy. By building a feedback loop with your consumers, where they feel heard and see their comments leading to beneficial improvements, you may develop deeper connections and drive customer loyalty. Loyal consumers are more likely to give regular feedback, alert you to possible barriers, and become brand advocates.

6. input methods: There are several methods via which you may obtain client input, including online surveys, feedback forms on your website, social media listening, customer service encounters, or even focus groups. Choose mediums that are handy and accessible to your target audience and promote active involvement. Regularly examine and analyze the input received to detect trends, repeating themes, and possible impediments.

Foster Collaboration and Knowledge Sharing

Fostering cooperation and information exchange inside your business is a great strategy for recognizing possible roadblocks and generating inventive solutions. Collaboration brings together varied views, talents, and knowledge, allowing your team to cooperatively handle difficulties and foresee hurdles. By cultivating a culture of collaboration and information sharing, you can leverage the collective wisdom of your staff and remain ahead in a fast-changing business world.

Here are crucial aspects to grasp about encouraging teamwork and information sharing:

1. Cross-Departmental Communication: Encourage open communication and cooperation across various departments and teams within your business. Breaking down barriers and increasing cross-departmental communication gives a comprehensive knowledge of the company and its operations. When workers from multiple departments share their views and experiences, it becomes simpler to detect possible impediments that may occur at the junction of different activities.

2. Regular Team Meetings and Brainstorming Sessions: Schedule regular team meetings and brainstorming sessions to bring together personnel from diverse roles and levels. These seminars give a chance for exchanging ideas, opinions, and information. By encouraging open talks, you may expose possible roadblocks and explore inventive solutions as a group. Encourage active engagement and establish a safe area for workers to voice their thoughts and recommendations.

3. Sharing Best Practices and Lessons gained: Encourage workers to share their best practices and lessons gained from

prior experiences. This information sharing helps others to benefit from established ways and avoid possible problems. By encouraging a culture of sharing achievements and mistakes, you create an atmosphere where workers can collectively learn and develop, eventually leading to enhanced problem-solving capacities and obstacle anticipation.

4. Learning and Development Initiatives: Invest in learning and development initiatives that foster teamwork and information exchange. Provide opportunities for workers to increase their skills, knowledge, and expertise via training programs, workshops, and seminars. By equipping workers with new skills and information, you enable them to better foresee challenges and contribute to the general development and success of the firm.

5. Technology Platforms for Collaboration: Leverage technology platforms that encourage collaboration and information exchange. Tools like project management software, collaborative document-sharing platforms, and internal communication tools may promote cross-functional cooperation and make knowledge exchange more efficient. These systems allow teams to interact in real time, exchange information, and access resources that aid in recognizing possible roadblocks and developing effective solutions.

6. Encouraging Feedback and ideas: Create a culture where workers feel comfortable sharing feedback and expressing their ideas. Actively solicit their perspectives and suggestions on possible challenges and solutions. Encourage constructive

criticism and develop outlets for anonymous input to encourage open and honest conversation. By appreciating employee feedback, you tap into their collective expertise and receive useful insights that may expose possible roadblocks that were previously overlooked.

7. Recognition and Rewards: Recognize and reward workers who actively contribute to cooperation and information-sharing activities. This promotes the significance of teamwork and creates a culture of constant learning and sharing. Celebrate successes stemming from joint efforts, and highlight success stories to motivate others to embrace cooperation and offer their expertise and ideas.

Monitor Competitors

Monitoring rivals is a vital activity for spotting possible roadblocks and keeping ahead in the competitive business scene. Understanding what your rivals are doing, their plans, and their market positioning gives significant information that may help you foresee issues and make educated choices to keep your competitive advantage.

Here are crucial aspects to learn about monitoring competitors:

1. Competitive Analysis: Monitoring rivals entails doing a detailed competitive analysis. This study analyzes the strengths, weaknesses, opportunities, and dangers offered by your rivals. It helps you comprehend their product offers, pricing methods, marketing approaches, customer

involvement, and total market share. By studying this information, you may anticipate possible impediments that may develop from your rivals' behavior.

2. Market Positioning: Monitoring rivals helps you to determine how your firm is positioned in contrast to others in the market. By studying how your rivals distinguish themselves, target certain consumer categories, or use distinct value propositions, you may identify possible challenges that may result from their market positioning. This understanding helps you enhance your strategy and identify ways to distinguish from competitors.

3. Identifying Competitive risks: By watching your rivals, you may uncover possible competitive risks that may damage your market share or client base. This includes following new product launches, marketing initiatives, or growth into new areas. By anticipating these dangers, you can proactively design ways to fight them and lessen any possible barriers they may provide to your firm.

4. Capitalizing on possibilities: Monitoring rivals not only helps you identify hurdles but also allows you to find possibilities. By evaluating their behaviors and plans, you may find market gaps, underserved client categories, or rising trends that your rivals have not yet seized on. This helps you to aggressively grab these chances and acquire a competitive edge.

5. Industry Trends and Developments: Competitor monitoring gives insights into industry trends and developments. By studying your rivals, you may detect upcoming innovations, changes in client preferences, or adjustments in market dynamics. This understanding helps you predict any hurdles that may develop from these trends and change your plans appropriately.

6. Differentiation and Innovation: Monitoring rivals helps you to find areas where you can distinguish yourself and innovate. By studying your rivals' offers and methods, you may identify ways to add distinctive value to your consumers and remain ahead. This may mean improving your product features, boosting customer experience, or using new technology to distinguish your firm and overcome possible challenges.

7. Continuous Improvement: Competitor monitoring is a continual effort. It demands regularly keeping informed with industry news, watching rival actions, and assessing market trends. By regularly watching your competition, you can remain flexible, adjust fast to changes, and continuously enhance your methods to overcome barriers and retain a competitive edge.

Embrace Technology and Automation

Embracing technology and automation is a strong method for detecting possible roadblocks and boosting corporate efficiency. Technology may give essential tools and solutions that expedite operations, enhance decision-making, and help firms remain ahead of the curve. By adopting technology and automation, you may recognize and solve possible hurdles more efficiently, streamline processes, and promote innovation.

Here are crucial elements to realize about adopting technology and automation:

1. Data Analytics and Insights: Technology allows firms to gather and analyze massive volumes of data. By employing sophisticated analytics solutions, firms may acquire significant insights into consumer behavior, market trends, and operational performance. These insights assist identify possible impediments and enable data-driven decision-making, enabling firms to proactively manage difficulties and capture opportunities.

2. Predictive Analytics: Predictive analytics employs historical data and statistical models to estimate future results. By applying predictive analytics algorithms, firms may foresee future challenges and trends, allowing them to make educated choices and take pre-emptive actions to avoid risks. This proactive strategy helps organizations keep ahead of possible roadblocks and respond rapidly to developments in the market.

3. Process Automation: Automation technologies automate repetitive operations and simplify workflows, lowering the risk of mistakes and freeing up important human resources. By automating manual procedures, firms may decrease possible impediments stemming from human mistakes, increase operational efficiency, and dedicate resources to

more strategic projects. This automation allows people to concentrate on higher-value tasks that demand creativity and problem-solving abilities.

4. Artificial Intelligence (AI) and Machine Learning (ML): AI and ML technologies allow organizations to harness algorithms and models that learn from data and make predictions or judgments without explicit programming. These technologies may assist recognize trends, detect abnormalities, and foresee prospective difficulties with higher precision. By utilizing the potential of AI and ML, organizations may proactively solve bottlenecks and enhance their operations.

5. Enhanced Communication and Collaboration: Technology solutions such as project management software, virtual meeting platforms, and collaboration tools allow efficient communication and cooperation among teams, even in distant or scattered work contexts. These tools enhance information sharing, idea development, and real-time collaboration, enabling teams to detect possible problems and jointly build solutions.

6. Customer Experience Enhancement: Technology plays a significant part in boosting the customer experience. Customer relationship management (CRM) systems, chatbots, customized marketing automation, and other technologies allow firms to create tailored and efficient interactions with customers. By employing technology to identify consumer demands, preferences, and pain spots, organizations may

proactively eliminate possible impediments to create a flawless customer experience.

7. Competitive Advantage: Embracing technology and automation may provide firms with a competitive advantage. By remaining aware of technology changes and implementing creative solutions, organizations may distinguish themselves, enhance their operations, and adapt rapidly to changing market dynamics. This capacity to adapt and exploit technology helps organizations overcome possible roadblocks and remain ahead of their competition.

In the fast-paced and competitive corporate scene, anticipating difficulties is vital for keeping a competitive advantage. By developing a forward-thinking approach, remaining updated about market trends, doing risk assessments, obtaining consumer input, promoting teamwork, watching rivals, and employing technology, you may detect possible roadblocks and handle them effectively. By proactively tackling these challenges, you will position your organization for long-term success and development, ensuring you remain ahead in the ever-evolving industry.

CHAPTER 24:PROBLEM SOLVING

In today's quickly developing business market, where change is relentless and competition is severe, firms confront a myriad of complicated issues. To manage these challenges and prosper in the marketplace, firms must have the capacity to use creative ideas and new methods of problem-solving.

Gone are the days when basic, cookie-cutter solutions were adequate. The complexities of the corporate world necessitate a new viewpoint and a desire to explore the unexplored ground. This is when the power of creative problem-solving comes into play.

Creative problem-solving entails breaking out from standard thought patterns and exploring new pathways for discovering answers. It takes a change in mentality, from perceiving difficulties as impediments to embracing them as opportunities for development and advancement. By adopting this approach, organizations may unleash their creative potential and tap into a multitude of inventive ideas.

Moreover, in a highly competitive atmosphere, distinguishing from the throng is vital. Creative problem-solving gives a method to distinguish your organization and achieve a competitive advantage. It lets you tackle difficulties in a new and unexpected way, resulting in breakthrough solutions that set you apart from your competition.

Innovation sits at the core of creative problem-solving. By pushing your team to think differently, take measured chances, and question the existing quo, you establish an atmosphere where innovation may thrive. This, in turn, helps your firm to respond to changing market dynamics, exploit opportunities, and overcome hurdles with agility.

In this post, we will look into the numerous facets of implementing creative ideas and innovative ways to problem-solving in a commercial environment. We will discuss tactics that develop a growth mentality, stimulate out-of-the-box thinking, promote collaboration, harness technology, embrace experimentation, and emphasize customer-centric solutions. By adding these strategies to your problem-solving toolset, you may position your firm for success in today's competitive marketplace.

Embracing a Growth Mindset

A growth mindset is the concept that talents and intellect can be grown and enhanced through commitment, effort, and a desire to learn. In the context of problem-solving, having a growth mindset is vital for establishing a culture of innovation and continual development inside your firm.

Here are some crucial characteristics of developing a development mindset in problem-solving:

1. View issues as chances: Instead of perceiving issues as insurmountable impediments, urge your team to consider them as chances for development and learning. Help them realize that facing problems is a normal part of the problem-solving process and that it allows them to gain new skills and insights.

2. Encourage a Love for Learning: Cultivate a hunger for knowledge and encourage your team members to seek out learning opportunities. Provide tools, training programs, and seminars that strengthen their problem-solving ability. Emphasize that every setback or loss is a chance to learn and develop.

3. Foster a friendly atmosphere: Create a secure and friendly atmosphere where people feel comfortable taking chances and expressing their thoughts. Avoid blaming or condemning errors, since this may inhibit creativity and hinder exploration. Instead, encourage constructive comments and applaud efforts, even if they don't always lead to quick results.

4. Emphasize Effort and Resilience: Shift the attention from the final product to the process itself. Encourage your staff to value work and endurance above rapid achievement. Recognize and reward those who display resilience and a desire to confront challenging situations head-on.

5. Encourage Reflective Thinking: Foster a culture of reflection by encouraging your team to assess their problem-solving tactics. By reflecting on prior experiences,

triumphs, and failures, they may discover areas for development and adapt their strategy appropriately.

6. Lead by Example: As a leader, it's vital to exemplify a growth mentality and act as a role model for your team. Demonstrate a desire to learn, adapt, and take on problems with a positive and open perspective. Encourage and assist your team members in their personal development journeys.

Thinking Outside the Box

Thinking outside the box is an attitude that pushes people to break away from normal thinking patterns and seek alternate and unusual methods of problem-solving. It entails questioning assumptions, finding fresh views, and examining options that may not be immediately evident.

Here are some major components of thinking outside the box in problem-solving:

1. Challenge Assumptions: Encourage your team to examine assumptions and preconceived views about the topic at hand. Often, we approach problem-solving with set beliefs or assumptions about what is feasible or successful. By questioning these assumptions, you open up the chance for fresh and creative solutions to emerge.

2. Embrace Divergent Thinking: Divergent thinking means producing a broad variety of thoughts and possibilities without judgment or constraint. Encourage brainstorming meetings where team members may openly discuss their

ideas, no matter how odd they may sound. Emphasize quantity over quality in the beginning phases to stimulate a flow of ideas.

3. Seek Unconventional opinions: Encourage your team to seek feedback and opinions from varied sources. This might mean engaging colleagues from various departments, consulting experts from outside your firm, or even getting thoughts from adjacent sectors. Different viewpoints may bring new insights and stimulate inventive ideas that may not have been explored otherwise.

4. Break Down Mental hurdles: Help your team overcome mental hurdles and constraints that hamper creative thinking. Encourage them to let go of self-imposed limits and explore ideas that may appear first impractical or far-fetched. Foster an environment where crazy and inventive ideas are embraced, since they may frequently act as catalysts for innovative problem-solving.

5. Foster a Culture of Curiosity: Cultivate a culture of curiosity and a quest for knowledge among your team. Encourage them to explore new topics, learn from other disciplines, and seek inspiration outside their current work setting. Curiosity fosters creativity and brings up new options for alternative problem-solving techniques.

6. Encourage Experimentation and Risk-Taking: Provide your team with the flexibility and encouragement to experiment and take measured risks. Encourage them to try out new ideas,

even if they may not guarantee instant success. Create a secure atmosphere where failures are recognized as learning opportunities and stepping stones toward creative solutions.

Emphasizing Collaboration and Diversity

Collaboration and diversity play a significant role in problem-solving by bringing together various viewpoints, experiences, and skills. When people from varied backgrounds work together in a collaborative setting, they may harness their unique ideas to produce new and successful solutions.

Here are some crucial characteristics of promoting teamwork and diversity in problem-solving:

1. Harnessing Collective Intelligence: Collaboration allows for the pooling of ideas, information, and abilities from various team members. By building an atmosphere that supports open communication and cooperation, you may tap into the collective intellect of your team. Each employee provides a distinct viewpoint and skill, which, when combined, may lead to more thorough and innovative problem-solving results.

2. Cross-Pollination of Ideas: When individuals with varied backgrounds and skill sets get together, they bring a diversity of perspectives and ways of thinking to the table. This variety helps break down mental boundaries and offers up fresh paths for problem-solving. By fostering the flow of ideas and views,

you may stimulate cross-pollination, when thoughts and solutions from one area inspire advances in another.

3. Encouraging Active Listening and Respect: Collaboration needs active listening and respect for others' opinions. Create an inclusive workplace where everyone's views are respected, and people feel safe expressing their perspectives. Encourage team members to actively listen and explore various ideas, especially if they vary from their own. This free and polite exchange of ideas may lead to the birth of unique and breakthrough solutions.

4. Multidisciplinary Approach: Seek to form teams with varied skill sets and experiences. By bringing together experts with diverse areas of expertise, you may attack challenges from many viewpoints. A multidisciplinary approach facilitates innovative problem-solving by relying on a breadth of knowledge and approaches. It allows for the integration of ideas and approaches from diverse domains, resulting in unique and comprehensive solutions.

5. Overcoming prejudices and Stereotypes: Emphasize the significance of overcoming prejudices and stereotypes that may hamper cooperation and restrict a variety of ideas. Create awareness about unconscious biases and foster an inclusive atmosphere where every team member feels appreciated and encouraged to participate. Overcoming prejudices allows for the free flow of ideas and guarantees that varied viewpoints are properly acknowledged.

6. Building Strong Interpersonal connections: Foster strong interpersonal connections among team members. Encourage social contacts, team-building events, and chances for cross-functional cooperation. Strong connections and a feeling of trust among team members increase communication, collaboration, and the desire to share and build upon each other's ideas.

Leveraging Technology

In today's digital era, technology provides a multitude of tools, resources, and skills that may dramatically boost problem-solving procedures. By utilizing the power of technology, organizations may simplify processes, get important insights, and uncover new opportunities for imaginative problem-solving.

Here are some major components of employing technology in problem-solving:

1. Data Analytics: Data is a significant commodity that may give insights into patterns, trends, and consumer behaviors. By applying data analytics tools and methodologies, firms may analyze vast amounts of data to reveal hidden patterns, identify core causes of issues, and make data-driven choices. Data analytics helps firms to obtain a better knowledge of the difficulties they face and design tailored solutions.

2. Artificial Intelligence (AI) and Machine Learning (ML): AI and ML technologies have the potential to transform problem-solving. These technologies may automate

monotonous operations, make predictions based on data trends, and even produce novel solutions. AI-powered algorithms can analyze large volumes of data and deliver significant insights, supplementing human intellect and allowing more efficient and effective problem-solving.

3. Automation and Workflow Optimization: Technology helps firms to automate tedious and repetitive operations, freeing up significant time and resources. By optimizing workflows and automating regular operations, firms may concentrate their attention on more strategic and complicated problem-solving activities. Automation not only increases efficiency but also lowers mistakes and promotes overall production.

4. Virtual Collaboration Platforms: Technology supports collaboration by allowing teams to work together smoothly, regardless of geographical constraints. Virtual collaboration systems include services like video conferencing, document sharing, and real-time collaboration tools. These systems enable teams to engage in real time, share ideas, and work on problem-solving projects jointly, regardless of their physical location.

5. Simulation and Modeling: Technology gives the tools to build virtual simulations and models that can imitate real-world circumstances. This lets firms try multiple problem-solving techniques in a controlled environment, without the need for costly or time-consuming physical tests. Simulations and models help firms to examine the possible

effect of alternative solutions, improve tactics, and make educated choices.

6. quick Prototyping and Iteration: Technology solutions, such as 3D printing and virtual prototyping software, allow quick prototyping and iteration. This helps firms swiftly design and test prototypes of viable solutions, receive feedback, and iterate depending on user insights. Rapid prototyping speeds the problem-solving process, lowering time-to-market and allowing firms to adapt rapidly to emerging obstacles.

Creating a Culture of Experimentation

A culture of experimentation is an atmosphere where people and teams are encouraged to explore new ideas, take measured risks, and learn from both triumphs and mistakes. It is a mentality that welcomes the concept of continual improvement and realizes that creativity frequently arises via experimenting.

Here are some critical characteristics of building a culture of experimenting in problem-solving:

1. Encouraging Risk-Taking: Foster an atmosphere where employees feel empowered to take chances and explore alternative solutions. Encourage calculated risk-taking by offering assistance, resources, and the flexibility to explore. This approach helps overcome the fear of failure and inspires people to think creatively and beyond their comfort zones.

2. Learning from mistakes: In a culture of experimentation, mistakes are considered learning opportunities rather than setbacks. Encourage team members to reflect on failures, extract useful insights, and apply those learnings to future problem-solving initiatives. Celebrate the process of learning and progress, supporting the concept that setbacks are stepping stones towards success.

3. Iterative Approach: Emphasize the role of iteration in problem-solving. Encourage your team to construct a prototype or minimal viable product (MVP) and receive feedback early on. Use the feedback to develop and iterate on the solution. Iterative problem-solving allows for continual learning, adaptation, and development, leading to more robust and successful solutions.

4. Setting Realistic Expectations: It is crucial to create realistic expectations when it comes to experimenting. Acknowledge that not every trial will result in instant success. Be open about the uncertainties and the hazards involved. By managing expectations, you create a supportive atmosphere where employees are inspired to take chances and learn from the consequences, regardless of the immediate outcome.

5. Providing Resources and Support: Ensure that your team has access to the required resources, tools, and support to run experiments successfully. This may involve offering time, funding, training, and mentoring. By investing in the infrastructure and support required for experimenting, you

show a commitment to promoting creativity and problem-solving.

Embracing Customer-Centric Solutions

Embracing customer-centric solutions involves placing the requirements, preferences, and experiences of customers at the center of problem-solving initiatives. It requires obtaining a comprehensive knowledge of your consumers, their pain spots, and their intended goals. By aligning problem-solving activities with consumer expectations, firms can distinguish themselves, develop strong customer connections, and generate long-term success.

Here are some major components of implementing customer-centric solutions in problem-solving:

1. Customer Research and Empathy: Invest in customer research to obtain insights into their requirements, issues, and goals. Use approaches such as surveys, interviews, and observational studies to identify their pain areas and experiences. Foster empathy among your team, pushing them to put themselves in the consumers' shoes and fully comprehend their viewpoints.

2. Define the Customer issue: Clearly define the issue from the customer's viewpoint. This requires going beyond surface-level symptoms and identifying the fundamental reasons for their issues. By identifying the issue from the customer's point of view, you may concentrate

problem-solving efforts on addressing the core causes and offering meaningful solutions.

3. Co-Creation and cooperation: Involve consumers in the problem-solving process via co-creation and cooperation. Seek their opinion, thoughts, and suggestions to comprehend their unique views and viewpoints. Collaborative problem-solving enables the creation of solutions that directly meet consumer wants and preferences, leading to increased levels of satisfaction and loyalty.

4. Iterative Feedback Loops: Implement feedback loops with consumers to constantly develop and enhance solutions. Regularly gather feedback on the efficacy and usability of your solutions, and utilize that input to improve and enhance the customer experience. This iterative approach guarantees that solutions are constantly adjusted to suit changing client requirements.

5. Design Thinking Approach: Adopt a design thinking approach, which stresses a deep knowledge of client requirements and a focus on producing new solutions. This human-centered method incorporates steps such as empathizing, defining, ideating, prototyping, and testing. By applying design thinking concepts, organizations can build customer-centric products that connect with their target audience.

6. Personalization and Customization: Tailor solutions to particular client preferences wherever feasible. Embrace

personalization and customization to create distinct and relevant experiences. Leverage technology and data insights to create customized solutions that answer individual client demands, generating a feeling of value and difference.

7. Continuous Customer interaction: Maintain continuing interaction with customers beyond problem-solving activities. Regularly engage with clients to get feedback, understand their shifting requirements, and proactively handle any developing difficulties. By remaining connected with consumers, you may create strong connections, promote loyalty, and acquire useful insights for future problem-solving attempts.

Innovation and innovative problem-solving have become vital in today's competitive corporate world. By adopting a growth mentality, supporting out-of-the-box thinking, fostering collaboration, using technology, embracing innovation, and emphasizing customer-centric solutions, organizations may unleash their full potential. Don't shy away from obstacles; instead, consider them as chances to apply creative ideas and unique methods that can set your organization apart from the competition and drive success in the long term.

CHAPTER 25: BUILDING RESILIENCE

In the dynamic world of business, setbacks, and failures are sure to occur. They may be depressing, demoralizing, and even risk the very life of a corporation. However, the actual measure of success resides not in avoiding failure totally, but in how successfully we recover and bounce back from it. Building resilience is the way to turn setbacks and failures into opportunities for development and success. In this post, we will look into the techniques and attitude necessary to reinvent resilience inside your organization, allowing you to emerge stronger, smarter, and more successful than ever before.

Every entrepreneur and company leader confronts hurdles along the road. It might be a product launch that falls short of expectations, a strategy decision that doesn't generate the intended outcomes, or unforeseen market issues that undermine the roots of a firm. These losses may be depressing and may drive people to doubt their ability or even contemplate abandoning up. However, it is crucial to remember that setbacks are not symptomatic of failure; they are stepping stones on the route to achievement.

Resilience is the capacity to bounce back from adversity, setbacks, and failures. It is about keeping a positive perspective, learning from errors, adjusting to change, and pressing on with newfound drive. Resilient entrepreneurs consider setbacks as chances for development and self-improvement. They recognize that failure is not an endpoint but a stimulus for creativity and growth.

In the face of setbacks, cultivating resilience becomes vital. It is a process of reinventing yourself and your company to endure setbacks and emerge stronger on the other side. Resilience is not just about enduring the storm; it's about embracing the storm as a chance to develop and prosper.

Throughout this essay, we will discuss the mentality and tactics that successful entrepreneurs adopt to create resilience. We will go into the significance of accepting failure as a stepping stone, creating a growth mentality, learning from the past, fostering a supportive and adaptable staff, and discovering opportunities in times of crisis. By implementing these tactics, you may convert failures into springboards for success, enabling your firm to bounce back stronger and more adaptive than ever before.

Remember, setbacks and failures are not indicators of weakness; they are the tests that mold us and define our path. By creating resilience, you may navigate through adversity, surmount problems, and change the story of your company. It's time to redefine resilience and begin on a road of development, innovation, and sustainable success.

Embrace Failure as a Stepping Stone

Failure has long been stigmatized in society, typically connected with humiliation, sadness, and a feeling of defeat. However, resilient entrepreneurs recognize that failure is not the end of the road but a stepping stone on the journey to success. Instead of dreading failure, they embrace it as a chance for development and learning.

When setbacks occur, it is vital to adjust your attitude and regard failure as great teaching. Each failure gives insights into what went wrong, what techniques didn't succeed, and what improvements need to be made. By accepting failure, you open yourself up to crucial lessons that may affect your future choices and behaviors.

Resilient entrepreneurs recognize that failure is not a reflection of their value or ability. They divorce their self-esteem from the success of their companies and accept that failure is a normal part of the entrepreneurial process. This perspective permits individuals to bounce back more swiftly and with a greater commitment.

By reframing failure as a stepping stone, entrepreneurs can take learning from their experiences and utilize it to move their enterprises forward. They study the causes behind the failure, identify the errors committed, and explore other alternatives. This process of self-reflection and learning helps people to develop their methods, enhance their talents, and improve their decision-making.

Furthermore, accepting failure cultivates resilience by creating a willingness to take chances. When entrepreneurs are not frightened of failure, they are more inclined to travel into unexplored territory, explore novel ideas, and push the frontiers of what is feasible. They recognize that failure is an inevitable result of daring greatly and pushing beyond their comfort zones.

It is vital to stress that accepting failure does not entail soliciting failure or being complacent in the face of setbacks. Rather, it implies accepting that failure is a possibility, but it should not prevent you from pursuing your ambitions. Resilient entrepreneurs recognize that failure is not the reverse of success; it is a stepping stone toward it.

Cultivate a Growth Mindset

A growth mindset is a strong mentality that feeds resilience and generates a continual desire for learning, development, and achievement. Resilient entrepreneurs realize the necessity of maintaining a development mentality within themselves and their staff. They think that talents and intellect can be cultivated by devotion, effort, and a willingness to learn from failure.

Here are the major characteristics and advantages of having a development mindset:

1. Embracing problems: Resilient entrepreneurs perceive problems as opportunities for progress rather than hurdles to be avoided. They recognize that encountering and conquering

problems leads to personal and professional growth. Instead of shying away from challenging circumstances, they pursue them with curiosity, persistence, and conviction in their capacity to learn and adapt.

2. perseverance and Effort: A growth mindset stresses the value of perseverance and effort in obtaining achievement. Resilient entrepreneurs know that setbacks and failures are not indications of their ability but rather feedback about their existing methods. They recognize the importance of hard work, tenacity, and devotion, realizing that success frequently involves ongoing effort and a willingness to explore new techniques.

3. Learning from Failure: A growth mindset encourages entrepreneurs to consider failure as an opportunity for learning and progress. Rather than being disappointed or dismayed by failure, they embrace it as a normal part of the road toward achievement. They examine their failures, extract useful lessons, and utilize them to enhance their tactics and decision-making processes. Failures become stepping stones toward progress and creativity.

4. Embracing input: Resilient entrepreneurs aggressively seek and embrace input from others. They recognize that feedback gives vital insights and views that may help them develop and improve. Rather than taking critique personally or defensively, they welcome it as a chance for development and self-reflection. Constructive criticism is considered an

opportunity to find areas for progress and make required modifications.

5. applauding Others' Success: Cultivating a development mindset entails recognizing and applauding the successes of others. Resilient entrepreneurs do not regard the success of others as a threat or a reflection of their shortcomings. Instead, they celebrate the successes of their peers and seek inspiration from their travels. They recognize that success is not a limitless resource and that by helping and learning from others, they may improve their progress.

Learn from the Past, Plan for the Future

Resilient entrepreneurs realize the necessity of learning from previous events and applying that information to prepare for the future. They know that the past provides rich insights and lessons that may guide their decision-making and help them handle future issues with more wisdom and readiness.

Here are crucial parts of learning from the past and preparing for the future:

1. Analyzing prior Setbacks and Failures: Resilient entrepreneurs take the time to study prior setbacks and failures. They evaluate what went wrong, identify the core causes, and grasp the elements that led to the adverse consequences. This study helps them develop a greater knowledge of the issues they experienced and allows them to learn from their errors.

2. Identifying Patterns and Trends: By reviewing prior experiences, entrepreneurs may uncover patterns and trends that may have affected their successes or failures. They seek repeating themes, market trends, client preferences, and industry dynamics. This knowledge helps them to make better-educated judgments and predict possible obstacles or opportunities in the future.

3. Leveraging Lessons Learned: Learning from the past is not only about reflecting on errors; it's about collecting meaningful lessons and insights. Resilient entrepreneurs utilize these lessons to influence their strategy, enhance their methods, and avoid repeating the same errors. By harnessing the insight garnered from prior events, individuals may make more successful and proactive choices in the future.

4. Proactive Risk Management: Armed with the information obtained from examining the past, resilient entrepreneurs engage in proactive risk management. They assess possible risks and uncertainties, make contingency plans, and take efforts to reduce such risks. This proactive strategy helps them navigate through uncertain times more successfully and reduce the potential impact of unanticipated issues.

5. Strategic Planning and Adaptability: Learning from the past helps entrepreneurs to participate in strategic planning for the future. They establish realistic goals, develop clear tactics, and build practical plans to attain their objectives. However, they also appreciate the significance of flexibility and adaptation. They know that plans may need to be altered or

updated when circumstances change, and they are prepared to pivot and modify their strategy appropriately.

6. Embracing Innovation and Continuous Improvement: Resilient entrepreneurs know that the business environment is continuously altering. They accept innovation and constant improvement as major drivers of success. By learning from the past, they find opportunities for innovation and explore new methods to remain ahead of the competition. They are open to embracing new technology, procedures, and business models that can provide them with a competitive advantage in the future.

Foster a Supportive and Agile Workforce

Resilient entrepreneurs recognize that establishing a supportive and adaptive staff is vital for overcoming setbacks and failures. They know that the success of their organization is inextricably related to the collective resilience and flexibility of its personnel. By building a friendly and adaptive work environment, entrepreneurs may develop a culture that flourishes in the face of adversity and welcomes change.

Here are crucial factors in developing a supportive and adaptable workforce:

1. Open Communication and cooperation: Resilient entrepreneurs promote open communication and cooperation among their teams. They establish a climate where workers feel comfortable expressing their ideas, problems, and criticism. This open communication generates a feeling of

belonging, encourages cooperation, and allows the collective intellect of the workforce to grow. It also enables the identification and resolution of difficulties at an early stage.

2. Empowerment and Autonomy: Resilient entrepreneurs empower their staff by giving them autonomy and decision-making authority. They trust their staff to make educated judgments and take responsibility for their job. This empowerment develops a feeling of duty, accountability, and resilience. When workers feel trusted and respected, they are more willing to accept challenges, take prudent risks, and adjust swiftly to changing circumstances.

3. Continual Learning and Skill Development: Resilient entrepreneurs promote continual learning and skill development within their staff. They invest in training programs, mentoring opportunities, and professional development activities. By training workers with the required information and abilities, they guarantee that their teams are equipped to navigate through setbacks and failures. Continuous learning also cultivates a growth mentality and a culture of resilience.

4. Flexibility and adaptation: Resilient entrepreneurs appreciate the significance of flexibility and adaptation in today's fast-paced business climate. They promote a workforce that is nimble and sensitive to change. This flexibility helps personnel to change their methods, accept new technology or procedures, and pivot as required. It helps

the firm to swiftly adjust to market fluctuations and exploit chances that result from setbacks or unforeseen occurrences.

5. Recognition and Support: Resilient entrepreneurs realize the necessity of recognizing and supporting their personnel. They celebrate triumphs, praise hard effort, and give support during trying times. By providing a supportive work environment, they promote a feeling of camaraderie and resilience among the team. Employees feel respected, motivated, and more inclined to bounce back from setbacks with resolve.

6. Encouraging Innovation and Creativity: Resilient entrepreneurs promote innovation and creativity within their workforce. They offer room for workers to explore new ideas, experiment with alternative ways, and take prudent risks. This supports a culture of innovation and builds resilience by supporting out-of-the-box thinking and the capacity to adapt to changing market conditions.

Seek Opportunities in Crisis

Resilient entrepreneurs recognize that crises and tough times may also bring hidden chances for development and innovation. Rather than being overwhelmed by the turmoil or negativity, they actively seek and capitalize on possibilities that come during these situations. By adopting a mentality of pursuing opportunities amid crises, entrepreneurs may convert setbacks into catalysts for good change and growth.

Here are crucial characteristics of finding chances amid a crisis:

1. Identifying Unmet Needs: Crises typically alter current systems, processes, and consumer behaviors. Resilient entrepreneurs perceive these upheavals as opportunities to find unmet needs or rising trends. They carefully study changes in consumer behavior, market dynamics, and societal expectations. By analyzing the dynamic environment, they may find holes in the market and create new possibilities for goods, services, or solutions.

2. Adapting and Innovating: Crises compel entrepreneurs to modify their strategy, business models, and operations. Resilient entrepreneurs regard these changes as chances to innovate and develop. They explore methods to reinvent their services, establish more efficient procedures, or generate new income sources. By embracing change and harnessing their ingenuity, companies may convert crisis-induced obstacles into opportunities for distinction and development.

3. Market Expansion and Diversification: Crises may lead to adjustments in consumer preferences, economic situations, and industry dynamics. Resilient businesses exploit these adjustments to seek new markets or expand their offers. They examine how their goods or services might be changed or extended to meet increasing client requirements or new sectors. By going into uncharted areas or broadening their consumer base, businesses might uncover new opportunities for development and resilience.

4. Strategic Partnerships and Collaborations: Crises typically need collaboration and cooperation across enterprises and sectors. Resilient entrepreneurs aggressively seek strategic alliances or collaborations with complementing firms. By combining resources, knowledge, and networks, they may harness collective strengths to navigate through hard times. Collaborations may lead to creative solutions, improved market reach, and shared knowledge, eventually leading to enhanced resilience.

5. Embracing Digital Transformation: Crises typically drive the demand for digital transformation across sectors. Resilient entrepreneurs perceive this as a chance to embrace technology improvements and automate their business. They invest in digital infrastructure, online platforms, and e-commerce skills. By embracing digital tools and channels, businesses may reach new consumers, streamline operations, and boost their agility in adjusting to constantly changing conditions.

6. Reinventing the company Model: Crises may push entrepreneurs to rethink and redesign their company concepts. Resilient entrepreneurs analyze their present models and discover possibilities for development or adaptation. They examine alternate income sources, subscription models, or innovative pricing techniques. By questioning established beliefs and embracing innovation, businesses may develop a more robust and sustainable company model.

:

Building resilience is not a one-time activity; it is a continual process that takes commitment, adaptation, and a development mentality. By accepting failure, establishing a development mentality, learning from the past, building a supportive staff, and discovering opportunities amid crises, you can reinvent resilience inside your firm. Setbacks and failures will no longer be obstacles but stepping stones to success. Remember, resilience is not only about rebounding back; it's about bouncing back stronger, smarter, and more determined than ever before.

CHAPTER 26: EMPOWERING ACTION-ORIENTED CULTURE

In the fast-paced and ever-changing world of business, keeping a static and conventional strategy is no longer adequate. Instead, firms must build a culture that inspires people to take action, question the status quo, and promote significant change. An action-oriented culture encompasses the attitude of proactive problem-solving, creativity, and a feeling of ownership among workers. It encourages employees to go beyond their allocated roles and actively contribute to the development and success of the business.

By allowing workers to take action, companies tap into a great resource - the pooled creativity, knowledge, and insights of their workforce. When workers feel empowered, they become more engaged, motivated, and devoted to attaining company objectives. They take responsibility for their job and accept accountability for their actions. This leads to enhanced productivity, higher levels of creativity, and a greater readiness to adapt and react to altering market needs.

Furthermore, an action-oriented culture develops an atmosphere where people are not hesitant to take chances. They are encouraged to experiment, learn from mistakes, and always explore possibilities for growth. This mentality encourages a culture of continual learning and progress, where people are not confined by fear or complacency but are driven to push limits and discover new possibilities.

In addition to fostering internal innovation, an action-oriented culture also fosters cooperation and teamwork. When workers are empowered to take action, they are more likely to actively engage, offer their unique insights, and cooperate with others to accomplish common objectives. This collaborative synergy leads to the production of new ideas, more efficient problem-solving, and the capacity to handle complicated issues jointly.

Moreover, an action-oriented culture produces a pleasant work atmosphere that attracts and keeps top personnel. Ambitious people are attracted to companies that appreciate and promote their passion to make a difference. They prefer environments where they can actively participate, take ownership of their job, and see the effect of their efforts. By building an empowering culture, firms may present themselves as attractive employers, capable of offering meaningful employment that gives chances for personal growth and professional development.

Cultivating a Growth Mindset

Cultivating a development mentality is a vital part of establishing an action-oriented culture inside a business. A growth mindset is the concept that people can develop and enhance their talents through commitment, effort, and a desire to learn. It is about accepting difficulties, continuing in the face of setbacks, and viewing failures as chances for development and learning.

In an action-oriented culture, leaders and managers play a critical role in encouraging and supporting a development mentality among workers. They inspire people to consider issues as opportunities for progress rather than barriers to conquer. By reframing failures as learning experiences, people are encouraged to stretch their limits and go out of their comfort zones to explore creative ideas and solutions.

To create a growth mindset inside the business, it is vital to offer workers the tools, support, and motivation to increase their skills and knowledge. This may be done via training programs, seminars, mentorship, and coaching activities. By investing in staff development, firms show their commitment to promoting growth and continual progress.

Creating a comfortable and non-judgmental atmosphere is also vital in creating a development mentality. Employees should feel safe taking chances and expressing their ideas, knowing that their efforts will be acknowledged and valued, regardless of the result. Encouraging open communication, constructive criticism, and recognizing both accomplishments and mistakes fosters a culture where employees are driven to learn from their experiences and strive for personal and professional progress.

In a development mindset society, people are not bound by their existing talents or abilities. They are encouraged to extend themselves, accept new challenges, and always seek chances for growth and development. This attitude encourages a feeling of curiosity, flexibility, and resilience, helping people to solve complicated issues and generate innovation inside the firm.

By creating a growth mindset, firms may cultivate a workforce that is open to change, flexible to new technology and market trends, and capable of taking on new tasks and positions. Employees with a growth mindset are more likely to seek out new ideas, communicate successfully, and take responsibility for their job, leading to better productivity and performance.

Ultimately, a growth mindset produces a culture of continual progress, where individuals are encouraged to explore their full potential, gain new abilities, and accept setbacks as chances for growth. By developing this attitude, firms may build a competitive edge by unleashing the latent potential and inventive thinking of their employees.

Building Trust and Collaboration

Building trust and promoting cooperation are crucial components of an action-oriented culture inside a business. Trust creates the cornerstone of good cooperation, open communication, and a supportive work environment. Collaboration, on the other hand, facilitates the pooling of varied views, expertise, and talents to accomplish shared objectives. Together, trust and cooperation create a culture where people feel respected, empowered, and inspired to deliver their best efforts.

To develop confidence inside the company, leaders must establish clear and open channels of communication. This requires actively listening to staff, offering chances for input, and ensuring that information flows openly and honestly. By establishing a culture of open communication, leaders show their readiness to listen to concerns, handle difficulties, and include staff in decision-making processes. This promotes a feeling of trust, where workers feel appreciated and respected, and are more inclined to take ownership of their job and share their ideas.

Another crucial part of gaining trust is leading by example. Leaders should display honesty, and consistency, and follow through on their pledges. By being trustworthy and responsible, they inspire confidence and trust among team members. Additionally, recognizing and praising individual and team efforts is vital in creating trust. Celebrating successes and delivering appreciation for a job well done maintains the perception that each employee's efforts are respected and appreciated.

Collaboration is equally crucial in developing an action-oriented culture. It entails establishing an atmosphere where people feel comfortable working together, exchanging ideas, and seeking opinions from others. Collaboration helps people to harness their combined knowledge and skills to solve challenges, make informed choices, and create innovation.

To enhance cooperation, companies should break down silos and stimulate cross-functional connections. This may be done via team-building activities, project-based projects, and providing venues for exchanging ideas and information. By encouraging individuals from various departments or teams to cooperate, businesses generate opportunities for new views and fresh ideas, leading to more inventive solutions.

Leaders may also enhance collaboration by creating clear objectives and expectations that need the participation of various people or teams. When workers have common objectives and understand the collective effect of their work, they are more inclined to cooperate and assist one another to attain those goals.

Furthermore, providing a psychologically comfortable setting is vital for successful teamwork. Employees should feel safe expressing their thoughts, debating ideas, and participating in constructive arguments without fear of criticism or retaliation. When people feel psychologically comfortable, they are more ready to share their unique ideas, which may lead to more innovative problem-solving and better decision-making.

Ultimately, developing trust and promoting cooperation create a culture where workers feel encouraged to offer their ideas, take chances, and support one another. This collaborative atmosphere stimulates the sharing of information, spurs creativity, and leads to improved results for the business as a whole. By emphasizing trust and cooperation, firms may generate a competitive edge by tapping into the collective expertise and capacities of their workforce.

Providing Autonomy and Ownership

Providing autonomy and ownership to workers is a vital feature of an action-oriented culture. Autonomy refers to allowing people the flexibility and power to make choices and take action within their jobs, whereas ownership implies creating a feeling of duty and accountability for the consequences of their work. By offering autonomy and ownership, businesses allow people to take initiative, be proactive, and generate genuine change.

When workers have autonomy, they are given the trust and liberty to select how they approach and perform their tasks. This implies letting people make choices, solve issues, and exercise their judgment based on their skills and knowledge. By abandoning control and empowering individuals with autonomy, businesses tap into their unique skills and insights, which may lead to new solutions and better results.

Autonomy also generates a feeling of empowerment and professional satisfaction. When people have the flexibility to use their creativity and make choices that directly affect their job, they are more engaged, driven, and involved in the results. They have a better feeling of ownership over their work and are more inclined to take pleasure in their successes. This, in turn, adds to increased levels of productivity, initiative, and a proactive mentality inside the firm.

Ownership goes hand in hand with autonomy and requires fostering a feeling of duty and accountability in workers. When employees feel a feeling of ownership over their work, they take personal responsibility for its success and are dedicated to providing high-quality outcomes. They go beyond fulfilling expectations and take the initiative to consistently improve and surpass benchmarks. Ownership promotes a culture where people take pride in their job, seek out chances for progress, and actively contribute to the organization's success.

To promote autonomy and ownership, firms might start by clearly outlining roles and duties while giving freedom to individuals to use their judgment and creativity. Establishing defined goals and objectives creates a framework within which workers may act freely and take responsibility for their job. By defining defined and quantifiable objectives, workers have a clear idea of what is expected of them and can align their activities appropriately.

Additionally, leaders should establish an atmosphere where people feel comfortable taking measured risks and exploring new ideas. Mistakes should be seen as learning opportunities rather than failures. By developing a growth mindset and establishing a culture that encourages experimentation and continual development, workers are more inclined to accept autonomy and take responsibility for their work.

Regular feedback and support from leaders are vital in promoting autonomy and ownership. By giving direction, tools, and constructive criticism, leaders can help workers overcome problems and make educated choices. This assistance underscores the concept that autonomy is not about working in solitude but rather about giving people the necessary tools and support to succeed.

Ultimately, granting autonomy and ownership fosters a culture where people are empowered to take initiative, make choices, and drive genuine change. It develops a feeling of ownership, responsibility, and a proactive mentality inside the business. By offering workers the autonomy and ownership they require, firms can unleash their full potential and harness their inventive thinking, leading to higher productivity, flexibility, and competitive advantage.

Recognizing and Celebrating Achievements

Recognizing and celebrating successes is an important component of an action-oriented culture inside a business. It entails recognizing and praising the efforts, growth, and successes of people and teams. By recognizing and celebrating successes, companies create a good and encouraging work environment that develops a feeling of pride, enhances morale, and encourages continuous performance.

One of the primary advantages of acknowledging successes is the reinforcement of desirable behaviors and results. When workers' efforts and successes are recognized, it reaffirms the value and significance of their job. This acknowledgment acts as positive reinforcement, pushing employees to continue aiming for excellence and taking responsibility for their work. It also conveys to other workers the sorts of actions and accomplishments that are appreciated inside the company.

Celebrating successes goes beyond mere acknowledgment and entails establishing a culture of gratitude and enthusiasm. It may take numerous forms, such as public acknowledgment at team meetings, appreciation emails or texts, certificates, rewards, or even celebratory activities. The idea is to make workers feel unique and appreciated for their efforts.

Celebrations give an occasion for the whole business to come together and jointly honor the successes of individuals or teams. They provide a forum to publicly express thanks and promote the successes, building a feeling of camaraderie and solidarity among workers. Celebratory events and activities generate a pleasant and pleasurable environment, which may help establish deeper connections, promote team spirit, and raise employee morale.

Recognizing and celebrating successes also has a big influence on employee engagement and motivation. When workers feel that their efforts are recognized and acknowledged, they create a feeling of pride in their job. This feeling of success and acknowledgment creates intrinsic motivation, leading to higher work satisfaction and a desire to continue succeeding. Employees who feel appreciated and acknowledged are more inclined to go above and beyond, putting their best efforts into the organization's success.

Furthermore, honoring successes helps develop a culture of excellence and ongoing progress. When workers' successes are honored, it creates a baseline for performance and inspires others to aim for equal levels of success. It generates healthy competition, stimulates people to set greater objectives, and provides an atmosphere where everyone is encouraged to attain their full potential.

To properly acknowledge and celebrate successes, businesses should adopt a disciplined and consistent strategy. This might involve adopting official recognition programs, building a mechanism for peer-to-peer recognition, or integrating accomplishment celebrations into regular team meetings or company-wide events. It is crucial to ensure that recognition is timely, relevant, and tailored to each individual, emphasizing their unique achievements and impact.

Leaders and managers have a key role in recognizing and celebrating successes. By actively watching and appreciating workers' efforts, they convey their support and gratitude. Leaders should also foster a culture of acknowledgment and enable staff to recognize and celebrate one another's successes. Peer appreciation may be as influential as official acknowledgment from leaders, generating a feeling of camaraderie and cooperation among teams.

In conclusion, recognizing and celebrating successes is a significant tool in developing an action-oriented society. It promotes desirable behaviors, enhances morale, and inspires staff to continue performing. By developing a culture of appreciation and celebration, businesses build an atmosphere where employees feel appreciated, engaged, and encouraged to take ownership of their work. Ultimately, recognizing and celebrating successes adds to a healthy and high-performing corporate culture, leading to greater productivity, creativity, and a competitive edge.

Embracing Continuous Learning

Embracing continuous learning is a critical part of an action-oriented culture inside a business. It entails building an atmosphere that appreciates and supports continual growth, development, and the learning of new information and skills. By promoting a culture of continuous learning, firms empower people to adapt to change, remain ahead of market trends, and promote innovation.

In today's fast-paced and ever-evolving business market, firms must prioritize learning to stay competitive. Embracing continuous learning helps people to enhance their talents, remain relevant in their professions, and gain the skills required to confront new problems. It motivates people to seek out possibilities for advancement and take the initiative in gaining new information and abilities.

Continuous learning may take different forms, including official training programs, seminars, conferences, online courses, mentorship, and self-directed learning initiatives. Organizations may give resources and assistance to workers, allowing them to access relevant learning opportunities and keep current on industry changes. By investing in employee development, firms show their commitment to maintaining their personnel equipped with the newest skills and knowledge.

In an action-oriented culture, learning is not restricted to formal training sessions or organized programs. It develops an attitude that penetrates daily work. Employees are encouraged to learn from their experiences, reflect on their achievements and disappointments, and share information and best practices with their colleagues. This encourages a culture of continuous development, where employees are continuously finding ways to increase their performance, innovate, and discover better solutions.

Leaders have a critical role in building a culture of continual learning. They should set the example by being lifelong learners themselves and exhibiting a commitment to personal and professional progress. Leaders may foster learning by offering frequent feedback, coaching, and mentoring, as well as by devoting time and resources to learning activities. They should establish an atmosphere where errors are recognized as learning opportunities and where curiosity, experimentation, and invention are appreciated.

Recognizing and recognizing learning and development successes is also vital in establishing a culture of continual learning. Organizations might celebrate workers' completion of training programs, the learning of new skills, or the effective deployment of new information. By praising and rewarding workers' dedication to learning, firms stress the value of continuous improvement and urge others to follow suit.

Embracing continuous learning provides several advantages for both people and companies. It encourages personal and professional development, boosts employee engagement and work happiness, and strengthens the organization's potential for creativity and adaptation. Continuous learners are more inclined to be proactive, take responsibility for their job, and seek ways to make a good influence.

Finally, changing the corporate world, developing an action-oriented culture is important for keeping ahead of the competition. By cultivating a development mindset, developing trust and cooperation, granting autonomy, rewarding successes, and embracing continuous learning, you enable people to become catalysts for change from within. Such a culture not only fosters creativity, agility, and productivity but also generates a work environment that attracts and keeps top personnel. So, empower your team, inspire action, and move your organization toward sustainable success in the face of relentless change.

CHAPTER 27:LEADERSHIP INFLUENCE

Leaders who understand the power of influence know that a culture of action is not something that arises spontaneously; it takes conscious effort and strategic leadership. By establishing a culture that rewards action, decisiveness, and creativity, CEOs may gain a huge competitive edge for their firms.

In this chapter, we will dig into the notion of leadership influence and investigate how it may be utilized to build a culture of action. We will emphasize the important aspects that contribute to such a culture and share insights into how executives may harness them to move their enterprises ahead.

By grasping the significance of inspiring a shared vision, empowering decision-making, encouraging risk-taking, boosting cooperation and communication, leading by example, and recognizing and rewarding action, leaders can set the scene for a dynamic and proactive work environment. This, in turn, generates a culture where people feel inspired, empowered, and engaged, leading to greater productivity, creativity, and ultimately, company success.

So, whether you are a seasoned leader looking to enhance your organization's competitive edge or an aspiring leader aiming to cultivate a culture of action from the outset, this article will equip you with the knowledge and strategies to create an environment where action thrives and drives your organization's growth and prosperity.

Inspiring a Shared Vision

Inspiring a common vision is a vital part of leadership influence that plays a critical role in developing a culture of action inside an organization. When leaders can successfully convey a compelling vision, they inspire a feeling of purpose and direction among their staff, pushing people to take action and strive towards a shared objective.

To inspire a common vision, leaders must first have a clear and well-defined vision themselves. This vision should define the expected future condition of the company, covering its objectives, values, and purpose. It should be communicated in a style that connects with people, underlining the potential impact and advantages of realizing that goal.

When expressing the vision, leaders should stress the "why" behind the activities and choices that need to be done. They should present a clear image of what success looks like, enabling people to view themselves as part of something important and valuable. By tying workers' work to a broader mission, leaders generate a feeling of urgency and significance, encouraging people to take action.

In addition to good communication, leaders should actively include their staff in the vision-building process. This may be done by requesting opinions, seeking comments, and fostering debate. When workers feel that their ideas and viewpoints are acknowledged and included in the vision, they acquire a feeling of ownership and commitment, further driving their enthusiasm to take action.

Furthermore, leaders must regularly reaffirm and remind staff of the agreed goal. This may be accomplished via frequent communication channels such as team meetings, newsletters, or company-wide updates. By continually connecting activities and choices with the overall vision, leaders stress the necessity of taking action in pursuit of common objectives.

Inspiring a common vision goes beyond merely expressing goals; it entails developing an emotional connection that motivates and mobilizes workers to take action. When workers understand and believe in the vision, they become proactive problem solvers, searching for ways to contribute and have a meaningful effect on the organization's success.

Empowering Decision-Making

Empowering decision-making is a vital part of leadership influence that leads to the formation of a culture of action inside an organization. When leaders empower their teams to make choices, they build a feeling of ownership, responsibility, and proactivity among workers, encouraging them to take action and drive development.

To empower decision-making, leaders need to develop a culture of trust and confidence in their staff. They must trust in the talents and knowledge of their workers and empower them with the autonomy and authority to make choices within their areas of responsibility. By delegating decision-making authority, leaders not only alleviate their burden but also enable people to take ownership of their job and share their unique viewpoints and skills.

Effective leaders also ensure that workers have access to the knowledge and tools required to make educated choices. They give explicit standards, objectives, and limits to govern decision-making processes, while also promoting innovation and critical thinking. By educating workers with the appropriate skills and information, leaders empower individuals to make confident judgments and take action without continual monitoring or micromanagement.

In addition to empowering people, leaders may also create communal decision-making procedures. This might entail promoting collaborative talks, encouraging multiple opinions, and requesting feedback from different team members. By integrating diverse viewpoints in the decision-making process, leaders tap into the collective knowledge of their teams and foster a culture of inclusion and cooperation.

To further empower decision-making, leaders should adopt a growth mentality and foster a readiness to learn from both achievements and mistakes. They should establish an atmosphere where errors are perceived as chances for development and progress rather than failures. When workers feel supported and encouraged to take calculated risks, they are more inclined to make choices and take action without fear of negative consequences.

Furthermore, leaders should give feedback and acknowledgement for the choices made by their employees. The positive reward for proactive decision-making and excellent results supports the culture of action and encourages people to continue taking initiative.

By empowering decision-making, leaders establish a culture where people feel trusted, respected, and capable of making important contributions. This culture of action promotes employees to take initiative, make timely choices, and grab possibilities for innovation and progress. It eventually leads to a more agile and responsive firm that can adjust swiftly to changes in the business environment and retain a competitive advantage.

Encouraging Risk-Taking

Encouraging risk-taking is a critical part of leadership influence in developing a culture of action inside a business. When leaders establish an atmosphere where calculated risks are respected and accepted, they allow people to think outside the box, explore new ideas, and take daring actions that may lead to innovation and development.

To promote risk-taking, leaders must first develop psychological safety among their employees. This includes fostering an environment where people feel secure to share their ideas, take chances, and learn from both achievements and mistakes without fear of negative repercussions. When workers feel supported and encouraged to take calculated risks, they are more inclined to go out of their comfort zones and explore creative ideas.

Effective leaders also convey the value of risk-taking by stressing the possible rewards and advantages that may come from taking controlled risks. They assist workers realize that innovation and success may entail walking into unfamiliar areas and accepting uncertainty. By reframing risk as an opportunity rather than a threat, leaders influence the attitude inside the business and inspire people to consider risk-taking as a natural part of the road toward success.

Furthermore, leaders should lead by example and exhibit their readiness to take risks. When workers observe their leaders taking calculated risks and managing the repercussions, whether good or poor, with resilience and adaptation, it motivates others to do the same. By demonstrating that risk-taking is not only acceptable but also appreciated, leaders establish a culture that pushes people to push boundaries and question the status quo.

To enable risk-taking, leaders may also give the appropriate resources, support, and direction to avoid any hazards. This involves giving funding for experimentation, fostering cooperation and knowledge-sharing to decrease individual risk, and offering mentoring or coaching to assist staff overcome uncertainty. By giving a safety net and support structure, leaders create confidence in their teams and encourage them to accept risk in pursuit of innovation and success.

It is vital to stress that promoting risk-taking does not equal condoning irresponsible or uneducated decision-making. Leaders should highlight the need of undertaking rigorous study, analysis, and assessment of risks before making choices. By encouraging a culture of educated risk-taking, executives ensure that risks are assessed, aligned with company objectives, and have a greater probability of generating good results.

Promoting Collaboration and Communication

Promoting cooperation and communication is a critical component of leadership influence in developing a culture of action inside a company. When leaders emphasize and encourage successful collaboration and communication, they create a climate that promotes cooperation,
knowledge-sharing, and collaborative action, leading to higher productivity and creativity.

To foster cooperation, leaders should develop a culture that appreciates and promotes teamwork. They encourage people to work together, break down silos, and harness the varied talents and viewpoints inside the business. By developing a feeling of collective responsibility and highlighting the value of cooperation, leaders create an environment where employees are compelled to share ideas, seek advice from others, and work towards shared objectives.

Effective leaders also give the essential venues and instruments for cooperation. This might involve installing project management tools, collaboration software, or constructing physical venues that enable informal contacts and the exchange of ideas. By allowing seamless communication and cooperation, leaders eliminate obstacles and empower workers to work together more successfully, regardless of their physical location or departmental boundaries.

In addition to cooperation, leaders must highlight the value of open and transparent communication inside the business. They establish a culture where information flows easily, ensuring that workers have access to the knowledge and tools required to make educated choices and take action. Regular and regular communication channels, such as team meetings, newsletters, and digital platforms, keep workers informed about company objectives, progress, and difficulties.

Moreover, leaders should actively listen to their teams and promote active engagement in talks. They establish an atmosphere where everyone's opinion is respected and heard, providing a feeling of psychological safety that encourages workers to express their ideas, problems, and criticism. Leaders should create chances for workers to share their skills and viewpoints, which not only increases the quality of decision-making but also promotes a feeling of ownership and commitment among team members.
To further increase cooperation and communication, leaders should enable cross-functional projects and encourage

knowledge-sharing. They foster cooperation across departments and teams, allowing employees with varied skill sets to work together and exploit their combined capabilities. This cross-pollination of ideas and knowledge inspires creativity and helps break down silos inside the business.

Effective leaders also lead by example by actively engaging in collaborative activities, asking for ideas from their colleagues, and exhibiting honest communication. When workers experience their leaders appreciating and exercising teamwork and communication, they are more inclined to adopt these practices themselves.

Leading by Example

Leading by example is a vital part of leadership's impact in developing a culture of action inside an organization. When leaders model the behaviors and activities they demand from their teams, they inspire and encourage people to follow suit, establishing a culture of proactive involvement, responsibility, and initiative.

Leading by example begins with living the beliefs, ideals, and work ethic that leaders desire to see reflected in their business. It entails continually displaying the attitudes and activities that correspond with the intended culture. When leaders set a good example, it provides a clear standard for conduct and fosters a feeling of confidence and trust among workers.

One key part of leading by example is being proactive and taking initiative. Leaders who take the initiative to identify and solve difficulties, provide solutions, and grasp opportunities display a feeling of ownership and a predisposition for action. When workers watch their leaders being proactive, it motivates others to do the same, promoting a culture of action and a proactive attitude.

Responsiveness is another crucial quality of leading by example. Leaders that value timely communication, feedback, and follow-up show their commitment to cooperation and responsibility. They create the expectation that promptness and responsiveness are valued throughout the business, encouraging individuals to be proactive and take action in their respective areas of responsibility.

Problem-solving and decision-making abilities are also crucial areas where leaders may lead by example. By confronting issues with a solution-oriented perspective, leaders show the significance of critical thinking, creativity, and resilience. When workers see their leaders actively pursuing answers and making educated choices, they are encouraged to do the same, leading to a culture of action and continual progress.

Leading by example also includes exhibiting flexibility and accepting change. Leaders that are open to new ideas, ready to adjust to developing conditions, and demonstrate a growth mindset creates an atmosphere where people feel empowered to accept change and take sensible risks. This flexibility and eagerness to learn enable people to move beyond their comfort zones, experiment with new techniques, and create creativity.

Furthermore, leaders should display ethical behavior and integrity in their acts. When leaders continuously display honesty, openness, and ethical conduct, it develops a culture of trust and promotes an atmosphere where people feel secure and inspired to take action.

It's crucial to recognize that leading by example is not about being flawless or infallible. Leaders should also be upfront about their own mistakes and learning experiences since this supports a growth mentality and encourages people to accept difficulties and learn from setbacks.

Recognizing and Rewarding Action

Recognizing and rewarding activity is a vital part of leadership influence in developing a culture of action within a company. When leaders praise and encourage proactive conduct and initiative, they reaffirm the value of action and urge people to continue taking ownership and pushing for success.

Recognition and incentives serve as strong instruments for reinforcing desirable actions and establishing a culture of activity. By identifying and publicly applauding people or teams that display proactive involvement, leaders establish a positive feedback loop. This award not only raises morale but also sends a clear message that taking action and going above and beyond expectations is respected and appreciated inside the workplace.Recognition may take different forms, including personal praise, written thanks, or public acknowledgment during team meetings or company-wide communications. By spotlighting particular activities and the good effect they have had, leaders present concrete examples of what is valued and wanted inside the business, pushing others to follow suit.

In addition to acknowledgement, leaders can also consider awarding prizes for activity and effort. Rewards might include bonuses, promotions, unique initiatives, or chances for professional growth. By tying incentives to action, leaders reinforce the concept that proactive conduct is not only acknowledged but also directly related to career development and progress within the business. This motivates individuals to consistently explore chances for improvement and take initiative in their job.

Leaders must ensure that the recognition and awards are fair, consistent, and transparent. Employees should grasp the requirements for recognition and be aware of the possible incentives offered. Transparency and consistency in the recognition and awards process generate a feeling of fairness and drive people to strive for action and greatness.

Leaders may also promote peer-to-peer appreciation when workers acknowledge and appreciate each other's proactive efforts and accomplishments. This generates a good and collaborative work atmosphere, where workers feel appreciated by their colleagues and driven to support and reward each other's efforts.

Moreover, leaders should consider offering constructive comments and assistance to help workers further improve their skills and competencies. Feedback should be immediate, detailed, and focused on development and progress. By delivering constructive criticism, leaders enable people to develop their performance and continue taking action in more effective and meaningful ways.

Leadership impact has a crucial role in developing a culture of action that promotes organizational success. By inspiring a common vision, empowering decision-making, encouraging risk-taking, supporting cooperation, leading by example, and recognizing action, leaders can develop a culture that thrives on proactive behavior, decisiveness, and creativity.

Embracing such a culture will provide firms with a substantial competitive edge by keeping ahead of the curve, adjusting to change, and driving development in today's changing business world.

CHAPTER 28: COMMUNICATION AND COLLABORATION

One essential feature that sets successful organizations apart is their ability to communicate effectively and create cooperation among employees. However, many firms confront a common obstacle known as "silos." Silos refer to the barriers that exist inside an organization, where departments or teams function in isolation, restricting the flow of information and preventing cooperation. To solve this difficulty, firms must concentrate on breaking down silos and promoting alignment across the company.

Silos may have a severe influence on an organization's performance. They contribute to a lack of coordination, duplication of efforts, and a fragmented approach to problem-solving. Moreover, silos may develop a culture of distrust, where departments labor in isolation, hoard information, and avoid sharing resources. Such an atmosphere stifles creativity, slows down decision-making, and eventually inhibits corporate development.

In contrast, firms that value communication and cooperation flourish in today's fast-paced and interconnected world. By breaking down divisions and creating alignment, organizations establish a cohesive environment where teams work together towards common objectives. This method supports the open flow of information, stimulates knowledge-sharing, and promotes cross-departmental collaboration.

Breaking down barriers and creating alignment is not only a phrase; it is a strategic need for firms that wish to stay competitive. The capacity to communicate effectively across all levels of the business ensures that everyone is on the same page, avoiding misunderstandings and enhancing overall efficiency. Collaboration, on the other hand, brings together varied views, skills, and knowledge, allowing teams to solve difficult issues and promote innovation.

In this essay, we explore further the necessity of successful communication and teamwork in the corporate setting. We address practical techniques to break down silos, such as building a culture of open communication, promoting cross-functional cooperation, using technology, and empowering leadership. By adopting these ideas, organizations can build a collaborative atmosphere that releases the full potential of their employees and prepares them for success in the competitive marketplace.

So, let us begin on a trip to explore how communication and collaboration, when combined seamlessly, can revolutionize businesses, break down silos, and drive alignment toward producing remarkable results.

Building a Culture of Open Communication

Silos within an organization sometimes form owing to a lack of adequate communication routes. To break down these divisions and encourage cooperation, firms must emphasize developing a culture of open communication. This requires fostering an atmosphere where workers feel comfortable expressing their ideas, exchanging information, and offering feedback across departments.

1. Encouraging Dialogue and Feedback:
One of the main parts of developing open communication is encouraging debate and feedback at all levels of the company. Employees should feel empowered to speak their thoughts, ask questions, and contribute feedback without fear of reprisal or condemnation. This may be done by creating an open-door policy, arranging frequent team meetings, and implementing feedback channels such as suggestion boxes or anonymous surveys. By actively soliciting and respecting advice from workers, firms may break down communication barriers and guarantee that information flows easily across the company.

2. Establishing Transparent Communication Channels:
Transparent communication channels are vital for developing a culture of open communication. Organizations may employ numerous methods and platforms to enable the exchange of information and ideas. Internal messaging systems, intranets, and project management software may serve as centralized platforms for sharing updates, documents, and communications. These channels should be widely available to all workers, fostering openness, and ensuring that essential information reaches the correct individuals in a timely way.

3. Embracing Active Listening:
Open communication is a two-way street. It entails not just expressing thoughts but also actively listening to others. Encourage staff to practice active listening by intently participating in discussions, striving to comprehend diverse views, and delivering insightful replies. Active listening increases empathy, understanding, and trust among team members, leading to increased cooperation and problem-solving.

4. Promoting Cross-Departmental Collaboration:
Breaking down barriers needs cooperation not just inside departments but also across various functional areas. Encourage staff to cooperate with colleagues from diverse departments, establishing a feeling of unity and shared purpose. This may be done via cross-departmental initiatives, joint meetings, or even social activities that bring workers from various teams together. By breaking down the boundaries between departments, businesses may enable the interchange of ideas, foster cross-pollination of information, and boost overall teamwork.

5. Recognizing and Rewarding Open Communication:
To underscore the significance of open communication, firms should recognize and reward individuals who actively contribute to a culture of openness and cooperation. This may be done via performance assessments, staff appreciation programs, or even by integrating communication and cooperation skills into career growth chances. By showcasing the advantages of open communication, organizations

encourage workers to actively engage, share ideas, and cooperate efficiently.

Building a culture of open communication requires time and work, but the advantages are far-reaching. It fosters an atmosphere where workers feel appreciated, stimulates creativity, increases problem-solving capacities, and boosts overall productivity. By breaking down silos via open communication, businesses build the framework for effective cooperation and alignment throughout the whole company.

Breaking Down Barriers via Cross-Functional Collaboration

Silos within an organization sometimes result in hurdles that prevent successful cooperation. These obstacles might result from departmental boundaries, opposing goals, or simply a lack of awareness of other teams' roles and duties. To break down these barriers and encourage cooperation, firms must embrace cross-functional collaboration, which entails bringing together employees from varied backgrounds and areas of expertise to work towards common objectives.

Here's a closer look at how cross-functional teamwork might assist overcome silos:

1. Harnessing Diverse Perspectives and Expertise:
Cross-functional cooperation helps businesses to tap into the unique views, talents, and knowledge of employees from other departments. Each department brings a distinct set of information and experiences to the table. By merging these

varied viewpoints, teams may obtain a more thorough knowledge of complicated challenges and generate new solutions. This collaborative approach stimulates creativity, encourages out-of-the-box thinking, and boosts problem-solving talents.

2. Breaking Down Information Silos:
Silos sometimes result in information gaps, when essential knowledge is limited inside specialized departments. Cross-functional cooperation helps down these information silos by facilitating the sharing and exchange of knowledge across various teams. Through open communication channels and collaborative platforms, employees from multiple departments may exchange ideas, best practices, and lessons learned. This offers a more comprehensive view of organizational difficulties and supports improved decision-making.

3. Enhancing Communication and Coordination:
Cross-functional cooperation enhances communication and coordination across departments. By working together on projects or initiatives, teams are compelled to communicate effectively, align their efforts, and coordinate their activities. Regular meetings, progress reports, and collaborative decision-making sessions ensure that all departments are on the same page and working towards common goals. This alignment avoids misconceptions, lowers duplication of resources, and supports a more effective workflow throughout the business.

4. Encouraging Interdepartmental Relationships and Trust:
Collaborating across departments supports the establishment of interdepartmental connections and trust. When employees from various teams work together, they get a greater grasp of each other's responsibilities, difficulties, and talents. This knowledge promotes empathy and trust, strengthening collaboration and promoting a feeling of oneness. As trust builds, the boundaries between departments lessen, and communication becomes more smooth, further breaking down divisions within the business.

5. Aligning Goals and Priorities:
Cross-functional cooperation helps unify objectives and priorities across various departments. By working together towards common goals, teams may overcome opposing agendas and synchronize their efforts to achieve collective achievement. This alignment guarantees that all departments are working towards the same goal, reducing conflicting objectives and boosting organizational performance.

6. Empowering Cross-Functional Teams:
To encourage cross-functional cooperation, businesses might form dedicated cross-functional teams or project groups. These teams comprise professionals from various departments who join together to work on particular projects or initiatives. By giving these teams the authority and resources required to fulfill their objectives, businesses build a framework that encourages cooperation, responsibility, and ownership.

Harnessing Technology for Seamless Collaboration

In today's digital era, technology plays a critical role in breaking down walls and facilitating seamless communication across enterprises. With the appropriate tools and platforms, organizations can overcome geographical obstacles, expedite communication, and boost cooperation.

Here are crucial factors of utilizing technology for smooth collaboration:

1. Collaboration Platforms & Tools:

Collaboration platforms and technologies serve as digital workplaces where teams may interact, exchange information, and work together on projects. These platforms offer a single area for storing and accessing data, having conversations, assigning tasks, and measuring progress. Examples of collaboration technologies include project management software, team chat applications, shared document repositories, and virtual whiteboards. By embracing these tools, enterprises may promote real-time collaboration, even when team members are geographically distant.

2. Video Conferencing and Virtual Meetings:

Video conferencing and virtual meeting solutions have become vital for smooth communication in today's distant work environment. These solutions enable teams to hold face-to-face meetings, brainstorming sessions, and presentations regardless of their physical locations. Video conferencing promotes collaboration by giving visual clues and establishing a feeling of closeness among team members.

It also enables real-time collaboration on papers, screen sharing, and recording meetings for future reference.

3. Cloud-Based Storage and File Sharing:
Cloud-based storage and file-sharing services provide a safe and accessible method to save, distribute, and collaborate on documents. These systems enable teams to collaborate on the same files concurrently, avoiding version control difficulties and guaranteeing that everyone has access to the newest modifications. Cloud storage also allows the freedom to view files from any device with an internet connection, allowing remote collaboration and facilitating cooperation across multiple locations and time zones.

4. Workflow Automation and Task Management:
Technology may automate tedious processes and optimize operations, allowing teams to concentrate on more strategic and collaborative work. Workflow automation systems automate common procedures, such as approvals, alerts, and data input, decreasing human work and minimizing mistakes. Task management systems let teams plan and prioritize work, assign projects, create deadlines, and measure progress. By automating processes and handling tasks effectively, teams may interact smoothly and boost overall productivity.

5. Virtual Collaboration Spaces:
Virtual collaboration spaces provide dynamic and immersive settings for teams to work and explore ideas. These spaces may feature virtual reality (VR) or augmented reality (AR) technology that imitates actual meetings or workshops,

enabling participants to interact with virtual items, visualize ideas, and communicate in a more engaging and inventive way. Virtual collaboration spaces stimulate innovation, break down geographical borders, and increase cooperation among team members.

6. Mobile Applications:
Mobile apps allow teams to interact on the move, offering access to collaboration platforms, communication tools, and crucial documents. With mobile applications, team members can remain connected, engage in conversations, get real-time information, and contribute to projects, regardless of their location. Mobile collaboration enables distant employees, promotes agility, and facilitates seamless communication across diverse devices and operating systems.

Empowering Leadership to Drive Alignment

Effective leadership is vital for breaking down divisions and achieving alignment within a company. Leaders play a critical role in developing a collaborative culture, defining clear objectives, and providing the necessary support and resources for success.

Here's a closer look at how leadership may empower teams and promote alignment:

1. Setting a Clear Vision and Goals:
Leadership determines the direction and vision of the company. By clearly conveying the mission, values, and objectives, leaders give a feeling of purpose and direct teams

towards a single target. A clear vision helps integrate individual efforts with the greater corporate objectives, ensuring that everyone is working towards the same destination. Effective leaders also break down barriers by encouraging the awareness that teamwork is crucial for accomplishing those objectives.

2. Leading by Example:
Leaders that lead by example and display collaborative behaviors motivate their employees to follow suit. When leaders actively participate in cross-departmental communication, seek opinions from other teams, and foster knowledge sharing, they inspire others to do the same. By demonstrating collaborative behavior, leaders build a culture where cooperation and alignment are valued and practiced across the business.

3. Fostering Open Communication and Feedback:
Leadership has a crucial role in establishing free communication and feedback inside the business. Leaders should establish an atmosphere where workers feel comfortable sharing their thoughts, problems, and recommendations. They should actively listen to staff, promote open debate, and ensure that communication channels are available and transparent. By establishing a culture of open communication, executives break down boundaries across departments and build alignment via common knowledge.

4. Providing Resources and Support:
Empowering leaders gives the essential resources, tools, and support for teams to cooperate successfully. This involves investing in collaborative tools, training programs, and cross-functional efforts. Leaders ensure that teams have the necessary resources to communicate, cooperate, and exchange information smoothly. They also give direction, coaching, and support to assist teams to manage issues and establish alignment.

5. Establishing Shared Objectives and Key Performance Indicators (KPIs):
Leadership plays a significant role in creating agreed goals and key performance indicators (KPIs) that foster cooperation and alignment. By creating clear measures for success that cover several departments, leaders inspire teams to work together towards similar objectives. These shared goals promote a feeling of collective responsibility, enabling departments to work and help one another to accomplish the intended results.

6. Recognizing and Rewarding Collaborative Efforts:
Leadership should recognize and reward collaborative initiatives inside the business. By identifying and praising people and teams who actively contribute to breaking down silos and achieving alignment, leaders highlight the significance of cooperation. Recognition might take the shape of rewards, performance assessments, or public acclaim, reaffirming the importance of cooperation and pushing others to follow suit.

7. Promoting Cross-Departmental Collaboration:
Leadership has a critical role in fostering and enabling cross-departmental cooperation. Leaders might plan cross-functional initiatives, seminars, or team-building events that bring staff from various departments together. By encouraging chances for collaboration, leaders empower teams to form connections, exchange knowledge, and acquire a better grasp of each other's responsibilities and viewpoints.

In a competitive corporate world, good communication and teamwork are vital for success. Breaking down divisions and promoting alignment within a company may unleash the full potential of cooperation, leading to higher productivity, creativity, and better results. By developing a culture of open communication, promoting cross-functional cooperation, embracing technology, and empowering leadership, organizations may revolutionize their operations and achieve a competitive advantage in today's fast-shifting market. Embrace the power of communication and cooperation, and watch your company grow in the age of teamwork and synergy.

CHAPTER 29: REWARDING INITIATIVE

In today's fast-paced corporate world, businesses are continuously exploring methods to establish a proactive and results-driven workplace. One of the most successful techniques to do this is by introducing a rewarding program. By recognizing and encouraging workers' hard work and successes, firms may unleash latent potential, enhance productivity, and build a culture of excellence. In this essay, we look into the advantages of a rewarding initiative and investigate how it may build a dynamic and flourishing workplace.

Fueling Motivation for Excellence

A rewarding endeavor acts as a spark for fuelling enthusiasm among workers, pushing them to strive for excellence in their job.

Here are some crucial aspects to further clarify how a rewarding project fosters motivation for excellence:

1. Recognition and gratitude: A rewarding effort offers workers the recognition and gratitude they deserve for their hard work and successes. When people feel recognized for their accomplishments, it enhances their self-esteem and confidence, providing a feeling of pride in their job. This award functions as a potent incentive, motivating staff to

maintain their high-performance levels and surpass expectations.

2. Incentives and prizes: In addition to recognition, a rewarding project generally includes tangible incentives and prizes. These may take numerous forms, such as money bonuses, gift cards, additional time off, or unique privileges. By delivering these incentives, workers are inspired to go the additional mile, knowing that their efforts will be appreciated. The promise of receiving rich prizes becomes a motivating factor behind their drive to achieve excellent outcomes.

3. Career progression chances: A well-designed rewarding endeavor also integrates career progression chances as a source of incentive. When workers perceive a clear route for growth and development inside the firm, they feel driven to achieve in their existing jobs. The potential of gaining promotions, accepting larger responsibilities, or acquiring new abilities provides a compelling motivator to consistently develop and display excellence.

4. Goal defining and Progress measuring: A worthwhile project frequently entails defining explicit objectives and measuring progress towards their realization. This goal-oriented strategy gives a feeling of purpose and direction to workers, fostering a motivation to perform at their best to attain their aims. Regular feedback and progress evaluations give workers a feeling of success and push them to continually strive for greatness.

5. Healthy rivalry: A rewarding effort may also foster healthy rivalry among workers. Recognizing and rewarding top performers promotes a friendly competition that drives people to exceed their boundaries and surpass their colleagues. This healthy rivalry drives workers to consistently improve their abilities, knowledge, and performance, propelling them toward perfection.

6. Personal and Professional Development: A rewarding effort might be devised to assist workers' personal and professional development. By giving chances for training, mentorship, or attending conferences and seminars, employers show their involvement in their workers' growth. This not only boosts their motivation but also allows them to gain new abilities, extend their knowledge, and attain new levels of excellence in their profession.

Enhancing Employee Engagement

Employee engagement is a vital aspect of generating organizational performance and establishing a great work environment. A rewarding endeavor plays a key role in promoting employee engagement.

Here are some essential aspects to further clarify how a rewarding program helps to improve employee engagement:

1. Meaningful Recognition: A rewarding program guarantees that workers' contributions and successes are acknowledged and appreciated in a meaningful manner. When workers feel that their efforts are appreciated and respected, it produces a

feeling of pride and pleasure in their job. This award not only enhances their morale but also builds a stronger connection and loyalty to the institution.

2. Sense of Belonging: A rewarding program develops a sense of belonging among workers. When people are recognized for their hard work, it fosters a pleasant and inclusive culture where everyone feels like a valued part of the team. This feeling of belonging develops a strong emotional connection to the company, leading to enhanced involvement and devotion to group objectives.

3. Aligning awards with Performance: A well-designed rewarding endeavor ties awards with key performance indicators and intended goals. This guarantees that people are engaged in their job and focused on attaining quantifiable outcomes. When awards are related to performance, workers realize the clear relationship between their efforts and the influence on their development and recognition, further improving their engagement.

4. Increased Job contentment: A satisfying project greatly leads to job contentment. When workers are acknowledged and rewarded for their successes, it boosts their overall job satisfaction levels. Satisfied workers are more likely to be engaged in their job, devoted to the business, and inspired to perform at their best. This positive loop of job satisfaction and engagement generates a more productive and peaceful work environment.

5. Empowerment and Autonomy: A rewarding endeavor may empower workers and give them a feeling of autonomy in their positions. When workers can contribute their ideas, make choices, and take ownership of their job, it enhances their engagement and drive. By recognizing and rewarding their accomplishments, employers promote this feeling of empowerment and autonomy, further improving employee engagement.

6. Open Communication and Feedback: A rewarding project fosters open communication and frequent feedback between workers and management. This fosters a friendly atmosphere where workers feel comfortable expressing their ideas, problems, and objectives. Managers may give positive criticism and direction, helping workers grow and develop in their positions. Such continual communication develops trust, improves relationships, and promotes employee engagement.

Fostering Healthy Competition
Competition, when directed healthily and constructively, can be a tremendous motivator of development and innovation inside a business. A rewarding initiative plays a significant role in encouraging healthy competition among workers.

Here are some crucial aspects to further clarify how a rewarding effort assists in developing healthy competition:

1. Performance Recognition: A rewarding endeavor acknowledges and rewards excellent performance and accomplishments. When workers observe their colleagues

being recognized and rewarded for their great performance, it promotes a healthy feeling of rivalry. Seeing others thrive pushes people to push their limits and strive for perfection, resulting in continual growth and greater performance levels.

2. Setting Performance Standards: A rewarding project generally entails setting performance standards or objectives. These standards operate as benchmarks for workers to assess their performance against their peers. This direct comparison creates healthy rivalry as people seek to outperform their colleagues and attain or beyond the defined norms. It pushes people to move outside their comfort zones and explore new ways to get greater outcomes.

3. Encouraging Continuous Improvement: Healthy competition drives workers to consistently enhance their skills, knowledge, and performance. When people witness their colleagues performing and getting recognized, it establishes a baseline for greatness. Employees are driven to explore personal and professional development opportunities, gain new skills, and increase their performance to stay competitive within the firm.

4. Promoting Innovation and Creativity: A rewarding project may encourage innovation and creativity inside the workplace. Healthy competition drives workers to think outside the box, explore new ideas, and discover more effective methods to reach their objectives. The desire to stand out and be acknowledged may lead to the creation of creative

ideas, procedures, and strategies that propel the business ahead.

5. Collaboration and Knowledge Sharing: Healthy competition does not imply people working in isolation. A rewarding project may build a collaborative atmosphere where workers share their expertise, experiences, and best practices. This cooperation creates healthy rivalry as people learn from one another and attempt to integrate those learnings into their work. It encourages a culture of continual learning and progress, benefitting both people and the company as a whole.

6. pleasant Work Environment: Fostering healthy competition via a rewarding project generates a pleasant work environment. Employees are pushed by a similar ambition for development and achievement, which improves camaraderie and collaboration. Instead of generating a cut-throat or confrontational culture, healthy competition stimulates mutual support, encouragement, and celebration of each other's successes. This pleasant work atmosphere drives motivation, engagement, and overall job happiness.

Retaining Top Talent

In today's competitive labor market, acquiring and maintaining top personnel is vital for the long-term success of any firm. A well-executed incentive effort plays a significant role in keeping top workers.

Here are some essential aspects to further clarify how a rewarding endeavor aids in keeping top talent:

1. Recognition and gratitude: A rewarding campaign guarantees that top achievers get the recognition and gratitude they deserve. When workers' hard work and successes are recognized and appreciated, it reaffirms their worth in the business. This acknowledgment fosters a feeling of loyalty and commitment, making individuals more inclined to remain with the organization rather than explore possibilities elsewhere.

2. rewards for Excellence: A rewarding project provides attractive rewards for top performers. These incentives might include cash awards, bonuses, unique benefits, or further professional progression chances. By offering concrete awards that acknowledge their remarkable accomplishments, firms establish a compelling motivation for top individuals to stay dedicated and motivated in their employment.

3. Career Growth and Development: A rewarding project that focuses on giving top employees the opportunity for career growth and development. This might entail giving training programs, mentoring opportunities, or initiatives that enable them to enhance their skills and expertise. By investing in their professional development, firms show their commitment to the long-term success and promotion of their best performers.

4. Competitive pay Packages: A rewarding project might involve competitive pay packages for top individuals. While incentives and recognition are vital, delivering competitive pay and perks is also key to keeping top workers. A well-designed rewarding effort ensures that top personnel is paid properly for their talents, expertise, and extraordinary performance.

5. tough Assignments and Autonomy: Retaining top talent frequently demands delivering tough and important assignments that enable them to demonstrate their strengths and make a major contribution. A rewarding endeavor ensures that top performers are allowed to take on new tasks, lead key initiatives, and have a measure of autonomy in their job. This allows people to succeed, encourages their professional progress, and keeps them interested and happy in their positions.

6. pleasant Work Environment and Culture: A rewarding effort leads to a pleasant work environment and culture that is appealing to top personnel. When workers witness their colleagues being acknowledged and rewarded for their successes, it fosters a supportive and encouraging culture. A favorable work culture, paired with a rewarding endeavor, encourages cooperation, collaboration, and a feeling of belonging that top talent desires in a business.

Building a Positive Work Culture

A healthy work culture is a vital basis for supporting employee engagement, productivity, and overall company success. A well-executed rewarding program plays a key part in developing and fostering a pleasant work culture. Here are some essential aspects to further clarify how a rewarding initiative helps to develop a pleasant work culture:

1. Recognition & Appreciation: A rewarding endeavor guarantees that workers' efforts and successes are acknowledged and appreciated. When people feel appreciated and recognized for their work, it promotes a good and supportive culture. This acknowledgment develops a culture of gratitude, where workers celebrate one another's triumphs and feel driven to perform at their best.

2. Collaboration and Teamwork: A worthwhile effort fosters collaboration and teamwork. When workers are acknowledged and rewarded jointly for their combined efforts and successes, it deepens ties and develops a feeling of togetherness. This collaborative culture emphasizes open communication, information sharing, and mutual support, producing a happy work atmosphere where everyone feels committed to the team's success.

3. Trust and openness: A rewarding endeavor creates trust and openness inside the company. When incentives and recognition are matched with performance and properly stated, it improves trust among workers. They regard the process as fair and transparent, knowing that their hard effort would be recognized and rewarded properly. This trust helps to a strong work atmosphere where people feel appreciated, respected, and driven to make their best efforts.

4. continual Learning and growth: A rewarding endeavor may encourage a culture of continual learning and growth. By offering chances for training, mentoring, and skill advancement, firms demonstrate their commitment to workers' progress. When workers perceive that their development is encouraged and supported, it generates a culture of continual improvement, creativity, and personal progress.

5. Work-Life Balance and Well-being: A rewarding program may also contribute to a good work culture by encouraging work-life balance and employee well-being. By recognizing and rewarding workers' hard work, firms stress the necessity of maintaining a good work-life balance. This might include giving flexible work arrangements, fitness programs, or extra time off as incentives. A healthy work culture emphasizes workers' well-being, resulting in increased job satisfaction and improved general morale.

In a competitive company landscape, maintaining a proactive and results-driven workplace is key to attaining success. A rewarding program may be the key to unlocking the full potential of your team, sparking motivation, improving engagement, and establishing a culture of excellence. By recognizing and rewarding hard work and success, firms can retain top personnel, promote productivity, and build a workplace that lives on success. Embrace the power of a rewarding endeavor and observe your company fly to new heights of accomplishment.

www.ingramcontent.com/pod-product-compliance
Lightning Source LLC
Chambersburg PA
CBHW070917260726
48661CB00003B/739